Jackie Moffat is a Londoner, born and bred, but in 1982 moved to the Eden Valley in Cumbria, where she still lives and farms. As well as breeding Manx Loghtans (a rare breed of sheep, originating from the Isle of Man), she also writes a column for *Cumbria and Lake District Life* magazine.

www.booksattransworld.co.uk

The Funny Farm

THE LAUGHTER AND TEARS OF ONE WOMAN'S FARM IN CUMBRIA

Jackie Moffat

BANTAM BOOKS

LONDON • NEW YORK • TORONTO • SYDNEY • AUCKLAND

THE FUNNY FARM
A BANTAM BOOK: 0553816551
9780553816556

Originally published in Great Britain by Cumbria and Lake
District Life Magazine, part of the CN Group Limited

PRINTING HISTORY
Cumbria and Lake District Life Magazine edition published 2002
Bantam edition published 2004

9 10 8

Photographs taken by:
Val Corbett, Johnny Becker, Paula Paisley, Ashley Cooper, Jane Fay and Jackie
Moffat. Photos courtesy of Cumbria & Lake District Life Magazine – in-text:
84, 114, 234, 235; colour section: author with Tess, lamb in Rayburn, Manx
Loghtan, Large Black sow, Lady, Micky and Kareima, Give us a kiss!, Frederic.

Set in 11/13.5pt Sabon by
Falcon Oast Graphic Art Ltd.

Bantam Books are published by Transworld Publishers,
61–63 Uxbridge Road, London W5 5SA,
a division of The Random House Group Ltd,
in Australia by Random House Australia (Pty) Ltd,
20 Alfred Street, Milsons Point, Sydney, NSW 2061, Australia,
in New Zealand by Random House New Zealand Ltd,
18 Poland Road, Glenfield, Auckland 10, New Zealand
and in South Africa by Random House (Pty) Ltd, Isle of Houghton,
Corner of Boundary Road & Carse O'Gowrie, Houghton 2198, South Africa.

Printed and bound in Great Britain by
Cox & Wyman Ltd, Reading, Berkshire.

Papers used by Transworld Publishers are natural, recyclable products
made from wood grown in sustainable forests. The manufacturing processes
conform to the environmental regulations of the country of origin.

For Malcolm

*Without whose support and encouragement,
I would never have written anything but a shopping list.*

Foreword

Jackie Moffat is a very special person. A redhead, she makes me laugh not only because of her personality but also because she is a superb writer with a wacky sense of humour and an at times bizarre outlook on life.

The articles which she has written for every edition of *Cumbria and Lake District Life* for the last 10 years or more, and which I have had the enormous pleasure of preparing for publication in the magazine, are the main basis for this book. In addition there is a lot of new material which Jackie has produced especially for the book.

In my not so humble opinion this book is brilliant; not only for the humorous insight it gives to a one woman farm in Cumbria, deep in the rich greenery of the Eden Valley, but also because of its astute observation and the manner in which it is written and presented.

Unfortunately, it is not all laughter. The way in which Jackie describes the impact upon her and the farming community of the foot and mouth epidemic is colossal. The chapter headed 'Apocalypse in Eden' is for me one of the most emotional and superbly written pieces I have ever read on the entire foot and mouth disaster. It is an exceptional piece of writing from the heart.

But my overriding feeling after completing this book is of a wonderfully warm publication with a great deal more joy than sorrow. It will, I promise, make you laugh out loud as it takes you to The Funny Farm ... where the animals are infinitely saner than the humans. But then perhaps that's true of animals everywhere. With the possible exception of lemmings.

Keith Richardson

Introduction 11
The Milky Bar Kid 17
A Little Bundle of Joy 23
Muck Spreading 27
Pinky and Stinky 33
Double Trouble at Lambing Time 37
Chinese Whispers 41
Where There's Muck 45
The Millie Goat 49
Rodeo Time at Rowfoot 53
The Pale Rider 57
Blood, Sweat and Butter 61
It Ain't Half Hot Mum 65
Why Sheep are the Villains 71
The Lamb's Tale 77
My Rut and I Like It 81
Gyp and Tess 85
Take a Walk on the Wild Side 91
Merry Christmas 97
Julie the Smiling Dog 101
Kareima the Wonder Horse 109
Lady with the Film Star Eyes 115
It's Good to Talk 121
Acid House 125
A Spent Force 129
The Little Red Tractor 133
Extracting the Michael 137
An Awful Lot of Pigs 141
And a Merry EEC 145
Nutcracker Suite 149
Not Such a Silly Old Moo After All 153
Golden Fleece 159
Memories are Made of This 163
Counting Sheep 169
Calving Time 173

Dogs are Hard Work 179
Great Balls of Fire 183
Homeward Bound 187
1066 And All That 191
Frederic, frae Tow Law 195
Squeaky Clean 199
The Old Dairy Cottage 205
The End Game 209
Guilty as Charged 213
Rowfoot Revisited 217
Gnashing of Teeth 221
Apocalypse in Eden 227
Experts Set the World on Fire 237
Running Away to the Sun 243
Chestnuts Roasting on an Open Fire 249
Diary of a Lottery Winner 253
One Year on After Foot and Mouth 257
Percy's Progress 261
I Wool Never Find Another Ewe 265
Taking Stock 271
Sheep Terrorise Terrier 275
The Gateway to London 279
A Perfect Day 283
Epilogue 287

Introduction

'Well, dog, we've really done it now.' Julie the collie looked inscrutably ahead through slightly narrowed eyes. Unimpressed.

There was something affecting about getting north of Birmingham on the M6, a definite feeling that there was no going back. None that involved solvency anyway.

The dog and I were in my motorised sardine tin, a Fiat 126 with dodgy brakes and chugging along in our wake in the safety of the Land Rover, with our remaining worldly goods were my husband, Malcolm and Sara his youngest daughter. For Sara, The Move was an adventure, for Malcolm a homecoming. For me it was like emigrating.

That we would move to the country at some unspecified point in the future had always been understood. I had country blood in my veins and a distaste of metropolitan life in my heart and anyway, as my dad had insisted on my middle name being Elizabeth, after the Queen, I felt I should echo the monarch's well documented desire to 'live in the country with lots of dogs and horses.' Even if I didn't much fancy all the palaces and houses, mainly because of all the miles of hoovering it involved.

Malcolm was a Cumbrian. No, that's not strictly true, he started life as a Lancastrian but someone in the ordnance office played about with boundaries and he became

11

a Cumbrian at the stroke of a civil servant's pen. His family, though, were authentic time-served Cumbrians having farmed at Threlkeld and Eaglesfield. While I was rootless, he had live relatives scattered over the north of the county and dead ones entombed there, so Cumbria and a house with five acres was always the plan.

What wasn't in the script was the timing. The fantasy became reality when Malcolm fell off a horse onto the impacted sand at Bardsea and spifflicated both his back and his career in one go. We thought we had at least another five years of shivering and sheltering in estate agents' doorways on family holidays in Cumbria saying 'oh, we could afford that one' or 'ooh, look at that – it's got land/stabling/weird wallpaper/rising damp/damp that's been that high for years.'

Suddenly, we hadn't and our house in Surrey went on the market.

Our first 'buyer' wanted us out by March 7th. The date came and went, as did the buyer; we neither saw nor heard from him again. Our second 'buyers' offered our asking price and claimed to be first timers, which we thought was odd. That deal fell to bits when their 'buyers' could not sell their house. Still, third time lucky. Our eventual purchaser made two appointments to view the house at ten o'clock through one agent and at twelve with a different one. She arrived at eleven. I still can't remember what we did about the commission, but at least an agreement was reached.

And in Cumbria we – Malcolm, Sara, the dog (whose approval was essential) and I – were doing our own house hunting. We never saw the one in Salkeld with a 'conversation pit' but the first of the others we viewed had very pretty red floral curtains but very suspect floors and its entire acreage (all five of them) was situated on a 43.8 degree hill. Great for tobogganing but not so hot for keeping a house cow. The second, Sara dismissed as 'deeply creepy' and that was before we heard the legend of the local vampire. It smelt foisty too. In fact, foist lurked hidden and unbidden like anthrax in every corner. Nasty stuff, foist. The third had an impressive fabric feature incorporated into the ceiling which may have been an early piece of installation art but more likely was there to catch falling plaster – suspended ceilings are one thing, suspended sheeting quite another. Another had a wonderful view. Of electricity pylons, sadly.

Then we came to Rowfoot. Malcolm stood on the barn steps and looked curiously at home. Sara said it was a happy house. The dog liked it. The land was good old pasture, the buildings had character – OK, they probably had mice too but we wanted livestock and at least these came free. The garage yielded up a metal man trap and a huge gasunder while there was a single seater kharzi in a Lilliputian sandstone and slate building in the garden. Shamefully, during my mother's first visit to our country idyll, we encouraged her to think that the kharzi and the gasunder constituted the extent of the sanitary arrangements, only introducing her to the flushing porcelain sort when she started squealing for train timetables.

We all agreed. Rowfoot it had to be.

We sold our house at the beginning of June. For the next month, until we completed the purchase, we lived like gypsies, pitching camp with various friends for days at a time, then packing everything into the Land Rover and heading off again. It was probably as well that the two older girls had live-in jobs at that stage, one in Paris and one in London, or billets might not have been as easy to find.

Our first day at Rowfoot was memorable for all the wrong reasons. The dog went missing. I scooted down to Ainstable Hall and made suitable wailing noises, adding that said dog was a collie of the non-working variety. My wellie-booted, brawny audience was, to a man, underwhelmed. Half an hour later, feeling an even bigger nit than before, I scooted off there again, with good news – dog had surfaced, shut in an upstairs room by mistake. Terribly sorry and all that. Slammed door, you see. As a means of introducing yourself to your new neighbours, it was one of peerless idiocy. Just to test our resolve, soon after our arrival they took the lambs from their mothers and lifted the top from the silage pit, working on the assumption that if we coped with such audible and olfactory assaults without complaint, we might pass muster. We were, frankly, much too delighted to have found the dog to bother.

Malcolm enrolled at Newton Rigg and became a student alongside a bunch of battle-hardened 18 year olds, the idea being that he would be the 'brains' behind whatever we ended up doing and I would supply the brawn. At home, I completed my apprenticeship as brickie's mate as floors came out and central heating went in, southern cissies that we were. When the third skip went away, the little guy over the road was moved to enquire whether we were 'making it all open plan.'

We weren't, I assured him. During the next few months, we became accustomed to plaster dust in our coffee and began to wonder exactly why we needed wooden wardrobes like everyone else when the Pickford's cardboard jobs were just as serviceable if not particularly decorative.

By Autumn we needed stock. The grass-letting season was approaching its end, and in spite of paying close attention to all those episodes of *The Good Life* we had absolutely no idea what we should buy and even less idea of how much we should pay for it, so we asked our neighbour Nathan to go off sheep shopping for us. He came back with 25 fine Cheviot hoggs. My mother always thought that sheep were a licence to print money.

'What, you just put them out in the fields, they keep the grass down and then you make money when you sell them?' she had spluttered as if sheep farming were easily as disreputable a way of earning a crust as arms dealing or slave trafficking. She pointed out that in a sheepless world, farmers would need to buy extremely long cables for their hover mowers and venture into inhospitable territory cutting grass. She was dead right, I thought, at least about the money printing bit of this when they all graded and cleared a tenner a head the following Spring.

Fired with enthusiasm, and a profound desire to separate ourselves from our ill-gotten gains, we thought a cow might be a good idea and acquired Lady, a Jersey with limpid eyes, pendulous teats and endless patience. Two cows might be double the fun. And so it went on and in no time at all we acquired half a dozen Jerseys, a milking machine, a butter worker, a cheese press, backache and an accountant. We even managed to get into profit, due mainly to the fact that we never had a day off and were enjoying life so much that a salary seemed an irrelevance.

One or two horses came and went during the first few years. In 1985, my Granny passed on to that great distillery in the sky (at least that is, I believe, what she hoped to find beyond the stars) and left me some money; enough to consider realising a dream which had hovered in and out of my consciousness since I was old enough to spell consciousness. An Arab mare. Ideally, a chestnut, flashy, stunningly beautiful, wise and kind mare. I found her. She was called Kareima.

They were quite a trilogy – Julie, Lady and Kareima. Each unique, utterly irreplaceable and unforgettable. As only girls of the species can be.

We returned from a week dodging electric storms in the south of France. The ritual of an annual holiday had re-entered our lives after several years of not leaving Rowfoot even for a weekend break. We must have been too busy, I suppose, or maybe too contented to bother about such inessentials.

The Milky Bar Kid

In 1993 I started to commit my rants and ramblings to print.

A quick squint at the Internet reveals that in the same year The Queen celebrated forty years on the throne and agreed to pay Income Tax; Nelson Mandela and F W de Klerk shared the Nobel Peace Prize; Mr Blobby had an eponymous hit record; bombs were going off all over the place, damaging Harrods in London, the Uffizi in Florence and the World Trade Centre in New York, yet curiously peace processes in Northern Ireland and the Middle East were recorded as having made good progress. Oh, and some nice people from Cambridge went on holiday to South Africa; it wasn't their first choice destination you understand – that was Kenya – and they finished the extension to their dining room with which they were well pleased, you will be glad to hear. Isn't it nice that the Internet takes due cognisance of this even if it does not mention me and the print?

By 1993, we had lived at Rowfoot, a small stockrearing farm in the Eden Valley for about eleven years and my apprenticeship as a Cumbrian was well under way. Back then, we ran a flock of Mules with a Suffolk tup to produce lambs to be either sold as stores or finished for the butcher. Mules incidentally, are not things with long ears and aggressive kicking skills, but a crossbred sheep with moderately configured lugs and the footballing skills of Newbiggin Under the Fell Reserves. The theory is that crossing hardy little hill bred Swaledales with prolific yet wussy Leicesters produces a sheep with the best qualities of both sides of its pedigree. As theories go, it's plausible enough but any sheep farmer will confirm that it is by no means infallible.

In addition, we kept three Jersey cows to provide us with milk, cheese and butter; we fed surplus milk to a veal calf or to pigs either or both of which ended up in the domestic freezer. The cows suckled their calves until 10–12 weeks of age when they became too much of a handful for a mere female such as my delicate self and were despatched to the local auction mart in return for some filthy lucre.

Our only mechanisation was a superannuated Massey Ferguson 135 tractor and a muck spreader; other than that it was all a gripe and barrow operation as all the buildings were and still are traditional stone with all its attendant inconvenience and narrow doors. In estate-agent-speak, this is called 'character'.

Even in 1993, we had abandoned making our own hay, finding the correlation between the UK's gin sales and hay time too close for the comfort of our long term health. Instead, we bought from neighbours Eric and his brother David who make far better stuff than we ever managed to do, a practice we continue to this day.

For fun, I had Kareima, my Arab mare to ride, her three-year-old home bred daughter and a retired Lancashire police horse, who never managed to find a publisher for his memoirs.

None of this appears on the Internet either, nor does the fact that in 1993 we didn't go to South Africa or to Kenya.

We went to France: it had been a very good holiday. We

had seen Rouges in l'Ouest, Blondes in Aquitaine, Limousins in Limoges (I cannot claim to have actually seen a bull in a china shop but I did see one grazing in very close proximity to a porcelain factory) and most bizarrely of all, we saw a Titterington's of Penrith coach in the village where we stayed. I confess that we both cowered behind a wall until it had disappeared from sight; I am still not quite clear why.

It was raining hard on our last evening in France as we awaited the homeward bound ferry. French rain is much the same as the Cumbrian variety – it is all pretty cold, wet, dismal stuff. Strange, it wasn't the rain which engendered acute homesickness but the sight of the container (refrigerated, articulated) on the quayside. 'La Vache qui Rit' screamed the legend on the side, accompanied by an incongruous bright red bovine physiognomy. For those whose fluency in French is comparable with my own, roughly translated this means The Cow Wot Smiles. It was a very enigmatic smile. A right Mona Lisa of a smile and it set me thinking with an embarrassing excess of sentimentality about my 'girls' at home at Rowfoot.

Caroline, who is not, as her name might first suggest, an escaped Sloane Ranger but a Jersey cow of advancing years; the divine Lady, Island-bred beauty queen, fine of bone and limpid of eye and jumpy old Yelper in constant need of stress management counselling. Caroline I mused, would be in the final stages of pregnancy and probably by now resembled a beached barrage balloon rather than a cow.

I was confident that our return would precede the arrival of the calf, having consulted the Oracle (well, the Breeders' Tables at the back of the NFU diary anyway). I should have known better, shouldn't I?

The return to Rowfoot may sound like a second rate movie but it was infinitely more exciting. Caroline had said Ya Moo to the wisdom of the Breeders' Tables and produced her calf two weeks early and in a good Cumbrian downpour. Malcolm, the kind and expert neighbour who stock-watches for us in our rare absences and whose seat in heaven is assured somewhere between Noah and Dr Dolittle, had brought mother and wobbly infant in and bedded them down in deep warm straw. Malcolm ensured that the calf had the vital colostrums, or first milk containing protective natural antibodies but the little bull remained reluctant to suckle his enthusiasm for life dampened by the climatic conditions attending his arrival. He probably wished he had stayed in the relative comfort of the womb.

I discarded the tidy clothes and climbed into dung-bunging kit. 'The time has come' I told the calf solemnly, 'for a bit of creative input on your part, pal.'

Somewhat unceremoniously, I manoeuvred Titch into position at the udder and stuck a teat in his mouth. He sucked. Hooray. I knelt at his side for encouragement and prayed that Caroline would not move. She didn't. But this is where the good news ends. My left knee felt ominously wet. And warm. Yes, it was securely embedded in a nice juicy cow pat. By this time the Snoopy bobble hat – an absolutely essential accessory for all seriously well dressed livestock farmers of either sex – was at a rather eccentric angle. Caroline swished her tail. My face now looked as if a rampant tribesman had run amok with a Dulux Matchpot of warpaint. Ah well. And only six hours ago, I had been prancing around in three inch heels in one of the finest country house hotels in the Cotswolds indulging in a luxurious last night on holiday, friendly staff there asking me whether I would prefer Earl Grey or some freshly ground coffee instead . . .

I looked at Caroline. Do you know what: there was a distinct 'Rit' on her face.

Titch thrives. He ought to be rechristened Torment because that is what he is. He acts as a self appointed Reveille Monitor; any sheep who settles down for a brief 'toes up' – as opposed to the permanent one to which all sheep ultimately aspire – can expect to be disturbed within minutes. He has even taken on Kareima my Arab mare, which given the disparity in their sizes I have to admire him for.

Having located his mother's milk bar, he wondered whether Kareima might oblige with an extra ration of Gold Top. She was grazing contentedly, with her back to him flicking her tail in a desultory manner when this brainwave occurred to him. He crept up and deftly stuck his wet little snout between her back legs. She took off at a speed which would have made Desert Orchid seem a bit of a laggard. Titch looked mildly disappointed at the failure of his mission and set off in search of something else to annoy.

Holidays are all right, but there's nowhere quite like home.

Calving time is always fraught, especially if your herd numbers so few that you regard them all as close personal friends. That Jerseys are particularly susceptible to milk fever which results from the sudden demand on the cow's system for calcium, means that at calving time tension rises to a level best described as 'fraught with bells on.'

A Little Bundle of Joy

She has a great sense of theatre for a cow, does Yelper. And timing, in theatre, they tell me, is everything. It certainly was to Yelper. Any cow who calves at four in the morning during a week when your mother is visiting can be said to have done her fair share of boning up in the timing department.

I had been due to collect mother from the London train. There I was, dressed in clean clothes in honour of her imminent arrival – mother's arrival that is, not the calf's – since mother has an inexplicable aversion to my preferred garb of jeans, sweater with a very inventive ventilation system (holes) and wellies, not so much green as sort of khaki. Do I make myself clear? She also objects to the delicate aroma of wet cow, wet horse and wet dog which is the natural accompaniment to such an ensemble. Can't think why. So, I had splashed myself with something fragrant; it might have been Chanel but I doubt it. More likely it was aftershave or possibly furniture polish but whatever it was it seemed to smell OK. Mind you, after mucking out cows, pretty well anything smells OK.

Then it was that I chanced to look out of the window. Yelper was lying almost on her side, looking dangerously near calving. Call me devious if you like, but that is how it looked at the time. Honestly. So my other half departed for sunny Carlisle to collect mother from the train, assuming, of course that she had done her bit and managed to get on the right one at Euston. I stayed at home in the jeans etc. and maintained discreet surveillance of Yelper having persuaded her into the calving shed.

Only a few days previously she had stood in the field in the evening looking pathetic and pleading and imminent as only a Jersey cow can. My defences crumbled and I had a look at the unfriendly threatening sky overhead and made a policy decision that she and the expected offspring would be better off indoors. Once housed, I could creep out any time during the night to see her. It would relieve me of the possible embarrassment of skulking about the field in the nightdress and wellies, a sight which my next door neighbour has become used to over the years but which still might cause concern – offence even – to other residents. And I had no wish to be responsible for a car accident, a highly relevant factor given that Yelper's field adjoins the road.

She must have just fancied bed and breakfast, though, because for a week I dutifully brought her in, inspected her frequently, put the alarm clock on at intervals through the night and generally did all the things which good stock keepers do. And where do you think that got me? Quite right. I need not have bothered. Our Yelper has an odd sense of humour in my opinion. Still, what do I know? I'm only a brainless biped.

The calf arrived eventually. At four o'clock one morning. By then I was suffering something akin to jet lag – absolutely no idea which day of the week it was at all. Yelper grunted and groaned and moaned and then just for a final dramatic flourish went down with a spectacular case of milk fever and threatened to turn up her bovine little toes. Happily, she was persuaded otherwise and mother and baby are both doing nicely now, thank you.

Incidentally, you may like to know that Yelper is unique among Cumbrian dairy cows. I have never been a gambling girl but I would wager a whole wadge of the hard earned folding stuff that no other cows in Cumbria received a card from a couple of nutters called Tracy and Warren who live in Shepherd's Bush, London (somewhere, I believe, south of Junction 39 on the M6), congratulating her on the arrival of her 'little bundle of joy.'

I wonder about the company I keep sometimes.

Of course, now that it is so much colder, the cows come in to the byre at nights. The procedure for gathering them in is one I commend to your attention if you are travelling along the Armathwaite to Ainstable road at about 4.30pm and fancy a bit of live entertainment. It usually involves three calves doing a couple of circuits of the field pursued by a redhead screaming abuse and uttering dire threats (such activity does wonders for fitness but not a great deal for the temper), watched by three geriatric Jerseys all wondering whether their own infant or the human is the dafter.

Meanwhile, the ewes are suffering their annual bout of glazed eye syndrome. This is not as nasty as some other sheep afflictions, such as the graphically named blackleg, scrapie or orf (pronounced as in the high class insult 'bog orf'). It is peculiar to Rowfoot ewes, delivered as they are each year of a toy boy tup. As I have a small flock I am able to borrow a ram of Suffolk origin from a friend. The hapless sheep arrives uninitiated in the ways of the flesh, a shortcoming which the old girls soon remedy. They regard him rather as a group of ladies of a certain age might look at a bunch of Chippendales and then they tutor him accordingly. Hence the glazed eyes.

All in a day's farming.

By March, you are really hoping that winter is over. Just about bottom of your list of Things To Cheer You Up are a period of unremitting rain, a busted ballcock, some frozen diesel in the tractor and having to come up with sensible answers to stupid questions on Ministry forms. You are entitled to Sense of Humour Failure, at the very least.

Muck Spreading

It was not so much Beijing Flu as Ainstable Ague and very nasty it proved to be. The most noticeable side effect of the Ague is a profound sense of feeling very sorry for yourself, a luxury not often afforded us tillers of the soil. Whilst I felt sorry for myself none of the other residents of Rowfoot did. The cows, sheep, horses and dogs were unimpressed. The Man of the House was completely unmoved.

'Go forth and muck out the cowshed,' quoth He of Little Sympathy.

Ainstable Ague alone is possibly just bearable but when it coincides with a busted ballcock, a mutinous muck spreader and a demented dog (well, does your dog eat a red biro pen and a wooden spoon in one sitting? No, I thought not. I did try mixing another ground up pen – blue this time just to introduce a little variety – in with the Winalot but Dog just shot me a withering look and I was forced to replace it with the more conventional Chum).

The ballcock shattered on the coldest day of the year to date. Well, it would, wouldn't it? I shan't even be able to moan about that in future, since the word 'ballcock' is to be erased from our vocabulary because of its sexist connotations. Quite where that leaves Cockermouth I cannot imagine. And the muckspreader – are you sitting comfortably with a large drink within easy reach of your right hand? Then I'll begin.

The spreader is pivotal to my winter existence. Happiness is a freshly emptied spreader. As it fills up, my nerves wobble. I dread rain which will make the field soggy and jeopardise access. I live in fear of hard frost which will make all the diesel in the tractor turn to sludge and make starting difficult. I pray it won't be windy because Murphy's Law states that whichever way you set off to spread the muck half way through the wind will change and you will end up with five per cent spread nicely on the field and the remaining 95 per cent decorating your coat, your wellies and worst of all, your Snoopy bobble hat.

Those farmers owning high-tech machines with in-cab stereo and air conditioning will not have this problem but I don't even have a cab on mine let alone all the fancy accessories. Open top tractors lack the comfort as well as the sex appeal of open top sports cars, you see.

There was nothing for it but to call up reinforcements, so debilitated was I by the beastly bug. Tom, kind neighbour that he is, turned up and relieved the muck spreader of its cargo. I breathed a mighty sigh of relief and as soon as I felt half human again, made Tom and his family a cheesecake to express my heartfelt appreciation. Cheesecakes are a bit of a speciality of mine as I have unfettered access to thick, rich coronary-inducing cream and I make my own cream cheese. I can personally guarantee that my cheesecakes contain a minimum of 3,000 calories a slice and are dreadfully bad for you. But I have no shame.

I am afraid that at this juncture this heart warming story of everyday country folk takes a turn for the worse.

I set off for Tom's, cheesecake in hand. It was a blustery evening. The first gust detached the cover from the plate. The second blast whipped off the creamy lemon topping and spread it, like so much flotsam, about the yard. I was left holding a denuded biscuit base. The cats descended for a feast and in seconds the confection was but a memory. I still went up to Tom and Pat's, sporting some tasty blobs on my sweatshirt just to convince them that the thought had been there, even if the cheesecake wasn't.

Spreading muck and being an efficient stockman are really incidental attributes for a farmer these days. The thing he really needs to be highly accomplished at is filling out forms. In triplicate, preferably, to satisfy the voracious appetites of MAFF as they once were, DEFRA as they have become and, naturally, the EEC as well. In a cunning attempt to circumvent this system, I took the calves to the mart. Once the little beasts reach the age of 12 weeks they require CID forms at the auction. These are nothing to do with undercover police work but Cattle Identification Documents.

So, when the eldest was eleven and a half weeks of age, off we went. Terry the Transporter arrived at the unholy hour of 7am to load them up. He examined the three carefully and jabbed an accusatory finger at the largest one.

'Might have to go to the stirks,' he announced.

My spirits sank. If he was right I could still be at Carlisle in 12 hours time. Besides, I have never worked out what, exactly, a stirk is, beyond the fact that it is anything you want it to be from an oversized calf to a prime beast.

'They have a bar,' said Terry.

My mind wandered off in the direction of gin and tonics and hot toddies but it was not that sort of bar apparently. Sad.

'They have to walk under it to be allowed in the calves,' Terry explained.

I toyed with the notion of shaving a bit off his hooves with a farrier's rasp and then, in no mood to spend a long cold day at the auction, said 'tell him to duck.'

When I arrived, joy of joys, they were all in the calf pens. They always look bigger at home, somehow. This left me with time to kill. I watched the pig sale. Trade was such that if you will forgive the awful pun, pigs were flying. I couldn't cope with the sheep at all. The auctioneer appeared to be speaking in tongues so I trailed off to see how the calf trade was progressing.

'On a form,' declared the auctioneer, 'good calf . . .'

What the devil did 'on a form mean'? When in doubt, find out, I have always reckoned, so I sought a friendly face and asked.

'Have you had Mad Cow disease?' the face enquired. You will be glad to learn that I refrained from any smart replies, partly because I only ever think of them three weeks later and partly because of my naturally retiring disposition. Now, I may question their sanity as well as my own on occasions but thankfully Rowfoot has remained unsullied by BSE. So, I needed to complete the supporting paperwork – there was bound to be a form to fill in somewhere wasn't there?

Time was dragging. I went in search of Jos in whose company I can happily spend an hour or three sorting out the world. Our remedies might make Vlad the Impaler look a liberal free-thinking sort of chap but we'd get things fixed, Jos and I. He was nowhere to be found. As fellows rarely are when you need them most.

Eventually my turn came and the calves sold exceptionally well. In fact, it was a real effort not to smile. But you know how it is at the mart. It would be breaking with time honoured tradition if you didn't complain that trade was a bit back on last week, that they were worth a little more than you had got, that there really wasn't money in calves any longer. You know the kind of thing. I grinned only when I was safely out of sight. Then I banked the cheque.

Having sold the calves, I have now acquired two pigs to feed on the surplus milk. You have to be quick feeding pigs in case they sink their efficient little molars into something not intended for them at all. Such as your left leg. Once I had a pig who bit off the buckle on my Trendy Wellie. The wellie was never the same again but the pig suffered only mild indigestion. So you do have to be quick.

Pigs arc the last remaining prehistoric creatures to trot this earth. They grunt and snort and have truly appalling table manners. You could never take a pig to a restaurant or even to a pub with pretensions, come to that. But there is something endearing about them especially when they allow your oldest cat to share their feasts. It is quite a sight, old Lady Jane (she started off life as Dorian, being grey, but cat-sexing is not one of my strong points and I had to rechristen her) at one end of the trough and Pinky and Stinky (you didn't really expect me to stoop so low as clichéd Perky, did you?) at the other.

Elsewhere, the current bout of filthy weather has meant that shepherding on foot is only pleasurable for those who list the little known sport of Treacle Paddling high on their list of sporting activities and on my little Massey Ferguson, G-reg (first time round), it is only marginally better.

I'm off to Treacle Paddle again. If it ever becomes an Olympic sport, I'll be there, in amongst the medals.

If you have cows, plural, and are not in league with any of the major buyers who send tankers to your door, you will have more milk than you need. There is no obscure law on this planet which can possibly justify your wasting something so nutritious, so you can do one of two things – feed it to pigs or calves. We always favoured traditional breeds of pig for outside in summer and Jersey bulls for veal. The latter became readily available when their value dropped to sub-50p; they grow well until about three months, when they take on their adult appearance: all front and no backside. Eat them before then!

Pinky and Stinky

The pigs are no more. The demise of Pinky and Stinky may strike a chord of sadness in the hearts of some readers but those who visit or, more importantly, dine at Rowfoot, are rejoicing. Even those who are introduced to their dinner personally: 'Sara, meet Pinky,' or to be more specific, belly of Pinky, leg of Pinky or whatever, soon overcome their initial reservations when they taste the sublime meat.

Our pigs taste good because they enjoy a privileged lifestyle. They are bred by a fellow called Ivan up in the fells at Roadhead, where they can wander at will about the farm, the only areas out of bounds being the house and the hallowed ground of Ivan's leek bed. Other than that, they have free range. At most farms a collie dog will greet you with varying degrees of pleasure or hostility depending on what sort of a dance its sheep are leading it at the time but at Ivan's the Welcome Committee is usually a pig. Sometimes, a very large pig indeed, which may explain why Ivan doesn't have the problem with itinerant worm reps that many other farmers seem to have.

Now, Ivan is that rare thing these days, a character. Ivan is uninhibited by the iniquitous 20th century obsession with conformity and his cheery eccentricity shines out like a beacon. He always brings the pigs to their new home at Rowfoot, having of course, first filled out the obligatory forms for Movement of Pigs. He likes to see them settled in and then we can get down to the serious business of the evening, namely gossip and dinner. Never pork, though. No, that would smack of cannibalism somehow.

From the time they arrive (the pigs that is) they feast on nothing but the best: Jersey milk and a soupcon of barley with a few interesting additions to tempt even the pickiest pig. They mooch and root. They are happy pigs. When the time comes, they are despatched at home and for as long as it remains legal to do so this will be our practice because it minimises stress. This way, they are neither subjected to hanging about in the slaughterhouse nor to the trauma of travel. Pigs do not like travelling. I am certain of this because one rarely sees a pig on the London underground or languishing in the departure lounge at Gatwick Airport during a strike of French air traffic controllers.

No, the pig is happiest at home and that is where he should end his days. When I end mine, it will be at home too. My plan is to leave Rowfoot in a box (or possibly a Herdwick shroud if I am persuaded to be planted in the new environmentally sound cemetery in Carlisle) but before then I am sure life will continue to throw up assorted problems.

Problems like the milking machine going into meltdown, as it did last Tuesday. I knew it was serious because of the noticeable absence of Red Indians in Ainstable. Why should this be significant? Well, if there are no Red Indians, then why should smoke signals emanate from the machine other than to herald serious trouble? The plume of smoke rose upwards from the round thingy and liquid gunge dripped down on to the green metal. The resident village genius who usually waves his magic spanner and makes everything work again had gone AWOL leaving a tractor parked across his gateway. This is code for 'I have gone out and will not be back in time to solve your crisis so go find yourself another saviour.'

So, I summoned Bob Steele, purveyor of dairy and refrigeration equipment and the engineer did what all engineers do. He got technical. Talked about capacitators and motors instead of green bits and brown bits. Then realising that I am a mere woman, untutored in such niceties, he gave up and asked: 'You know when it hisses here' gesticulating towards one of the little green bits. I returned a blank stare, because frankly, I could not tell you whether it hissed, spat or did a passable rendition of Old Macdonald's Farm complete with all the sound effects, so great a clanking did the machine emit when in operation. It probably contravened all those worthy noise pollution levels but apart from myself and three Jersey cows, nothing live was ever near enough to notice. Anyway, the wretched thing is repaired now and very much quieter it is. I know because I can tell when it's hissing.

To say that I am relieved is an understatement of cosmic proportions as the prospect of milking three cows by hand was daunting. Lady was bulling and the chances of her standing still registered somewhere on the minus scale. Caroline would have been OK for she is a peaceful beast and there are few pleasanter things to do than sit on a three-legged stool divorced from human kind with your face tucked comfortably into the warmth of a cow's flanks, listening to the satisfying whoosh, whoosh of milk hitting bucket. But Yelper? It would not be so much Chief

Sitting Bull, to use the Red Indian analogy once more, but Chief Sitting Target. She has a left hook to equal any prize fighter's and an accuracy of aim which would leave the entire English soccer team gasping with admiration. So yes, I am hugely relieved.

A little Jersey bull is drinking the milk now. He will be veal when he grows up and before you even ask, he is not kept in the dark nor is he confined to a crate, nor is he force fed. We are talking happy veal here. He is loose housed with a deep straw bed, he can run about freely, and socialises with his three surrogate mothers, four if you count dopey Gyp the collie who licks him with what can only be described as dogged devotion. He gets bucketfuls of fresh milk and Bob's Mix which is like muesli only a darned sight more expensive, so he has a good balanced diet. The resultant meat will not be quite so white as the Dutch stuff imported by the supermarket chains but at least I can eat it with a clear conscience.

Incidentally, the calf is called Bambi, for obvious reasons. But please, no tasteless jokes about 'you've seen the movie, now eat the burger.'

Whether your flock is thirty or three hundred, you have to watch over them with biblical assiduity. The trouble is that the weather in Cumbria is rarely biblical, except if you count the bit about Noah and the flood.

Double Trouble at Lambing Time

Traditionally, Spring is the time of year when shepherds up and down the land have been questioning their sanity and seriously considering applying for less arduous jobs such as perhaps, Chancellor of the Exchequer or Chairman of ICI. For Spring is lambing time.

City dwellers might see lambing as a time to celebrate the joy of the seasons and the miracle of birth. Personally, I see lambing as a time when I get very little sleep and what I do get is, I can assure you, not induced by counting anything of the woolly variety. A large gin does the trick rather better.

I confess to indolence this year. I moved the ewes on to the back field which, with any sort of luck ought to mean that the first round of shepherding could be done from the bedroom window with the pair of binoculars I normally use for watching what's going on in the back straight at Carlisle racecourse. Crafty, heh?

Needless to say, this ploy was a dismal failure. For one thing, two or three of the old girls refused to enter into the spirit of the thing. They skulked behind the barn where I could not see them even by performing some fairly elaborate contortions so I had to do a quick sprint out of the back door and up the barn steps to investigate their predicament. Or just watch them smirking, anyway.

For a first offence, I let them off with a caution but those who reoffended will be put through the dipper twice by way of revenge. As for the recidivists – they have been spray painted with their names. Not their number. We do not have numbers at Rowfoot. We are a little more personal than that. The other sheep regard the paintees as deplorably uncool. Well, wouldn't you feel silly with 'Ethelberta' sprayed on your bum in bright green letters?

The first to lamb did so as I was leaving for Penrith. Not to buy anything trivial such as food, you understand. Not human food anyway. I was off to stock up on Bob's Mix which is sustaining just about everything on the place at present – sheep, calf, horses – I can tell you. It looks and smells so good I am going to give it a go myself with a dollop of Jersey ice cream.

The ewe started prowling up and down the fence at about 6am. She did not look happy. You may contend that it is unusual to see a sheep in a state of delirium but this one looked noticeably unhappy even for a sheep. She sat down. She got up again. She sat down and wriggled about a bit. Agitated. I kept surveillance all morning mostly scampering up and down the stairs and peering through the bins. Also, it was raining – that special cats, dogs and several other varieties of domestic pet sort of rain. It would be though, wouldn't it, at lambing time? What self-respecting ewe lambs on a sunny day when just by hanging on a bit she can lamb in a decent downpour? Up and down, up and down, all morning the ewe and I.

By 4pm not a lot had happened except for the ewe having worn a path by the dyke but I was out of Bob's Mix and there was nothing for it but to set off for Penrith. As I turned the corner in the car I saw the feet of a lamb appearing. Anchors on, into reverse. Dash in to the house, change clothes, pull on waterproofs, grab crook and dive across the field. Twin lambs, up and drinking. Talk about blink and you miss it.

As has become the usual practice, I brought the new family into the warmth and comfort of a shed. By the time 24 hours had elapsed I had sheep in every building. And it was still raining.

If you were on the road next day and spied a figure draped in an oversized mackintosh (gents, fashionable – at least, it was fashionable in 1963) and wearing a Snoopy bobble hat, carrying what appeared to be a rag doll in each hand and pursued by a bleating ewe, I can now confirm that it was not an alien from the Planet Zog but me, moving sheep. I had changed clothes four times in one day and was running out of dry things to wear. I was about to start on the Armani and Chanel (I jest, I jest, when did you last meet a peasant who could afford much more than C&A – Coats and 'Ats – best offerings?). I have one of those hideous things which hangs over the Rayburn and dries clothes efficiently and for free. Like everything, it has its drawbacks not least of which is that any curious visitor has only to cast their eyes upwards to find out what colour knickers I wear. At lambing time I find myself completely unbothered by such considerations.

Another lambed late evening, just after I'd settled down with a G&T and two garlic sticks. It had been a stressful day and the normal ratio of G to T was probably a mite inverted so it was an eccentric path I weaved as I manoeuvred lambs and ewe towards the steading. The ewe kept shooting me reproachful glances, as if she adjudged me a completely unsuitable custodian for her precious new babies.

The next morning I peered out into an early dawn marred by a force eight gale and bouncing hailstones. There was a ewe on the hill with a lifeless heap either side of her. Pausing not even to dress properly – I won't go into details but suffice to say that it was a good thing there was no immediate prospect of being run over by a bus – and tore out into the inhospitable world. She saw me coming, got up, shook herself and wandered off into the arctic morning. The two heaps remained motionless. Why? Because they were heaps of horse shit, that's why.

A few days later, I was talking to a friend who farms up in the fells. My lambing had been hindered by bad weather; his had been catastrophic because of unseasonal blizzards and incessant, torrential, cold rain. Good and dedicated shepherd that he is, he was finding the level of losses hard to bear.

'If only,' he lamented, 'I could pretend that all the dead ones were live ones, I'd be able to afford a family holiday.' At least mine wasn't quite that bad.

Back home, I glanced out of the window. Several lambs were charging up and down joyously, others were sitting contentedly with their mothers. Funny, the horrors of lambing time seem to have dimmed a bit. I think I still enjoy it, but I'm not sure why. I'll have to see if I can work that one out next year.

Travel broadens the mind. And it makes you think. In 1994 we went to China, a land where agriculture was still labour intensive and where only Gentleman farmers had any sort of mechanisation – and that was a rotavator. Real toffs had ride-on rotavators and in spite of travelling extensively at harvest time we saw just one solitary hulk of antediluvian metal which may, or may not have been, an early combine harvester. All of this reawakened our respect for our Massey 135 no end.

Chinese Whispers

The prospect of a holiday induces strange and profound behavioural problems in this particular peasant. It is all to do with guilt I suppose. I mean, peasants aren't really entitled to any relaxation or enjoyment are they? Would I really have creosoted practically every gate on the place or tidied the muck heap had I stayed put for the next three weeks? I think not, because I clearly remember having overlooked both jobs last year. So what made me wield the brush with such messianic vigour? Answers on a postcard please.

Anyhow, with everything sprayed, stripped and creosoted (including the dogs) I felt justified in going on holiday. Holiday is a term I use loosely, since our tour of China made the Long March look like a Sunday afternoon perambulation around Ullswater, so frenetic was the pace.

China was an experience, not a holiday. I shall spare you the details of Chinese loos – let us just say that a Good Loo Guide to China would be an extremely slim volume indeed, nor shall I elaborate on the joys of internal air travel within China which is only for the truly intrepid explorer, steely of nerve and seriously keen on

Tuc biscuits. Let me explain. As you sit there squashed into an airline seat designed for a Chinaman – and a short Chinaman at that – expecting a beer and a sandwich (Chinese beer is actually rather good, not a patch on our home grown Jennings, but an amusing quaffable little number nevertheless), a stewardess hurls a pack – a family pack – of Tuc biscuits into your lap and disappears for the rest of the flight. That's it, in-flight catering, Chinese style.

Needless to say, it was rural life and agriculture which fascinated me most. It is all hands-on stuff, the only discernible power coming in the none too elegant shape of a water buffalo. But after a week or so I was suffering my customary withdrawal symptoms and I was very grateful to see anything remotely bovine, even if my girls would be deeply insulted if they thought that the pulchritudinously-challenged water buffalo reminded me in any way of them.

The other aspect of Chinese rural life pertinent to us Cumbrians was their method of fishing. Yes, they use good old nets and rods and reels of course. They also use cormorant. It's a spiffing wheeze, using cormorants. You tie a little necklace round the cormorant's neck which looks very fetching indeed and allows the bird to snack on small fry whilst ensuring that it has to surrender anything rather more dinner plate sized. Cormorants are great, but I can't see it catching on in a big way on the River Derwent.

And, as on any of our travels, there appeared the usual token Barrovian, proving conclusively the existence of a little known Law, closely related to those of Murphy and Sod, which decrees that if you go on a long haul holiday in the company of a Barrovian, sooner or later another of the species will pop up. I first became aware of this phenomenon on honeymoon in Tunisia where we met a rugby playing Barrovian called Len Stone. Then, some years later in Alaska – yes, Alaska – a chap sidled up to me outside our cabin on board ship and said: 'I see your cases are from Cumbria.'

Doubtless being a bright sort of chap – Barrovians are, you know – he deduced that the cases' owners enjoyed the same privileged provenance. He proceeded to wax lyrical about the joys of Walney on a Sunday afternoon. So, when my husband, looking very smug, emerged from the bar on board Chairman Mao's old tub, halfway up the Yangtze and uttered the introduction: 'This is Ken,' I knew what was coming next. Ken was from Barrow – he was bound to be.

Meanwhile, back at the ranch the cows were grazing peacefully, the sheep had probably not even noticed I was not around since they are not particular about the identity of the human bearing buckets so long as the buckets appear. The view from the hill behind the house across the valley grew ever more lush, more wonderful in our absence.

When we got home it was time for Rajah, our retired Lancashire Police horse, to celebrate his 30th birthday. How did he celebrate, I hear you ask? Being Rajah, who is unaware that most horses slow up a bit at 29 and a half, with a bucket of carrots, a roll, a squeal, a buck and a cacophonous breaking of wind, that's how.

The collie dogs seemed pleased enough to see us though they might have been just relieved to find that my threats had turned out to be empty ones. Before leaving, I had explained that the Chinese regarded dog as a delicacy and added that if I found any decent recipes while I was out there, their own futures were by no means assured. It was a cruel joke I know.

Predictably, behind the door was a veritable mountain of paper which if reconstituted would have accounted for at least half a rainforest. Leaflets, circulars and mail shots all exhorting us to purchase their products, everything from the offerings of Semen World – we are talking cattle here, just in case you were wondering – to the delights of a short break in the 'cosmopolitan kaleidoscope that is Hong Kong.' (Been there, done the booze cruise, got the hangover.)

I'm just about back in something of a routine and psyching myself up for the list of summer jobs – cleaning the muckspreader (I'm looking forward to that one), repainting the calf pens and creosoting the solitary gate which escaped my attention before the holiday.

I reflect on the trip to China when I'm sitting down with a cuppa, having been out for a ride and finished the mucking out. This strikes me as the most appropriate time since the Chinese popularised tea drinking, and invented both the foot stirrup and the wheelbarrow. My excellent little guide book assured me that the wheelbarrow first appeared in China in the 3rd century and that it took a thousand years to reach Europe.

Not the fastest things on earth, are they, wheelbarrows?

I began to understand why the Chinese hadn't been seduced into mechanisation. Machinery is fine when it is working but the trouble is when it doesn't. As someone once moaned when his combine packed up two weeks into harvesting: 'It's perfectly all right the other ten months of the year, it's just July and August it gets temperamental.' I still don't know if he was joking.

Where There's Muck

I have a perfectly reasonable excuse for only just having finished cleaning the muckspreader and repainting the calf pens. The lawn mower packed up. When? At the height of the grass growing season of course. Help was at hand, because I have a pal who is good with things mechanical. I phoned him and left a message with his cat – he has an answering machine with a message along the lines of 'There's only the cat in at the moment. Leave your message and the cat will have a pencil and paper ready.'

The mower departed Rowfoot at about the same time we went on holiday. When we got back, it hadn't. Several phone calls later – by which time I was developing quite a meaningful relationship with the cat – it reappeared but not before the garden looked like a jungle.

Our house is built into the hill so we have an eye level garden and the grass was so long that visibility from every window was severely impaired. When this problem began to afflict the upstairs windows immediate action was clearly called for. I thought of ringing the Army and seeing if they would like to rent the garden for manoeuvres – that would be a first in terms of farm diversification, now wouldn't it?

As soon as we got the mower back the monsoon which we had left behind in the Far East turned up in Ainstable creating another obstacle to my horticultural ambitions. To be honest my idea of a nice garden is half an acre of concrete and two hanging baskets but that would be letting the side down. It is all tidy now, absolutely triffidless. I think we'll designate it a 'wild-flower meadow' next year, which will obviate any need to mow anything. Ever.

So, on to the muckspreader. Or to be more accurate, into the muckspreader because when muckspreaders were designed the chap with the pencil and the graph paper neglected to consider the need for their cleaning out.

Picture the scene. The sun is beating down. The air is thick with the aroma of new mown hay and you're getting a tan to rival anything on the Costa Fortune. The warmth intensifies the gentle odours emanating from the interior, if you get my drift. If you don't, stand downwind a little. Then you are standing inside the beast, gouging off the detritus of the winter months with an undersized wall-paper scraper quite unequal to the task. The next bit is to hose it out. Remarkably, the hose is coil-free today. Great. You spray away merrily thinking that all is right with the world until you become aware of a previously undis-covered leak in your left welly. You can, at this point, safely assume that it is not your day save for the fact that the sun is beating down etc., etc. Next you find that the bung in the bottom is stuck fast. Many expletives and a grazed thumb later, you free it. In gratitude it disgorges filthy, smelly, dark brown water, as you crouch (unwisely) underneath. You climb back in, bearing no grudge because after all, the sun is beating down and all that.

You take up your brush. Most of its hairs have fallen out. Charitably, you refrain from drawing unkind paral-lels with one or two residents of the parish and you smear thick gluey used sump oil on its inner surface because this is the stuff that reaches parts of the spreader which other liquids do not reach. Not even a well-known brand of lager.

By now, you stink to high heaven, you look as if you have had a run-in with a north sea oil platform and you have to decide how best to prepare the cheesecakes for the parish bop without poisoning the entire population.

You leap head first into a shower, scrape the black gunge from your two remaining good fingernails (they took three weeks to grow on holiday and three days to break when you got home) and rinse the rust from your hair. No cracks about that please. And then what? You smile. You bloody well smile. Because we are, after all, jolly farmers. All the pub signs say so.

In recognition of my sterling efforts my husband bought me a present the other day. Flowers? Chocolates? Champagne? No a tub of Swarfega. Practical fellow isn't he?

Summer is a time for lovers and I fell in love this summer. The object of my affections was a pig. A posse of pigs to be precise, some very smart Saddlebacks. I have long thought that I wouldn't mind a sow or three about the place but I am not too sure about a boar. There is a way round this dilemma and it is this: Pig A.I. I asked a friend who works for the local Artificial Insemination centre about this; I think my timing could have been better because at the time I wanted to discuss pig A.I. she was preparing for her wedding but maybe it made a change from all that muppetry about bridesmaids and dresses and cakes. She gave me the full SP, even sent me the instructions for possible pig A.I. and in spite of considering myself willing to try anything at least once, I decided not to pursue this idea. Scenarios too bizarre to contemplate flashed before my eyes which then crossed abruptly. Perhaps I just have an over-active imagination but I simply could not see a pig standing still long enough for the operation to be completed satisfactorily.

Pig A.I., then, is not for me. So it is on to Plan B for the garth. A goat.

Goats are huge characters. Everyone should have at least one goat in a lifetime. I sometimes wonder what happened to Pip, mentioned in this piece. Did he marry a goat-loving model or was he doomed to be a goatless babe-magnet forever. If you're reading this, Pip . . .

The Millie Goat

It was our wedding anniversary recently. Now before you start objecting that this is a farming book not a gossip column, let me explain the connection. My anniversary present was a rather unconventional one. A goat.

She is a very nice goat and I have christened her Amelia, hence she is a Millie Goat as opposed to a Billy Goat. She came with two kids who were charming enough but the expense of constructing the twelve foot high security fence needed to curtail their mountaineering ambitions rendered keeping them too much of a financial liability.

Their first trick was to dance on the byre roof. 'Aye,' said my neighbour who has a goat of his own and is well up in the caprine field (or garth come to that) 'they'll be on the house roof next.'

He based this assumption on the fact that the byre roof leads neatly, for a goat, to the tin shed roof which in turn leads to the barn roof with a logical progression to the house roof. Now, goats on the skyline are something with which I am emotionally unequipped to deal and in any case they were taking all Millie's milk which I wanted for cheese, so they found their way into the classified ads and thence to a nice new home in Shap. If I could only find a horse able to jump in the same ratio to its own height as those kids could, I would be able to tear up my betting slips, pools coupons, Premium Bonds et al.

Millie is a most biddable creature. Her staple diet of Bob's Mix is supplemented with various tasty morsels from the kitchen such as boiled spud peelings (yum), banana skins sometimes but not always including the little stick-on labels (triple yum) and leeks which she dismissed as not-yum-at-all. Nor does she guzzle garlic or onion with any pleasure but in most respects she fills the role of domestic waste disposal unit with tremendous efficiency and enthusiasm.

She took one day to learn that she had to hop on and off her goat stand which my long suffering husband constructed from the remains of a redundant sideboard. Other component parts of the goat stand are some bits of an old piano and an old fence post which has probably been at Rowfoot for several hundred years in one guise or another before being reduced to its present humble usage. He is thinking of patenting the design so look out – there could be a real run on hitherto unfashionable G-Plan teak sideboards. Sometimes I ask my husband why he saves little bits of wood with all the assiduity of a squirrel preparing for hibernation. I shan't ask any more. I know now: it's for goat stands.

We have devised a system Millie and I. She hops on the stand and eats her breakfast and I milk her. It took her a day or so to come to terms with the business of yielding up her milk in response to a squeeze on her capacious teats, but she soon got the hang of it. It seems a fair enough deal to me. When she has finished, she chucks her food bowl on the floor. I pick it up (I know my place), then I put her on her lead and she goes out into the garth for the day if the weather is fine. From here, she can observe the world go by. She tells me that she has noticed the presence of a goat induces strange behaviour in passersby and she is at a loss to understand why seemingly intelligent adults peer at her and mockingly intone 'maaaaa.' She can only conclude that they are acting the goat. I've told her I'm not too sure either but I have seen them do it too. On balance, I consider the goat to be rather more sensible than the people in this little exchange.

Her only other reservation about humanity was clear when she met Roy. Now, Roy has a beard. Not a beard which could, at any stretch of the imagination, be described as goatee, nanny-goat or in any other way intruding into Millie's preserve but a beard nonetheless. She cocked her head on one side in the quizzical way that goats do and scrutinized him closely. Then she rolled her eyes heavenwards. A goat with attitude our Millie. It could only happen at Rowfoot.

I am making some goat cheeses and so far they are pretty good. I have a couple of small hard cheeses ripening in the dairy. Another, a semi-pressed peppered one has been shared with friends who have, you will be glad to hear, lived to tell the tale.

People fall into two distinct categories where goats are concerned. They are either committed goat lovers or they are goat haters. Indifference is not an option. I have had a soft spot for goats since my early teens when I lived in London. We were at number six and at number four was a guy called Pip, a frustrated country dweller if ever there was one. To mitigate his incarceration in suburbia he kept half a dozen chickens and a goat which he milked each morning while she stood on the dustbin. Pip may have lacked the sophistication of a goat stand but he had charisma. He was tall, dark and not so much handsome as drop dead gorgeous, something which I was just beginning to notice at that age. When he had milked the goat – a lovely Nubian – he changed into city slicker gear and roared off for the square mile in a purple TR6 which was, at that time, the sexiest car a man could drive. Unsurprisingly, he was pursued by a succession of leggy blondes, all of whom left, some within 24 hours, having made the acquaintance of the goat. Their spectacular failure to usurp the goat in Pip's affections had the effect of firstly, endearing the goat to me and secondly making me realise that even if you are a leggy blonde there are some things with which it is unwise to compete and a goat is top of that list.

Then there are the goat-hating brigade. 'Don't get a goat,' they tell you, 'they wreck trees, they're destructive.' Yes, exactly. Destruction, in the garth is precisely Millie's mission. It's in her job description to trample, then eat anything she can find. Elders grow like triffids in the garth, weeds spread apace and the good goat will keep on top of all of this for you, using it for fuel to manufacture milk from which you can fashion goat cheeses of staggering quality. Peppered if you like. Whilst cheese is a by-product of this process, the same cannot be said of any other land clearance system most of which are notable for their complete absence of cheese yielding characteristics. Millie has not yet fine tuned things to the point of providing her cheeses ready wrapped but give her time and I am confident she'll make some progress in that direction. So yes, I am a convert to the ranks of goat people.

Now that the anniversary present is a fully paid up member of the family, I am looking forward (that is to say planning for, as opposed to celebrating) my 40th birthday. I have taken the precaution of arranging to absent myself from the parish for the occasion because people play awful tricks round here on 40th birthdays. The only thing to commend staying in Ainstable would perhaps have been a party attended by my co-celebrants on the date, Billy Connolly, Ian Botham and the Marquis of Blandford. Just think what a knees up that would have been.

Calving time again. Winter again. There is a definite rhythm of life with livestock. And indeed, the downside of living with animals is that at some point, you lose them. We had come to regard Rajah – a negroid monster of a horse – as pretty well immortal, which he almost was, at the age of 31. He enjoyed a second, if not a third childhood with us here, discovering the joys of grass both to eat and to gallop on. In spite of – or perhaps because of – his life of strict discipline until he came to Rowfoot, it was absolutely impossible to stop him once he was in full flight.

Rodeo Time at Rowfoot

Three live calves. Three proud mothers. And oh, so little trouble. Sounds like a fairy story doesn't it? The calves are not just live but very much kicking as the condition of my left leg testifies. It closely resembles the experimental palette of a demented neo-pyschedelic painter with absolutely no sense of colour co-ordination, courtesy of a glancing blow by the Little White Bull. Delicate hues of purple, yellow and a sort of indeterminate but indubitably vile, green. Not attractive at all – I'll keep it well hidden don't worry – jeans and long skirts for the next week at least.

First to calve was scatty old Yelper who had ambitions to get in the Guinness Book of Records. She was the first cow in 13 years of bovine births at Rowfoot to calve on her correct due date. As the weather had been so mild I had not housed the cows although I was well into the nocturnal prowling sessions to check on progress. At midnight she looked perfectly happy – more than could be said for yours truly but no matter. At dawn, I drew the curtains and spied a wriggling white blob. Just as long as it's wriggling. It's when there is no wriggling that you have to panic. By the time I had the wellies and attendant clobber on the calf was up, drinking and almost licked dry. Yelper looked murderous, pawing the ground like a deranged fighting bull and shaking her head wildly at me in frantic cowy mime of 'you are welcome to come no closer if we are to stay on speaking terms.' Well, look on the bright side. At least she was showing no signs of rejecting the newborn.

The weather was now looking a bit grim so Yelper and her little heifer came into the nursery shed for a night or two. I watched her anxiously for signs of milk fever, old cows being particularly susceptible, Jerseys being particularly susceptible and old Jerseys just about guaranteed to succumb. The sudden demand on the newly calved cow's system for vast amounts of calcium is the cause. The trick is to get in before the cow goes 'down' which is to say they get down all right but they can't get up again. In some cases they never rise, ergo loss of cow. Getting in is easier said than done since administration of supplementary calcium by injection involves a needle about three and a half inches long and a temperamental piece of tubing called a flutter valve and a bottle of calcium suspended in glucose solution. Three vital bits of equipment but only two hands.

It is then a case of 'first catch your cow.' And old cows have seen it all before and have scant desire to be caught and then stabbed with a whopping great needle no matter how much you tell them it is for their own good. Signs of the onset of milk fever are loss of appetite, cold lugs, grinding teeth. Though come to think of it, my mum frequently grinds her teeth and I have never plunged a long needle into her backside. Yet.

Yelper continued to eat voraciously but at the first grind of teeth I grabbed the bottle. Three circuits of the shed and a bruised foot later I had her securely winched to the post in the corner, eyes rolling and emitting Neanderthal grunts. Yelper didn't take it too well either as I recall. I fed in the liquid calcium. Better safe than sorry.

Lady, due ten days later than Yelper, calved the next morning similarly with no difficulty. Maybe she felt left out. Another heifer, smaller for being on the early side and with joints not quite straight but alive and perfectly fit. Lady had the good sense not to grind her teeth and escaped the needle. Caroline had her little bull the following week again with no assistance, no drama and no milk fever. Superstitiously I kept a bottle of calcium in the kitchen at room temperature like a good Claret, for the next three weeks. Several Clarets came and went but the other bottle stayed; once the danger felt truly past it went back into the cold darkness of the medicine chest.

Of course, this halcyon interlude of trouble free livestock keeping was bound to come to an end and it did so abruptly when Lady kicked me. Now if Yelper kicks you, you just duck and dive a bit 'arry and consider it quite routine. But if Lady kicks there is a reason. Examination revealed that she had stood on one of her teats and not just stood on it but made a right royal mess of it, shearing it off about half way down. The danger here was that it was impossible to relieve that quarter of milk and if we didn't look out mastitis would set in. The vet had a bright idea – a drainage plug.

This was no ordinary plumbing job as became obvious when he extracted from his kit a thing shaped like a miniature corkscrew designed to engender immediate and comprehensive panic in a female of any species.

'Oh,' he said airily, 'don't worry, it's blunt at the end . . .'

I went green and thought about flaking out. Contrariwise, Lady looked like a pet pussycat on Prozac so doped was she. Just as well, I thought. She was duly plugged.

The cold snap had the effect of inspiring delinquency in the calves. They rushed about with their tails held aloft like masts, the little bull had a head banging session with one of the dustbins in the yard and when they weren't careering madly about they curled up all together in a multi-coloured heap. But there is cold and cold. A bit of frost never hurt anyone – a few thermal layers extra and you can cope with it. Usually.

But then there are what I call Two Kettles and a Pickaxe Mornings. This is not a follow-up to Four Weddings and a Funeral but my term of reference for those mornings when the temperature has plummeted to such an extent that the ice on the troughs can only be broken by clouting it firmly with a pickaxe and two kettles of water are needed to defrost the ice in the feeder pipes to the cows' drinkers. And that's when you find that titchy little hole in your gloves, isn't it?

FOOTNOTE: We have lost our beloved retired police horse Rajah, in his 31st year. He worked for 18 years in Lancashire Constabulary seeing service outside law courts – he was one of the few horses capable of ascending the steps to those in Lancaster – at football matches and on picket lines. He had only four days off due to illness in his entire career and there can be few people who can lay claim to an employment record like that. Rajah did not do 'sickies.' We had him for his last eight years during which time he enjoyed exploring the bridleways and forestry before retiring completely and living with a younger woman in the shape of the chestnut filly called Ziggy. He taught her a few manners; she kept him youthful. A good deal for both of them.

Rowfoot will not be the same without his big wise white face. We shall miss him.

Horses, eh? Just very sophisticated machines for turning expens-
ive hay and Bob's Mix into something which makes your roses
grow. If you're lucky. Still, they have always, as my father once
pointed out, kept me off the streets and perfume manufacturers
in business. I still haven't grown out of horses, though everyone
said I would.

The Pale Rider

Now that the days are longer I rather miss the rum old ritual of evening shepherding in the half light. There was something chimerical about the ill-defined faces of the sheep, eyes glinting eerily in the lengthening shadows, distant car headlamps snaking homewards along the lanes and Saddleback sinking into the darkness beyond. I can't, however, say that I shall miss fighting my way up the hill, bale on back and bucket in hand into the teeth of a force eight gale which hasn't paused for breath since it left the Arctic.

Like many folk working with livestock my recreation time simply involves livestock of a different type – horses – and with my home bred youngster I am looking forward to summer with a keen sense of anticipation. Riding in the sunshine instead of wading through clart will be a real pleasure. (OK, I am a Sagitarrian – didn't you know they are incurable optimists?)

I thought of sending the bills she has incurred recently to the vet since it was he who was responsible for concentrating my mind on the matter of keeping her. It could be argued that the vet in question was ever so slightly biased since it was he who attended Ziggy's arrival in the world back in 1990 but I prefer to believe that his motives were of the best sort.

Paul had come to do the annual round of injections for flu, tetanus and what have you and asked conversationally: 'What are you going to do with her?'

'She's for sale,' I responded, having drafted the advertisement that morning.

It ran: 'Anglo Arab filly, 4 years, Sire successful dual purpose racehorse, dam ridden show champion, competed successfully show jumping cross country long distance, dressage.' In the interests of protecting my reputation I omitted the bit about 'in spite of frequent and serious pilot error.' 'Sure to race or show.'

Paul looked at me in the way that people do when they think you are one pork pie short of a picnic.

'Why?' he asked simply.

'She didn't make the height I wanted.'

'How big did you expect her to be,' he asked his voice rising slightly with incredulity.

Then I looked at Ziggy. Properly. For the first time in perhaps two years. Ever felt silly? Wanted the ground to open up and swallow you? Yup, that was me.

She had, you see, been an impressive foal, a smart enough yearling, a mildly disappointing two year old and by the time she was three I had dismissed this breeding lark as a mug's game. She seemed to have stopped growing altogether and looked like an orange pony. So I planned to sell her. Someone out there must like orange ponies. But like her mother before her, she had had a late spurt of growth while I wasn't paying attention and now she was, when I looked properly, just as big as I had hoped she would be from the start – about 15.2 hands. I needed to confirm it so I measured her – first readings were taken using a blunt pencil, a length of slightly bent curtain rail and a length of broken fencing but a pukka measuring stick did, in fact confirm the findings of this suspect array of equipment. She had also become a very nice 'person' and I had never really wanted to part with her anyway in spite of the attraction of cash flowing in rather than out, itself a novel situation for anything to do with horses.

So, Ziggy's future was suddenly clear. Things happened quickly, then; she travelled, courtesy of neighbourly generosity, in five star luxury which I told her she need not get used to, to take up residence with Susan Bowman in Penrith. And so it came to pass that Susan broke Ziggy in. Now she's home and as they say 'riding out quietly,' alongside her mum. A kind friend turns up in all weathers so that Kareima can accompany her daughter on exercise, ostensibly to give her confidence but mostly, we are finding that it is Ziggy who insists on being the trailblazer, her dislike of being headed, even at a walk, confirming my belief that she would have made a smashing racehorse.

Although she has days when she is akin to Vesuvius on four legs and I make threatening allusions to the relationship between her future and a well-known brand of dog food, for the most part she is sensible, well adjusted and wonderful fun. Her appetite for work is insatiable; she adores exploring locally, sticky-beaking into other people's fields and exchanging neighing pleasantries with new acquaintances.

For those of you unfamiliar with the joys of being on horseback in motoring terms riding Ziggy is the equivalent of driving a Porsche. Only she goes marginally faster. Kareima, meanwhile, seems to regard her daughter rather as most parents regard their offspring – vicarious pride at times mingled with absolute horror.

Me, I hung up my competitive boots two years ago, sold the lorry, vowed never again to risk life, not to mention limb, doing daft things over fences at speed. Too old, you see, now that I've hit the big 40, but briefly the prospect of show jumping again tempted me. Common sense prevailed when I recall the number of obstacles I had negotiated in the past with my eyes wide shut, and reciting the Lord's Prayer. I dismissed the notion.

A Bright Young Thing will have to do that bit but I shall have a go at some local shows and maybe even attempt some dressage. If ever there is a dressage competition scheduled for Runway Three at Heathrow Airport you can rest assured we will be there, Ziggy being 100% jet proof. Having been born at Rowfoot, which lies on the direct line of every RAF training sortie there is, she is completely immune to aircraft however low, however noisy. There are one or two pilots I wave to when I see them, though the precise format of the gesture is sometimes not really what a proper, civil wave ought to be.

What next for Kareima then? She will visit (a wonderfully coy euphemism for something a great deal more basic) the boy next door, Geoff and Hazel's devastatingly handsome new acquisition, Irish Mickey. The Mikardo's latest trick is to absent himself from loose schooling sessions by hopping over the 5'2" arena gate. We can safely say he's got a bit of a jump in him, then. It will be interesting to see what he produces crossed with an Arab. Its whinny ought to have a distinctive accent if nothing else – Mickey's Irish lilt blended with Kareima's dulcet Middle Eastern tones.

So, if you are travelling around the Ainstable area before the stud season and you see two sassy chestnut mares, one of which is ridden by a character sporting a fluorescent jacket bearing the legend CAUTION – YOUNG HORSE and underneath, sewn on rather badly the additional words AGEING RIDER, slow down and give us a wave.

The depressing thing about the demise of my ducks was that I was just beginning to overcome my feather phobia. Perhaps it was Auntie Flo's canary that put me off feathers for good. Auntie Flo used to let the canary out to fly round her kitchen every Saturday; on its third orbit it habitually deposited something disgusting in the butter. It would have been better for my cholesterol levels if the deviant canary had left me with a butter phobia not a feather one.

Blood, Sweat and Butter

Since we last met Baby Horse inflicted an injury upon herself which made her stable look like the set of Chain Saw Massacre III, the nocturnal activities in the parish have ranged from murder (of my ducks) to theft (of my trailer), I've churned enough butter to last until the millennium – well, Christmas anyway, and I'm now at the gate-creosoting stage of the year. Whoever said that country life was dull?

Now I am quite willing to elaborate on all these matters with the exception of the trailer fiasco because if I get started on that one I shall spontaneously combust and make a nasty mess in my office. Suffice to say that the police declined my request to meet the perpetrators. I think it was my mention of justice, garden secateurs and that nice American Mr Bobbit in the same breath that worried them.

So, back to Ziggy who came in from the field one day carefree as usual, ate her lunch as usual, munched her hay as usual. But when I went down the stable to groom her an hour or so later there was blood everywhere. Blood is like spilt milk – it expands on impact so it made a ghoulish spectacle. Ziggy was unbothered, the site of the damage a titchy little nick on her coronet band, just where the hoof joins the flesh. It is an area liberally supplied with blood hence the horrifying sight. Once washed, clean and sprayed with wound powder it gave no further trouble at all but it upscuttled my nerves no end.

My poor ducks were never intended to provide a tasty takeaway for Mr Fox. It had to be a fox because only a fox goes in for decapitation as a leisure activity. Dido had disappeared from the face of the earth, only a sad heap of feathers remaining as her epitaph but Aeneas had been abandoned, headless, on the muckheap. I know that Dido and Aeneas might seem silly names for (ex) ducks, but Donald and Daffy struck me as much too ordinary for such lovely creatures so devoted to one another. The names of a pair of Great Lovers seemed far more appropriate.

Coincidentally, that week, there was a Wildlife on One documentary about winsome little Reynard, who was projected as a lovable rogue surviving against all odds in the face of adversity and all that kind of . . . er, nonsense. I was in no frame of mind to be sympathetic to the plight of four legged bandits and only in the interests of not inflicting GBH on my bank balance (two horses and sundry other unproductive mouths to feed), I forbore to put a brick through the screen.

As to the butter, I spend much of the winter churning worthy little nuggets of the stuff and stashing them in the freezer. It is beyond my ken that anyone in possession of the majority of their faculties is unable to distinguish this solidified nectar from margarine. If your taste buds are in that bad a state there is probably only one thing to do: book them in for relining at the earliest possible opportunity. Can there really be any confusion between luscious, golden, creamy butter and the axle grease masquerading as something worthy of adorning your toast? I think not.

It's an arduous process all right, making butter but well worth the effort. First of all you milk your cow, obviously. Then you separate the milk – I do mine using a super efficient electric separator which differs from the hand operated ones of the last century only in that you no longer wind a handle furiously but simply flick a switch. It drizzles thick Jersey cream into a waiting bowl and spills out the 'skim' into a waiting bucket. Supermarkets, you may have noticed, charge an extortionate price for white watery skim partly because it is so good for you and partly because they've made all that effort extracting something on your behalf – who do they think they are, for goodness sake, oil barons? At Rowfoot, this bucket is despatched to a pig or a calf; the people here drink real milk.

The health fascists will be pleased to know, though, that I have a system. I combat the damaging effects of cholesterol with an ample intake of garlic and red wine. If one glass is good for you, then two must be twice as good. That's right, isn't it?

The cream is heat-treated in the microwave to 75 degrees Centigrade. No doubt men will interpret the next bit as typically female logic but after cooling the cream overnight it is reheated to 98 degrees Fahrenheit (see what I mean) and whipped past the point of no return in cake making terms – it goes granular and sloshes about a bit as the grains of butter separate from the buttermilk.

The cats get the buttermilk or I use it for baking. Waste not, want not and all that. The butter is then washed; I don't mean in Lux, the twin tub or something kind to your hands but just in cold water. You do this until all the buttermilk is washed out and the water stays clear. Now, tip in the salt, stir it, squeeze it, belt the living daylights out of it with a pair of Scotch Hands and tap it into nice polite little shapes, wrap in greaseproof and refrigerate or freeze it.

Why do I bother? Because it tastes sublime, that's why. Even being someone with the sort of metabolism which puts on half a stone after making eye contact with a cream bum (sorry, bun!) I would rather have one slice of toast dripping with home made butter once a week than any amount piled high with disgusting margarine.

The colour of butter reflects the changing seasons. In winter it is almost white as the cows are eating hay and 'cake' but in summer with fresh grass, it changes to fluorescent yellow. Sorry to explode that quaint old myth about buttercups but there it is: that's the truth.

During winter I churn, during summer I cogitate. Freed from the constraints of wall to wall dung bunging and undeterred by the possibility of there being a directive in the corridors of the Health Department saying that the smell of creosote is a mind-altering substance, I can indulge my only deviant passion, creosoting gates. Gives me time to cogitate, creosoting.

Around me, the rest of the village has been losing its collective head making hay. There used to be a maxim for making hay in Ainstable which went something along the lines of 'when Eddie cuts his, cut yours,' Eddie being deemed to have a direct line to the Rain Fairy. Trouble is, Eddie's retired now and consequently everyone runs about looking horribly confused. The phrase headless chicken – or possibly duck – springs to mind.

Eric brought my hay down on Saturday, so I have considerable sympathy with Guy the Gorilla's younger sister because I feel as if my wrists are somewhere around my knees having mewed over 250 bales of the stuff. By way of compensation, the sitting room and my office are suffused with the heady aroma of sweet hay permeating the chimney breast on the dividing wall between the barn and the house. Lovely.

My mum never understood the ways of the countryside. She was baffled that her only daughter should, voluntarily, live in an area with no pavements, no street lights (then) and no Marks and Spencer within walking distance. When she first visited us in Ainstable she found the silence deafening. She came to love it, but never totally gave up hope that one day I might 'get a proper job.'

It Ain't Half Hot Mum

I suppose that 1995 will go down in the annals as the Long Hot Summer. It was certainly the first summer in England to turn me ever so slightly brown although in my case it is not so much a tan more a mass of joined up freckles. Nevertheless, it was a distinct improvement on my usual complexion which bears an uncanny resemblance to the colour of uncooked pastry. During this quasi-tropical interlude I've been skinny paddling (only up to the kneecaps, I've always been shy) at Walney and donned my Panama at Skelton.

The prolonged dry spell meant that hay or silage was fed not just early but in July and August and consequently hay prices escalated alarmingly. Stories circulated of panic buying at £9 and £10 a bale in the Cotswolds which testifies to the collective insanity of our southern friends. Must be something to do with living nearer the equator than we do.

And do you remember the bottomless clarts of January and February when we thought that God had gone out and left the tap on? I clearly recall muttering darkly then that any water shortages in the summer of 1995 would require suspension of disbelief on a grand scale.

When peasants come out to play in summer in Cumbria they do so at agricultural shows the length and breadth of the county. The most worrying trend this year has been nothing to do with the livestock exhibits, it has been the sartorial preferences of the Great British Public.

Now shorts are fine for aspirant Greek gods in their twenties – I'm all in favour of that – but this year there have been legions of folk wearing them who have ended up looking to be in need of an intensive course of style therapy.

That apart, I often wonder what visitors make of our strange rituals – beauty contests for cattle, sheep and goats, our unique Cumberland and Westmorland wrestling with its own inimitable dress code and the Industrial Tent. My favourite in there is that children's class for Creature Made from Fruit and Vegetables. It is probably the nearest some under tens get to a cabbage, but boy is it good. Tortuous tubers and ridiculous rhizomes are fashioned into monsters so awful that it makes one wonder what these kids read for bedtime stories. I just wish there was an adult section really. It would be such fun to stick those vicious little toothpicks into the really crucial areas.

Perhaps the show I enjoy the most is Skelton. The 1995 attractions included all the usual things – horses jumping and pulling carriages, sheep, cows and tradestands – plus some more unusual ones, a comprehensive display of working vintage machinery, ostriches and Angora goats. For the record the Angoras looked like the result of a clandestine liaison between a poodle and a llama and the ostriches unaccountably spent a great deal of time with their beaks open.

This year my mum came too as she was holidaying with us at the time. I should first explain that my mum is unfamiliar with many of our country ways. She has been known to comment on the baffling habit farmers have of putting their gates in the muddiest bits of their fields. Whether it was just that the intense heat was addling her wits or whether she saw her chance to carve herself a place in literary history we shall never know but as I turned my back to speculate on the forthcoming National Hunt season and lament the paucity of entries in the Jersey classes (Arnold's dodgy leg was cited as the main reason for this) my mum espied that great huge tree in the middle of the main ring. And it was VERY hot. Off she went, weaving between the Limousin cows competing for honours in the ring at the time and installed herself in the shade of its boughs. Thankfully, mother's excursion escaped the eagle eye and consequently the droll observational wit of Glen Tubman whose eloquence confers upon many a Cumbrian agricultural gathering a singular quirkiness or it could have well developed into My Most Embarrassing Moment. Ever. A lot of hissing and wild gesticulating from the ringside encouraged mum to retrace her steps. I should probably be grateful that no-one pinned a rosette on her before she left, I suppose.

Agricultural shows are fertile pastures for cultivating Most Embarrassing Moments. I recall witnessing someone else's once, though meanie that I am, I took the view that it was richly deserved. There was a little golden cherub riding a little golden pony. The cherub had the mandatory red ribbons in its hair, the pony was expensively dolled-up. They were in the practice area, trotting perfect little circles around the cherub's doting but ambitious mother.

'Sit up, Jennifer. Sit UP. UP. UP . . .'

The desperation level is rising.

'Shorten the reins . . . And sit UP.'

Jennifer scowls, the pony scowls.

'Push him ON Jennifer.'

You get the picture. The cherub looked pained, then dismounted, abandoned the pony which put its pretty little head down to graze. As it walked off, the cherub turned to its mother and trilled, 'you ride the f . . . pony.'

The mother turned a most unattractive shade of puce and began mumbling apologies. I, of course, found it all hugely entertaining.

Back home, the Pest Lamb (you thought it was pet lamb, didn't you but as in Fred, the 's' is silent) has been weaned. It had its last supper – a quart of Millie Goat Milk – some weeks ago so I have resumed cheesemaking and what's more I am relieved of the hazardous business of feeding the little brute. They are cute little things while fragile and exuding vulnerability but believe me, once past that stage they can deal you a blow at the back of the knee which, if deft enough and accurate enough, can fell you. By the time they are fed once or twice a day from a bottle out in the field you need to ensure that you have a sturdy pig netting fence between you and the sad little orphan. You will never know why its mother didn't want it and do not expect any support from the father either – tups are absent parents unimpressed by all that New Man Philosophy.

So, imagine the scenario. It is THAT side, you are THIS side. The trouble is that also this side is an inquisitive Jersey cow with an inexplicable homing instinct for your nether regions. At this point you can confidently expect a jab in the bum from behind and a crisis at the front end too, as the lamb sucks so furiously at the teat that it detaches it altogether from the bottle. A goat milk shower may have been of enormous cosmetic benefit to Cleopatra but it does nothing for the tightly curled coat of a Suffolk Mule cross. Worse, the rubber teat is rapidly disappearing down the gullet of a strong healthy lamb which you risked life and limb to snatch from the jaws of certain death at 2am on a freezing 'Spring' morning.

So now you understand why I am glad to be free of this task.

I tell you, it's a jungle out there in the fields of Eden.

This was back in the days when sheep had to be pawed and pummelled by the Grader. You were totally at the mercy of the Grader; the most feared of them all was Cloggie, tall, spare and with a permanently disappointed expression on his face. I tried inscrutability, I tried charm, I tried 'feek and weeble woman' tactics with Cloggie: none made the slightest bit of difference. I think whether your sheep graded depended on whether he had got out of bed the right side or not.

Why Sheep are the Villains

Do you want the good news or the bad news first? I'll start with the bad then at least things will improve. I have lost one of my lambs. This is not 'lost' as in the Bo Peep sense of mislaid. It is 'lost' as in the Monty Python Parrot sketch – ex, late, deceased, expired, would be pushing up the daisies sort of lost. I have no idea why it chose to keel over; it was there on Sunday morning but decidedly departed by Monday afternoon. I don't know why I persevere with sheep, they are ungrateful creatures.

When we first moved to Ainstable I had had a bit to do with cows but only a passing acquaintance with sheep. So it came as a shock to see my next door neighbour driving past on his tractor towing a trailer bearing a grisly load – two ovine corpses. When I offered my sincere condolences upon his losses, he just pushed his forefinger under his cap, scratched his head and said philosophically: 'Aye, Jackie, that's the thing with sheep. First sign of illness is generally death.' And off he went.

His indifference appalled me. He had seemed such a nice man. Now, of course, fourteen years of sheep keeping later I sympathise entirely with him. And yes, he is a thoroughly nice man. It's the sheep who are the villains of the piece.

I do my level best to thwart the sheep's propensity for dying unexpectedly, though with varying degrees of success. I become extremely suspicious if one of them is loitering in splendid isolation and staring absently into the middle distance instead of doing something useful like grazing, drinking or walking about.

It is particularly sinister if they are under a hedge as they are probably seeking a choice spot from which to depart this terrestrial life. If they lurk too long, I creep up on them to inspect them more closely. If I can catch the sheep I may as well give up there and then. It is obviously too far gone. And any sheep with the temerity to sleep in the daylight hours can expect a rude awakening; many a Rowfoot sheep has nearly been given instant heart failure by the rapid advance of welly on grass.

But every now and then one surprises me with its tenacity.

Many years ago we had some Swaledales attacked by creature or creatures unknown. Our old friend Mr Fox perhaps, or maybe even a brace of pet dogs having turned temporarily feral. It is not unknown. Of the several savaged, the very worst was a scrawny little lamb whose injuries were horrible. We lifted him gently into the pick-up and brought him down to the garth. We made him as comfortable as we could and gave him food and drink, more in the spirit of last rites than any genuine sense of optimism. He was too weak to stand, too damaged to bother. I did not actually dig his grave in front of his eyes but I didn't hold out much hope – and I had the spade handy.

But the miserable little git just hung on in there.

Every day, I expected to find him dead, every day he

astounded me by hanging on to life. And increasingly looking slightly less inclined to meet his Maker. One memorable day, slowly and bravely, he got to his cloven hooves and thereafter improved rapidly. In spite of having lost his fleece – a side effect of the penicillin injections he'd had – he thrived, eventually grading in the Mart. In those halcyon days, we even got the subsidy on him. So, sometimes when you least expect it, it does work out OK.

Whilst not wishing to dwell on the subject, even a sheep wot has shuffled off its mortal coil can bring a crinkle to the lips of the incurably cheerful. In France on holiday this year, the farm's prize ram pegged out. It hadn't looked at all well, so its demise hardly shocked me or put me off my croissant. But poor old Monsieur, mindful of the delicate sensibilities of Les Anglais, rushed out and covered the corpse with a bright green tarpaulin weighted down at each corner. Far more in-yer-face than any discreetly dead sheep, the heap now looked like nothing more than a battalion-sized portion of lime Dream Topping. When Monsieur, suitably depressed, announced that the elderly mouton was indeed as mort as could be, I told him it felt just like home . . .

In France you can't simply dig a hole and bury your dead (sheep) either. The municipal truck has to collect the cadaver and it has to be certified accordingly. I should have thought that the circumstantial evidence of it having remained inert for the duration of a weekend, exhibited a noticeable lack of appetite, not to mention breath would have been ample indication that it was a gonner but apparently not.

I thought it better not to investigate exactly why this system had become necessary lest I discovered something which might affect my fondness for roast lambs, but I guess that at least French peasants do not need to do O Level Gravedigging.

And where's the Good News, I hear you ask. Here: Kareima is pregnant. We know for sure because she had a scan. Fantastic things, scanners. Once upon a time you could count on the fingers of one hand how many of these things were available to vets in the UK; nowadays the vet turns up with a machine like a word processor crossed with a Polaroid camera in his car, you provide the necessary technical back up (two straw bales on which to balance the thing and a three pin plug) and away you go. With any sort of luck a photo of a black hole in a snowstorm pops out. For 'black hole' read foal. So, if ever in idle conversation I whip out the first Baby Picture and show it to you, the required response is: 'Oh, isn't he/she (not "it" please) gorgeous. Just like Mother.' Then we'll all be happy.

Of course, getting them in foal is quite a ticklish process, dependent upon such variables as timing, fertility and management. For a couple of weeks, Kareima and I ran the gauntlet of homeward bound commuters as we walked up to Dolphaz Stud each evening, evening being the best time to do the deed. Many a wag called out of a lowered car window witticisms along the lines of: 'I thought you were meant to ride them not take them for walks,' but we soldiered on.

Kareima just looked bored to tears when led up to Irish Mick's stable and often engaged in a bit of furniture kicking to emphasise her lack of desire to get up to anything naughty. Then we'd go home.

The threat of a needle-wielding vet with a hormone injection was all the encouragement she needed to bring her into season and she was covered with the minimum of romantic niceties. Stallions are not keen on foreplay, apparently. A fair bit of breath-holding went on during the next fortnight but she didn't come back in season. To be doubly sure we did a scan and all seems well.

I have never been in the business of counting chickens, foals or anything else so I have lots of things crossed, making everyday life even more of a challenge than usual. I look forward to Spring with a mixture of dread and excitement.

Sheep are funny things, by turns daft and intelligent, maternal and neglectful, worried and resigned. Bit like humans I suppose. At lambing time both species are fraying at the edges. Give them a week or so and they all calm down noticeably. And hindsight always wears rose coloured specs, doesn't it?

The Lamb's Tale

As the lambing season looms large on the horizon I've been reflecting on how things went last year. Thankfully, the work force was augmented in the shape of my old friend Kathy who came to stay. You will note that I do not use the word 'holiday' since heroically she turned out every single morning shepherding with me insisting she was having a good time. Mad? Course she is – but you surely wouldn't expect any friend of mine to be other than just a little eccentric would you?

Sets of twins here and there, between the Champion Hurdle and the Gold Cup, without incident. Spindly little lambs, wet and revolting, quickly metamorphose into sturdy playful creatures at two or three days old after a few drinks and a bit of sunshine. Like you and me on holiday, I guess.

It was all going swimmingly until the second Tuesday morning when the alarm wreaked its usual havoc on the early morning stillness and my semi-comatose husband said something helpful about there being a blizzard outside. Working on the principle that the worse the weather, the greater the likelihood of a population explosion, we dragged ourselves from under the duvet into a cold, bleak dawn.

I saw the twins first. They looked fine, unworried by

Mother Nature's fit of ill-humour; they were up, drinking and dry. Great. Then I saw the other old girl. With triplets. As a precautionary measure the twins and their mum came into a pen and off we went to retrieve the triplets. The ewe was happy enough and two of the lambs were on their feet but the third looked a dismal excuse for a sheep-to-be. It was – not surprisingly – shivering; its plight had failed to stimulate its mother's maternal instinct and she appeared ignorant of its existence. She was persuaded into a shed with the largest of the lambs following enthusiastically and the medium sized job more grudgingly in pursuit. I brought up the rear of this touching family picture clutching the slimy legs of the smallest. It could not stand on its own let alone walk.

Like generations before, she was rubbed dry with an old towel, wrapped and propped up in front of the Rayburn: every farmer's Intensive Care Unit. I generally reckon that they are recovering when they are well enough to stand and pee on the carpet. The nice salesman assured me when we bought the carpet that it was indestructible. Fourteen years of piddling lambs later, I'm beginning to believe that he wasn't exaggerating. Anyhow, there she sat for much of the day, getting colostrum at regular intervals through a tiny teat – I always take a bit of colostrum from the cows just after calving and freeze it for just this purpose. Encouragingly, she showed a strong desire to suck. And to stand. After crumpling pathetically on several attempts, eventually her funny little stick-like legs supported her bodyweight as she staggered drunkenly about. Rallying nicely. I transferred her to the recovery ward – a cardboard box by the fire bedded with old copies of *The Financial Times* to lend a certain gravitas to the proceedings.

By the time Small (her brothers having been christened, with consummate originality, Medium and Large) was restored to her mother, the ewe affected total amnesia regarding the third offspring. I made one or two absolutely pointless attempts to persuade her to accept Small. Most notable was an effort to restrain the ewe by standing astride her and gripping her fleece fore and aft whilst Kathy plugged Small onto a teat. The ewe took violent exception to this and set off at high speed round the shed with me clamped to her, fighting to stay on my feet, the lanolin in the fleece having bonded itself securely to my jeans. Judging by the peals of ghoulish laughter coming from Kathy's corner, it was quite a sight. You can go off people you know.

But ewe and lamb had been apart too long. I gave up. And accepted that I was lumbered with Small, as a pet lamb. The trouble is that when you have a lamb going spare, so does everyone else. So Small became a lamb with an identity crisis. She was looked after by a human, fed goat's milk, slept in a trough under the watchful gaze of two farm cats by night and had two daft dogs for friends. It would, of course, be impossible to round her up using a dog – she thought they were playmates not bosses. But she thrived, a testament to the restorative powers of an old Rayburn and a disparate army of other influences.

The day after Small's arrival, I sensed something else wrong when only two of the previous year's pet lambs arrived at the trough for food. There ought to have been three and they were all destined for the freezer. 'Where's the other store?' I asked Kathy. 'Down there on the bank. And it's got a lamb's head sticking out of its rear end . . .'

How could this be? When I had put the tup in the previous autumn I had sought advice from the local rural playboy, shepherd and acknowledged expert on the sex life of sheep whether it would be safe to leave the youngsters in with the ewes. 'No, no, quite safe,' he had told me with such confidence and a sly wink, 'they're too young to have such a notion . . .' Not this one, mate.

We did two circuits of the field during which time I reflected that firstly I should not be expected to keep up with a sheep since they are blessed with twice as many legs as I am and secondly that this was a less than ideal way to introduce the lamb to its new home. Reinforcements were necessary and finally, we struggled to deliver the lamb. I was adamant that it was dead by now but the rest of the birthing party had more faith than I. Sure enough, a handsome jet black lamb was safely delivered. The hogg looked first at me, then at the lamb; abject horror gave way to cautious investigation and she ventured up to him. She licked him experimentally. And thought a bit. She did it again, then again and as his breathing steadied and he tried to stand, she became keener. There's a happy ending to this tale: she is an adoring parent, he is a fine lamb. Aaah.

The last of the girls had resisted the temptations of the youthful tup first time round and was some time behind all the others lambing. Just as I was getting grumpy and bemoaning the likelihood of her having triplets, of which I had had my fill for one year – she lambed. Twins. Someone on high's way of restoring my equilibrium, I suppose.

And Kathy departed southwards for a decent rest. And that was it really, lambing over for another year.

Wonder what this season holds in store?

I loathe bureaucracy, partly because I always have to look up its spelling in the dictionary. But even so, I don't think when we moved here we ever envisaged quite how lengthy and complex the tangle with red tape would become. Still, as work colleagues go, give me a cow instead of a human any time.

My Rut and I Like It

Change, they say, is the only constant. In my previous incarnation my morning routine was to burrow down the London tube warren and pop up again like a sort of urban rabbit. I took the lift to my office on the 18th floor – odd, in hindsight, as I get vertigo much above Ladies Fashions these days. The crooks my work involved were more readily associated with sack emblazoned with the legend 'swag' and criminal records than any with Lakeland agricultural shows and nice carved horn handles.

A starker contrast of lifestyle is difficult to imagine.

Then, I was barely aware of the changing seasons. Now I am reassured by the certainty with which winter turns to spring and then into summer. I know for sure that the January weather will make brass monkeys stay by their own hearth if they are blessed with a modicum of good sense and that by March the first I shall be muttering about taking off for the Languedoc if a) this bloody weather persists and b) I win the Lottery. It has to be said that the former is rather more likely to come to pass than the latter since I understand one has to buy a ticket to stand even a remote chance of winning. I can look forward to lambing in April and May when it will all be over. Some might say my life is predictable now; predictability suits me just fine.

It's my rut and I like it.

Back in that other life – and you may find this difficult to believe – I held down a responsible job. I ran for trains in three inch heels – my balance is precarious in anything much above an elasticated plimsoll these days – I carried a spare pair of stockings (yes, stockings) in my handbag for emergencies – a small ladder was inconvenient, an entire fire escape a major emergency – and on my desk I had three trays, 'in', 'out' and 'GOK'.

What, I hear you ask is GOK? It's for all the things you don't put in 'in' or 'out' – it's the God Only Knows tray. As you might guess, it was always rather fuller than the other two. But it was, my mother said, a 'proper job.'

I had to look smart at work: suits, ladderless stockings and so on but here no-one gives a hoot what I wear. My current ensemble consists of a bright pink acrylic sweater with a crop of potatoes in the elbows, an emerald green and white stripy shirt (which I think Sara bought in the Hackney Branch of Save the Cats for ooh, as much as 50p), jeans which fly at half mast but no-one knows because they stick into my wellies, and odd gloves. I would not have got away with crimes against fashion like this in 1977 but here, the goat is colour blind and the dogs don't care.

It is all wonderfully liberating. I can even sing along to the radio in spite of having a singing voice which oscillates between the noise a polecat might make in the advanced stages of strangulation and a formula one racing car with a transmission defect. So appalling is my singing that I mime the National Anthem in public.

It's not just me, though, life was different fourteen years ago when we first came to Ainstable. The first week we moved in we bought the local paper. The front page carried a sorry little saga about an escaped ferret. This excited a warm glow of security – after all, it could hardly be the crime capital of Europe if that sort of thing was making headlines.

Farming was different too. We thought of the Min of Ag and Fish, not MAFF, of the Common Market not the EEC and CAP was something you wore on your head. Underneath your cap, now you get headaches trying to fill out IACS forms which hadn't even been dreamt up in the early eighties. Quotas were non-existent and BSE unknown – cows were never mad, they just got a little bit cross at times. It was all a deal simpler before we all became utterly obsessed with reducing our vocabulary to a range of acronyms.

The breeds of cattle have changed over the past fourteen years too but the one thing which hasn't is the undiminished pleasure I feel every day regardless of weather, when I draw back the curtains and look out on our own little piece of England, of Eden. The day that sight fails to lift my spirits, then I'll be off to the Languedoc.

This year's heifer is called Minnie. Why? It was the cat we heard of called Dennis because he is a menace that gave us the idea. Minnie, you see, is a minx.

Her piece de resistance was to jump up on to the muck-heap (vintage 1995). The purpose of the heap is to ensure that we have ample organic fertiliser enabling us to cultivate the biggest, juiciest, tastiest tomatoes in Ainstable. In case you had ever been deluded into thinking that 'organic' meant something wholesome and good let me tell you that, in truth all it means is that the tomatoes have been grown on poo and Other Rotted Matter. The details of ORM (another acronym for you) I shall not expand upon in case you are eating your tea while reading this. It would not be conducive to good digestion. Still, remember that the next time you are in your friendly local superstore selecting your good, wholesome 'organic' produce . . .

But I digress – we left Minnie on the muckheap didn't we? From there she cast me a devilish glance and hopped over the fence, nipped into the yard, slalomed between the tractor and the car, turned sharp right and headed for Ainstable Centre Ville under the ensign of a smartly raised tail.

Yes, I know I should have had the gates shut. I hissed at Lady: 'Go on, moo, please moo.' Desolate at seeing her offspring disappearing into the great grey yonder, she mooed obligingly and Minnie slunk back into the yard.

I shut the gates then.

Collie dogs are an integral feature of any Cumbrian farm. The only other breeds which appeal to me are Irish Setters and Lurchers, the former because they are engagingly bonkers and the latter because they always have a rakish, guilty look about them. The last time we visited our local animal rescue centre, I was especially taken by a lovely brindle lurcher bitch but my husband just glowered and said 'no, don't even think about it.' Fair enoughski, I suppose, since we already have two work-shy dogs to feed . . .

Gyp and Tess

G&T to their friends

If I asked you to picture the archetypal Cumbrian farmer I suspect that you would describe a gentleman not in the first flush of youth, craggy of stature and with a face bearing more lines than a contour map of Striding Edge, rather than a forty-something female with gold earrings and a keen interest in fourteenth century Hindustani glassblowing. Or something equally obscure.

But whatever your imaginary farmer in terms of age, gender, vital statistics and leisure pursuits there is one thing beyond doubt. He or she will have a collie dog at their feet because collie dogs and Cumbrian farmers are bound together by ties nearly as ancient as the landscape they inhabit.

I like collie dogs. I like all dogs come to that having only spent a few months of my life dogless. And the more I get to know people, the more I like my dogs. I heartily endorse a sign that hung in one of our local pubs and went something like: 'You ask if you can bring your dog to stay here. A dog has never left without paying its bill, a dog has never set light to the bedclothes with a cigarette and a dog has never nicked the towels. Yes, you can bring your dog and if he'll vouch for you, you can come too.'

And echoing that position, we decided even before we started on the conversion of the old byre into holiday accommodation that dogs would be welcome. Our canine visitors have included the matchless Moss, a rescue collie who sleeps upside down (it looks very peculiar and most uncomfortable), Duchess the greyhound who sat on the rug in front of the fire with her slender paws crossed elegantly for much of the week and when the magic word 'walkies' was mentioned, she would glance up as if to say 'why, exactly?', a matching pair of Dandy Dinmonts, a brace of Yorkies, several Springers – mad as gum trees full of galahs, Springers – Sophie a docile black Labrador with a coat of silk, Red the Staffie and his pal Vito the German Shepherd. When Red's and Vito's owners first telephoned and described their dogs, I envisaged a couple in black leather, with rings through most orifices. Not so – they wore hardly any leather at all, had no visible metal ornamentation and very prosaically turned out to be RSPCA volunteers with soft hearts who ended up homing the dogs no-one else wanted. Quite disappointing really.

Collie dogs like my own Gyp and Tess derive their name from rural Gaelic, 'collie' being something useful. In the case of my two this is stretching things, and the 'border' bit has more to do with their borderline usefulness than anything to do with their origins. G&T are eleven now and a very fine pair of dogs indeed, though not so fine, I fear, that my husband would ever contest for their custody.

Their arrival in this world was not without its own complications. On the way home from a half term holiday in Wales, their mother decided that she was done with pregnancy and when I phoned on their return to check on

Bonnie's progress, I received an unexpected, if commendably calm response: 'Oh, she's fine and so are the pups . . .' Pups? What pups? They had not been due for another week. 'She had six on the M6 and two at Charnock Richard.' Can you imagine it? Best not, really.

As the litter was so large, G&T had supplementary rations, some provided by our Jersey cows and some by the Bank House farm cat who had lost her own litter of kittens; consequently, G&T have never been too sure whether they are cats or dogs. At least they are absolutely sure they are not sheep though Tess spends quite a bit of time wondering what sheep are really *for* and neither she nor her sister can be bothered to summon up the energy to work them much less worry them.

Like all collies G&T are highly accomplished thieves and Tess herself presently faces a charge of larceny of a cheese and pickle sandwich. Her case comes up soon at Penrith Magistrates Court. The trouble with stealing is that it requires so much effort and Tess, Miss Indolence 1992, would rather curl up on a lap and watch television. Worryingly, she knows the theme music to *Coronation Street* (indeed, she is still mourning the demise of the collie dog that used to run up the street in the credits. Axed, now, that dog, but try telling TV Tess that), and *Animal Hospital* which she watches as people do *Casualty*, *ER* and any other programmes with large-scale blood spillage, like Rugby League. She especially likes Channel 4 Racing and runs up to the screen licking the winners. This is why we always have blobs of dog-snot on the telly and why our television weather map always indicates a dull front somewhere about Birmingham.

Unfortunately, Tess was in the wrong queue when God was giving the ears out and she got a coyote's set by mistake. They are unnecessarily huge ears and I fear she will never grow into them. Gyp is, quite frankly, lucky to have ears at all. Collies are apt to get little fur balls behind their ears; they are horrid so I snip them out. I nipped Gyp's tangle and she squealed. A couple of days later, I found a little scab on the denuded ear – to my utter horror, I had nearly lopped the poor dog's lug off. If I was Gyp, I wouldn't have come anywhere near me again but she is a very forgiving dog indeed and still craves my attention.

Oddly, Gyp likes children. With remarkable fortitude, she tolerates infants sticking their fingers up her nose, in her ears, in her eyes. This is all okay, I explain to the doting parents, as long as little Eglantyne or Egbert doesn't try the same trick with a Rottweiler tethered outside Sainsbury's next Saturday or the dear child could find itself minus a few digits.

G&T's sanctuary is their bed, the Doghouse, handily situated in a cosy corner of the kitchen twixt Rayburn and gas stove. Any child found trespassing on this territory can end up minus digits too although this is because I have frozen them off with a glacial stare rather than because a rabid hound has bitten them. A dog is entitled to some peace, after all.

Our first collie Julie, like G&T, was a shameless tea leaf. She stole chilli con carne with disastrous results: I'll just say 'H-Block Protest' and leave you to work the rest out for yourself. She was a bit of a bargain-basement dog setting us back just 15 guineas, probably because she had quite clear ideas about work: she didn't do work. Work was a four letter word to Julie.

But good collie dogs – proper working collie dogs – can change hands for sums of money which you and I would associate with a decent chunk of a round the world cruise. But when one considers what they can save in terms of man hours, worn out welly soles and frayed tempers they are worth their weight in gold.

I know a chap who had paid a sum of money for a dog

reflecting exactly that – its weight in bullion. He was most put out when his newly acquired pedigree chum refused to have anything to do with him much less take orders from him. Notwithstanding its substantial transfer fee it mutinied and was returned to its previous master where it continued to work happily and diligently until the end of the days.

Can't see transfers like that catching on in the Premier League can you?

Later, when we acquired the Manx sheep I put up a sign on the footpath, attempting to explain their origins and why they didn't look exactly like all the other sheep in the area. I added that if anyone was interested in finding out more, they were welcome to come and have a chat. And here's a thing – not one soul ever has, thus denying me the opportunity to bang the drum about our wonderful old breeds. Perhaps they knew what was in store . . .

Take a Walk on the Wild Side

A footpath crosses the field behind our house. This has some very definite drawbacks but it can also be great fun especially on a weekend when the racing is principally like Norfolk – very flat, and the cricket is going through a terminally depressing patch. You can watch an altogether new sport. What's more, it's live and it's called Walker Worrying. Ziggy has got it down to an art form.

Take the other week. I should really have been pounding the word processor but I was looking out of the window instead. It is a good thing that my desk does not face the window or I would never get anything done at all. I can watch the garden and the fields beyond for hours and never get in the least bit bored with the unfolding drama – lambs darting up and down the dykes, cattle arguing about the calf-sitting rota, the magnolia making valiant, if fruitless attempts to flower. It makes Shakespeare's plays look thin on plot by comparison.

Three walkers trudged into view, clad in cagouls and clutching plastic-covered maps. Not local then. They were heading for the stile. As usual, the horses were on the back pasture and Ziggy thought she had better go and greet her visitors. She dashed across at a pace one normally associates with winners of the Derby. Unfortunately, the prospect of her negotiating an effective emergency stop in time to avoid a serious accident is not something which people who don't know her have much confidence in and although I couldn't see the walkers' facial expressions, I suspect that the leader was gripped by a feeling of deep insecurity in the bowel region for he broke into a smart trot and hopped over the stile.

The two women appeared to have succumbed to Lot's Wife Syndrome and were motionless. Top of Ziggy's list of acceptable tit-bits are Polo Mints – oh, just be warned if you come walking on the Rowfoot path, she does not like the sugar-free variety and will spit them out if you offer her those instead of the real thing. I do not know how she can tell the difference but she can.

She snuffled about in the pocket region of the twin pillars of salt – an apple would go down nicely or a carrot, failing polo mints, perhaps. No? Nothing? A crust of bread for a starving horse? Anyone used to horses would have told her to buzz off but these ladies were not used to them. I could tell that much from the window. And the chap, of course, was safely the other side of the stile, having abandoned the womenfolk in a spirit of chivalry not dead, just resting. The thing with Ziggy is that she feels duty-bound to meet, greet and vet visitors – it's her field after all – before allowing them rite of passage.

She gave up eventually and the ladies clambered over the nice regulation stile no doubt relieved to be free of the attentions of half a ton of horseflesh. They thought it was all over but they had reckoned without the intervention of the sheep. The sheep called Small (you may recall that

Small suffers from a rare personality disorder as a result of her disturbed childhood) has acquired the dog-like habit of jumping up and licking people. She licked this group, every one of them.

So, by the time most walkers shut the last gate on Rowfoot land they are a) speedier of gait than they were when they opened the first one and b) confused and convinced that all the animals on the holding are completely barmy. They're right, of course.

Some walkers are friendlier than others. Once I was accosted by an irate yellow anorak in the farm yard. 'You,' accused the apprentice ayatollah, jabbing an angry finger in my direction and glowering at me from beneath eyebrows which closely resembled twin gerbils having a head-to-head confrontation, 'are breaking the law.'

I resisted the temptation to fling my fork load of muck at her, instead smiling sweetly and responding, 'really?' with Australian inflexion (I'd just been watching Neighbours).

'You have got a bull in that field. And you shouldn't have a bull in a field with a footpath going through it.' She looked formidable but there are limits to the things I will tolerate for a quiet life.

'I haven't got a bull.'

'Yes, you have.'

At this point, I did not want to get into a yes-you-have-no-I-haven't routine because I gave that up when I left Mixed Infants but I could not let such a palpably daft suggestion pass unchallenged. Partly as I'm terrified of bulls anyway. She put the finger away and added 'it's got horns.'

Well now, there's a thing.

'Did you, by any chance, inspect its undercarriage?' I enquired, cringing inwardly at the very idea of Lady being mistaken for a bull. Or, worse, referred to as an 'it.'

'If it's got horns then it's a bull,' persisted the anorak. Clearly she knew something I didn't because I had always believed that if 'it' had an udder then there was every probability 'it' was 'she' horns or no horns.

Gently, I explained that Lady being an Island bred cow had a full set of horns. I could have explained that they tether them by their horns on Jersey but I just couldn't be bothered. The anorak withdrew her tirade and apologised. But I have a nasty feeling she still had her doubts.

Of course, not all folk are so stupid. You've heard of a stuck pig. Well, how does a stuck sheep grab you?

Two ramblers appeared at the gate. The orange cagoul said that there was a sheep stuck in the hedge. I tried to establish what sort of a sheep and where, precisely, it was stuck. The blue cagoul took this as their starter for ten and said that it was three trees up from the boundary fence, East/North East of the stile. Smashing. But on the bonus question – what sort of a sheep – they were less sure. Sort of sheep shaped, sheep coloured was the best they could muster. Maybe it was bigger than the rest. Oh, and it had a black face . . . I didn't hang around for a photofit – that was George's prize tup, on loan to us. I could have given Linford a start and still beaten him up the hill.

The tup was strangely still but upright. Not dead then. Instead of grazing he was locked into the hedge leering lasciviously at the ewes in the next field who were admittedly, younger, more nubile than my lot. The intelligence quotient of the average Suffolk ram being what it is, he didn't simply move his great black skull downstream a bit releasing the vice like grip of the hedge but remained there in a frustrated voyeuristic trance. I flung a volley of unpleasant names in his direction, none of which bothered him in the slightest and released him. He gave a low grunt, curled his top lip at me insultingly and mooched off to his ageing harem.

Those walkers did me a big favour. Not so the varmints that came a mushrooming and left all the gates open, getting my heifers mixed up with Tom's bullocks. If I had ever got my hands on them I would be penning this clad in a little suit with arrows all over it.

Christmas. Things outside go on completely irrespective of the indoor festivities. All the same jobs have to be done and they take just as long as they do any other day of the year. Some might suggest they take rather longer . . . I can't imagine why.

Merry Christmas

What do you think of when someone says they are going to the country for Christmas? Things in mangers? Cattle lowing outside and humans raising glasses inside? Family all gathered round a vast log fire nibbling sausages on sticks (you know the sort, those which taste like condoms filled with Bisto-flavoured factory waste) and the tree in the corner already shedding its needles like so much dandruff. Yes, goodwill is all around. Or is that just an elaborate illusion?

If I am totally honest, I have to confess that I do not look forward to Christmas with unalloyed glee. For a start by the time I have been banged up with my nearest and dearest for three and a half days, the only time I would look forward to seeing them again would be as they drowned in a vat of gently simmering, double-strength Listerine. There is usually a loose ankle-biter amongst the throng. Don't get me wrong. I like children – they are particularly good gently braised in garlic butter with a side dish of roasted endive.

But at Christmas the cocktail of small child, hot pans and raised temper (mine) is potentially a lethal one, only compounded by visitors from the Great Metropolis. They, of course, arrive exhausted. Pressure, you see, stressed out. Poor darlings. Peasants do not fall prey to stress because their lifestyle is idyllic – all that fresh air and exercise means that they are in tune with the cosmos. So says my old schoolfriend, Moonbeam, anyway.

Those escaping the urban rat race regard BSE as a little local difficulty, the real problems are foreign exchange rates, negative equity and the erratic supplies of basil and garlic extra virgin olive oil at the local deli. They do not seem to comprehend that on Christmas Day, the pig farmer has just the same amount of piggy poo to contend with as he does on the other 364 days a year, the dairy farmer has found that signs saying 'no milk today. Thank you' have little effect on Daisy and her cohorts and that the shepherd has a hole of the same dimensions as always to dig if one of his flock decides to shuffle off into the ovine after life, Christmas or no Christmas.

The visitors collectively flop on to your sofa, clutching a medicinal glass each while you don waterproofs and several layers for it is time to shepherd the ewes on the top pasture. When you return, hopeful that something might have been peeled, chopped or stuffed in your absence, you shed the Scott of the Antarctic disguise and risk certain chilblains by placing your thighs against the welcome warmth of the Rayburn. It is then incumbent upon you to ask whether their glasses need recharging. They do. Manners demand that you smile while you do it. Goodwill, you decide, is not an elastic commodity. Yours is about to ping.

On top of this, last year, everything froze. The house froze. The exit pipe from the loo froze. The water troughs froze. When they did go out, the visitors themselves froze. Somebody, somewhere, chirruped 'ho, ho, ho' at that point. Can't think who.

As there were nine of us in the house, the first priority was to free the loo pipe. A ladder was propped up against the side of the house and several hot kettles administered. Nothing much happened. Then I had a Bright Idea. I aired it with caution since most of my BIs are met with snorts of derision and in truth are rarely workable. But as we were all getting a bit desperate in more ways than one, we gave it a try. A hairdryer and a very long extension lead were applied and lo! – the junction pipe gurgled happily and an orderly queue formed at the top of the stairs. I was less successful with the troughs outside. There is a theory that if you clout a frozen trough with a pick axe the ice will shatter. Not so. In my case, the ice broke the pick axe. The metal bit flew into orbit (I believe it is, at this very moment, circling Jupiter) and the handle remained resolutely in my hand. The ice remained, well, icy. It was about four inches thick and increasing daily in plunging temperatures. A gentleman in Armathwaite recorded minus 22 (!) on his greenhouse thermometer though the next day things warmed up to a Caribbean minus 19. So it wasn't all bad.

In between doing battle with troughs and in-lamb ewes there was the festive food to be sorted out. I reckon that we spend all year saving up for Christmas, six weeks preparing for it, all day cooking it and then a maximum of half an hour eating it. If Christmas Day lunch was a resounding success, Boxing Day was little short of a disaster area. I had intended feeding the starving masses pork but by mistake took a gammon out of the freezer. A home-cured gammon. Which we had not intended to share. They loved it of course and ate the lot. As a result of another faux pas they guzzled horse carrots with the gammon. Some you win, some you lose. Still, no one started to neigh so no lasting harm was done. I didn't bother to own up.

They all departed eventually back to their world of computers and mobile phones, Golf GTIs and aromatherapists (quite what a metropolitan aromawhatsit would make of the niff coming from the muck spreader, though, I can't think. Toxic, probably. Life threateningly so.) Two elected to let the train take the strain. It was then that I learned about stress, as I offered up silent prayers: 'Please God, let the trains run.' And in an irreligious attempt at bribery: 'If you do, I promise never to swear at the dogs again.' Stress? Blind panic, more like. The points on the line were frozen. Judging by the time it took to thaw them, that too was being done by a fellow with a hairdryer and a very long extension lead . . .

Back home, I leaned on a gate and looked across the valley. The gate gave a bit and I made a mental note to do something violent with a six inch nail, a course of action which fixes most things. I looked at the branches of the trees silhouetted against an ice blue sky; thin wintry rays of sun catching crystals of ice in the snow glistening like so many miniature stars in a frosty firmament. I thought of our visitors' lives and I thought of mine and I envied them not one jot. Golf GTIs and frozen troughs notwithstanding.

The spirit of Christmas is probably summed up best by my favourite present from last year: a little stone gargoyle who sits by the light at the back door, surreptitiously picking his nose and grinning, looking for all the world as if he is thoroughly enjoying the experience.

Merry Christmas one and all.

Once it dawned that humans became putty in her paws when she smiled, she did it increasingly often, revealing some truly startling teeth. With only a little encouragement, the smile turned into a full lip-curling beam, and a little black spot high up on her very pink gums emerged. The full performance involved wagging her tail furiously and inhaling noisily, all of which heightened the terrifying spectacle of the smiling dog.

Julie the Smiling Dog

Julie was a daft name for a sheepdog. It lacks the crisp monosyllabic barkability of Floss, Meg, Nell or just about any other human name hijacked for canine use. You just cannot imagine a shepherd on a windy hillside in Wasdale shouting 'Julie' somehow. Yet one did. His name was Tom Purdham and up in Wasdale they called him the Sheepdog Man. Officially the Biggest Liar in the World, he appeared later on Russell Harty's televisual tour of Britain, and do you know what? Julie, the sheepdog who never showed the slightest interest in anything on television however animated, awoke from her snooze, ran towards the screen and then ran round the back of it to see if she could find her erstwhile master. She looked a bit baffled for a while and then she went back to sleep.

At the start we thought we wanted two puppies, not one adolescent bitch. And just a word of warning here, if you are ever deluded enough to want to share your life with a dog – any dog – do not, ever, get two puppies together. The combined intellect of two diminutive canines fuses into one devastating weapon of mass destruction. Of furniture, carpets and newly planted bulbs mostly. They scheme, they plot, they connive, they egg one another on. You do not want them until they are three, when they will renounce evil and grow on you, rather like a wart. But then, back in August 1978, that is what I thought I needed although the search was hardly uppermost in our minds as we idled a day away at Muncaster Country Fair. Apart from the socking great Simmental bull on display (he may have been the centrepiece of a Guess the Weight competition, or that may just be my memory playing tricks), dogs of various sorts dominate my recollections of that day. First, there was the hound – trail, fox or I know not what. It loped elegantly around the show ring with its handler, then paused and thoughtfully cocked one of its rangy hind legs against that of a heavily trousered gentleman wearing a flat 'at and leaning on a fence post, deep in discussion with another who might have been his clone. From all the pipe sucking, head shaking and air prodding going on, they were doing a pretty fair job of setting the world to rights. It took a moment for both liquid and realisation to soak in. He looked about, in the way that only an Englishman can, wondering whether any vestige of decorum might be salvaged from the wreckage of his embarrassment, before scowling and stalking off.

Then there was the collie dog, which appeared by our sides as we ate a very fine pie (made, no doubt, by a member of a local Women's Institute) in the lee of the tent. We shared, naturally. Well, you do, with collie dogs don't you? He disappeared temporarily, playing havoc with his digestion, and materialised again minutes later. This sequence was repeated several times before we came to the end of our pies, got up and wandered round to the other side of the tent. And yes, there was another couple, sitting, eating, sharing – a pie if I'm not mistaken . . . The moral of this tale is: Never Trust a Collie Dog, Especially if he Claims to be Starving.

It was shortly after that that we saw the sign scrawled in the front window of a van 'collie bitch, 13 months, for sale' with a phone number. We found the nearest call box, dialled the number and reached Tom at Bengarth, his farm in the shadow of the mighty Wasdale screes. Tom had just got home from a wedding: it was not a long or especially coherent conversation. He invited us to come round. Now would be fine.

Julie was a canny dog and 'absolutely nae use at all. Yon dog's gone on Trade Union rates,' he explained. Seeking early retirement from Sheepdoggery, Julie had developed a persuasive exit strategy from employment: she ran precisely as far as she was whistled or shouted and then stopped. If a sheep lingered even two yards ahead, Julie, a right jobsworth of a dog, took the view that she had not been instructed to gather it, and as far as she was concerned, it could stay where it was. Up in the wild hills clad in bracken and strewn with hidy-places amidst the rocky outcrops, it was easy to see why Tom wanted – needed – dogs with a little more initiative. 'She'd do obedience,' he conjectured, though whether in a spirit of career advice or derision, it was difficult to divine, 'and she'll make a grand pet.'

Julie scampered about frantically: an engaging, friendly dog looking for an easier life. Call us bonkers, but we thought we had better find out if she liked us: a trial walk was arranged. She shot into the passenger well of the car, just as she had been trained to do in Tom's slightly smellier van and gazed up at me with an expression which said – no screamed 'you are the one I have waited for all my life.' She must have thought I was a right Muppet. She was right, though. Collie dogs usually are. Naturally, I fell for it.

Julie stood quietly for her blue baler twine lead to be affixed and trotted meekly by my side as if we had been together for ever. At carefully judged intervals she looked up at me beguilingly: that Open University course in Human Psychology was beginning to reap rich dividends. Then we came to the wooden bridge crossing the Ratty, the Ravenglass Railway. She stopped. She looked at the slatted bridge and declined to set paw on it. She quivered and affected a look of abject terror. She quivered again, just for emphasis. We picked her up and carried her across.

We returned to Bengarth and relayed the tale of Julie and the slatted bridge. Tom said that it was very odd indeed because Julie had never bothered about slatted bridges before, actually she was a bit of a whiz at slatted bridges. Julie looked the other way. But we were smitten and paid the asking price of fifteen guineas for Julie – 'only deal in Guineas, me,' Tom said, and she came back with us a week later, to suburban Surrey.

The first problem was her sleeping quarters. We had not strictly intended buying a dog on holiday and we hadn't had time to buy a dog bed. Never mind. She could sleep under the kitchen table on a blanket for a night. There was a rather nice jumper, drying flat on the kitchen table and conveniently for Julie that table was about the same height as the kennel – a converted guard's van with a raised platform to keep the dogs out of the draught – she had left behind in Wasdale. So she hopped up and snuggled up on the good blue sweater. Then she produced her master stroke. She smiled. She curled back her top lip as far as it would go, displaying a set of molars indicating that she was an eighty fags a day dog and breathed noisily through her teeth. Jumper or no jumper, no-one had the heart to dislodge her and there she stayed. Visitors thought it a tad strange of course, a dog on the kitchen table.

Eventually Julie transferred to a doggy bean bag. She

was a bridesmaid at a wedding sporting a huge satin bow the same colour as the other bridesmaids' dresses and she won a prize, a first prize at that, at Lowther Country Fair for the Dog With the Waggiest Tail. Tom would have cringed with embarrassment but it proved that he was absolutely right about Julie: she did make a grand pet.

It was all a very far cry from being a Sheepdog (Failed) in Wasdale.

Julie paid not the slightest attention to One Man And His Dog on television but condescended to amuse the locals by learning to jump park benches at the click of the fingers. She never slept in a kennel again, instead travelling with us wherever we went. She could, had she overcome the tiresome business of being unable to write, have produced a bestseller entitled 'A Hotel Guide For The Well-Travelled Dog' recommending the Palace at Buxton for its tasty biscuits but warning of the dangers of revolving doors if your tail is long and hairy, commending the service at Down Hall (tins opened on request and little chocolates in your favourite flavour supplied at night) and thanking the nice staff at the Forest and Vale for their attentive service, oh, and the extra biscuits.

Every Tuesday, Julie and I journeyed across London for lunch with my mother. With (almost) unfailing regularity, mother indulged Julie's passion for Cadbury's Dairy Milk and presented her with a bar every Tuesday. On the fateful singular occasion my poor mother forgot Julie's chocolate, instead of pressing her nose on the back window as we departed down Glebe Road, Julie stared resolutely forward, giving my mortified parent not a backward glance. She could be very cruel.

Yes, after a couple of years, she had us very well trained indeed.

When any of us hit rock bottom, for whatever reason, Julie would become a self-appointed minder. She sensed when she was needed and never once let any of us down even if such extended periods of attendance must have tested her bladder to its limits.

She was a dog in several million.

Julie, like us, was glad to leave the south. Many of her favourite parks and walks were earmarked for something mysteriously called 'development' though the mention of Ockham, a beautiful swathe of forest and commonland now depressingly criss-crossed by the M25 and the M3 caused her to prick up her ears for years after our departure. And anyway, by the time we moved we had acquired a Land Rover, from which a dog gets a far better view. She was thrilled. Though, naturally, she drew the line at chasing any of the Cheviots or going out in the rain. She thought about opening a Charm School but frankly, couldn't be bothered. Standards had to be maintained, after all.

Julie had two litters of puppies and proved a first class mother; from the first we kept Nell who had odd eyes, one blue and one brown and from the second the tricolour Bess. Both were very like their mother except in one respect: they both wanted to work. Nell would often sneak off and round up the sheep, just for something to do. Our sheep were underwhelmed by this trick because they could find themselves parked in the corner of the field for hours on end if Nell were not missed and retrieved.

Nell was no respecter of authority, particularly the misplaced sort. A southern friend of mine had the grievous misfortune to marry the first recipient of extensive charisma bypass surgery. He thought he knew everything there was to know about dogs and worse still, he was a pompous git.

'Collies,' he boomed at Nell, 'are renowned for obedience. SIT!' She stood. 'SIT!' Nell looked at him with her funny boss-eyes and walked off pausing briefly to look over her shoulder at him and break wind with devastating olfactory results.

We lost Nell to cancer at the lamentably early age of ten months. Julie herself succumbed to cancer at the age of thirteen and we lost Bess to the disease a year later. She was just seven.

They are buried together at home.

We were, after all, only a couple of amateurs and occasionally giving the professionals a bit of a trouncing was immensely gratifying. Since the age of nine I had dreamed of winning a prize in the main arena at the National Arab show. That it took me until I was 39 to achieve it only intensified my pride.

Kareima the Wonder Horse

You buy a horse with your head and your cheque book. Well, that's what I've always told people anyway. Falling in love with half a ton of unpredictable horseflesh is not just irrational, it can inflict terminal injuries on your bank balance. Taking your own advice is, though, a rather different matter.

It was the day West Tip won the Grand National. We were half way to Wales to look at this well bred chestnut Arab mare and pulled over into a lay-by to listen to the race. We were about to set off again, when my husband asked idly – indeed as if it hadn't actually crossed his mind before – 'how much do they want for this horse anyway?' It did not seem a good moment to tell him that I knew that she was on a Bloodstock Agent's books for in excess of £6,000. So I didn't. I have absolutely no idea of what I did say, but it assuredly was not that and we carried on, to Cardigan.

We had a whisky with Susan – the sun must have been over the yardarm or something – and she took us along to the stables. I took one look at Kareima and I knew I had to have her. I did not base this on any sustainable logic and I could hardly blame a small Scotch for addling my decision-making abilities. All I can say in my own defence is that she had eyes you could drown in and I knew – I just knew, all right – it was meant to be. There was something else too, something utterly beguiling, indefinable and elusive about her. She had style. And magic.

Her maternal half-brother was World Champion Arab Racehorse, Ibn Al Khalif and her father Silver Flame was a fairytale horse, a pure white fusion of power and elegance. The ethereal Silver Flame didn't trot, he floated, never touching the ground. It soon became apparent that his daughter did the same, though it would take time to persuade her to do it to order instead of when she felt like it. But once that was accomplished, she could bring houses down and entire showgrounds to a standstill. She was special, fantastic, flamboyant. And she knew it, luxuriated in it, revelled in it.

If Kareima's sheer speed and fire were exhilarating she was even more exciting when she was naughty. She was capable of the most furious paddies – mostly, these involved water. Out around the lanes she would flatly refuse to negotiate even a trickle of water across a road, much less a puddle. Once and only once, I was misguided enough to think that it was worth arguing with her about walking through water. This had the unintended result of a local farmer enjoying half an hour of unscheduled entertainment. He put his feet up on the tractor wheel, unwrapped his sandwiches and settled down to watch the cabaret. I lost, obviously. The maddening thing was that out on a long distance ride, or jumping cross country, Kareima was first into, through or over water with a 'come on chaps, follow me' spirit. But a puddle at Common House? I would still be there now if I hadn't given in.

We were, I suppose, a couple of mad redheads together. And somehow, I believed that we could do anything. We certainly had a crack at most things. In the early days, we did long distance rides, capitalising on her extraordinary stamina and toughness. She loved it.

Almost as soon as she came to Rowfoot, I realised that I needed help in educating her. So, every Tuesday, we had a lesson together at Blackdyke just outside Carlisle with John Collier. John understood us. He knew instinctively just how far he could push her temper and my nerve. We worked on the flat and over fences, growing in confidence, cementing our partnership.

Our first season on the show circuit was, however, an unmitigated disaster. Kareima hated travelling. She hated being away from home, refused to eat and shook in agitation. It was not a happy time. Mostly, I was incandescent with frustration. I had a horse with incredible ability and an equal disinclination to use it. Then we started jumping and strangely and slowly, we reached an accommodation. She would endure the sheer mind numbing boredom of standing quietly in a show line-up one weekend as long as we could go off jumping somewhere the next.

Occasionally, though, the needle on her tolerance bucket still strayed into the red zone. Then she lost it. Kareima especially disliked one judge on the circuit because she had rough hands. And Kareima, by then, expected to be asked nicely not told or bullied. She had – under sufferance – carted this lady a couple of circuits of a show field once, earlier in the season; to be required to do it again was just too much. She looked sideways at me – not difficult for a horse whose eyes are on the side of its head – twitched her expressive ears and delivered one almighty buck. More of a handstand really. Its devastating power sent the judge into a graceful arc and on to the grass. We did not win that class. Christine Bayman was different – Kareima wore an expression of benign co-operation whenever the quiet and tactful Mrs Bayman rode her.

So, when the Scottish Group of the Arab Horse Society appointed Mrs Bayman to officiate at their annual Inverness Show, the long trip seemed worthwhile. It was one of those rare, golden days when nothing at all went wrong. Kareima won the Ridden Mares, then, relatively unusually beat the stallions and geldings for the Ridden Pure Bred Arab title, going on to be Reserve Supreme of the show. Just for good measure, she also won the Working Hunters and came second in the show jumping. We brought our considerable booty back home to Rowfoot. It was the only time in my life I have actively enjoyed cleaning silverware.

About this time, the late Paolo Gucci instituted a show jumping championship at the National Arab Show, putting up the prizes, rosettes and indeed, jumps in his own Millfield Stud's livery. On our first foray, Kareima hardly touched a twig all weekend and came home dripping with ribbons, a feat she repeated with bells on the following year moving up a grade in the classes.

Given the deficit in my own technical ability, we had no right whatsoever to be among the prizewinners as often as we were. But as the saying goes there is no secret so close as that between a man (or a woman) and his horse. Some very special magic flows from that trust. And magic puts wings on dreams, makes them fly, soar into the realms of the utterly impossible.

We were, after all, only a couple of amateurs and occasionally giving the professionals a bit of a trouncing was immensely gratifying. Since the age of nine I had dreamed of winning a prize in the main arena at the National Arab show. That it took me until I was 39 to achieve it only intensified my pride and incidentally, Susan's too, for she continued to take a vicarious pleasure in basking in 'her' Kareima's reflected glory.

On a wing and a prayer, the saying goes. In my case it

was on a wondrous horse and with several prayers, not just the one.

The championships and rosettes and cups were great, of course. But they were as nothing compared with those summer mornings when we sneaked off in the cool of first light, galloping the full length of the back lane up to Longdales and clattered, ear-splittingly, through the hamlet as kettles boiled and coffee mugs filled. Or as we walked through the crepuscular stillness of the forest, waiting, hoping that we might meet a deer or catch a hawk on the wing. Those were the memorable times. The times I miss. And just seeing her – chiselled ears, bright and trusting eyes, looking over her box door, mistress of all she surveyed.

Kareima continued to queen it at Rowfoot long after she retired. During her last three years, I battled with her losing condition as she lost her teeth. Arthritis, mud fever and a failing immune system led us to the inevitable conclusion in December 2000. It was a dreadful time, made easier only by the compassion and kindness of our vet Paul May who had known Kareima much of her life.

She was the horse of a lifetime. I was immensely privileged to have her.

Lady prowled about her new fields by day, munching and sitting and thinking secret cowy thoughts and returned to the maternity unit – a stone shed deep with straw – by night. She regarded me, her new keeper, with some amusement from those huge soft, knowing eyes with film star lashes. She seemed to like having the little topknot between her ears rubbed and we had several meaningful, if slightly one-sided conversations on the subject of calves, the universe and the meaning of life. I could not have been happier with her.

Lady with the Film Star Eyes

A farm is not a farm, not even a very small one, without a cow. And anyway, a cow – a Jersey, or perhaps a Shorthorn – was always part of the plan. The Jersey is the ideal house cow; she will keep you, yours and a couple of pigs in milk, cheese, butter and ice cream. And show me a pig who doesn't like a nice vanilla cornet.

Finding a Jersey to hand milk is not an entirely straightforward matter. As well as being beautiful and biddable, she must have teats of a decent length. It is the very devil trying to milk a cow sans sufficiently pendulous teats, I can tell you. You squeeze, she kicks and no milk sploshes into your bucket at all. Sooner or later you will fall off your three-legged stool and find unpleasantly warm semi-solids soaking into your underwear.

We looked at the classifieds each week but they yielded little. There were plenty of pedigree Holsteins and Herefords but house cows, it seemed, were a thing of the past – too much trouble, too great a tie. The occasional

115

Jersey which ambled into the sale ring at the weekly auction had almost inevitably been machine-milked and was being discarded because she was ageing or 'three-titted' or deficient in both departments. If having three tits can ever be regarded as deficient, that is.

We passed the word around. Bush telegraph is a wonderful thing, especially in Cumbria and Paul from a few fields away suggested that we contacted Johnny Thompson, of Melmerby. Paul knew that Johnny, best known for some of the most highly regarded Limousin cattle this side of the Channel, had a house cow, but that a bout of poor health had led him to the conclusion that milking a cow was one job too many at the end of his working day. Paul thought that if Johnny could find the cow the right sort of home he would let her go. Lady was friendly, used to being handled and most importantly had teats like Smarties tubes. She was also in calf to one of Johnny's fabulous Hartside bulls. If you have ever had the dubious pleasure of standing very close indeed to a Limousin bull, this might sound an unpropitious mating but Johnny assured us that she would calve easily enough. She always had before. But we were not to be convinced and wimped out; we would buy her, but in three weeks time, after she had calved. We agreed a price, Johnny kindly threw in a stainless steel milking unit, offered to deliver her and we set off home. Then the doubts set in. Not that she wasn't absolutely the right cow rather the reverse. Why not have her now? After all, she knew what she was doing with this motherhood lark – far more than we did, certainly. What better cow to start with than one with previous experience? We rang Johnny, changed the plan and Lady came to Rowfoot that Saturday. He gave us a tenner luck money and set off home. We looked our Caramac coloured cow in the eye, and reflected that luck was never more needed.

Lady prowled about her new fields by day, munching and sitting and thinking secret cowy thoughts and returned to the maternity unit – a stone shed deep with straw – by night. She regarded me, her new keeper, with some amusement from those huge soft, knowing eyes with film star lashes. She seemed to like having the little topknot between her ears rubbed and we had several meaningful, if slightly one-sided conversations on the subject of calves, the universe and the meaning of life. I could not have been happier with her.

As her due date drew closer, her udder swelled and hardened. The more serene she became, the more our anxiety intensified. Then one morning, quite simply, there were two. Lady, plus a strong, lengthy calf with a short bullish head and an engaging wrinkly nose. He drank, he danced, he slept, he drank some more and three weeks later we sold him for £127. That price ensured that Rowfoot was amongst the Primestock listings in *The Cumberland News* and although we had very little to do with his breeding, arrival or nurture, we felt absurdly proud.

Lady quickly readjusted to her new routine. She would come to call, amble down the cobbled yard and into the shed and hoover up however much feed was in the trough while I sat on the stool, head tucked into her warm flanks and milk splashed generously into my bucket. As the weeks passed, her yield increased and my hands started to get cramp after the first three gallons. We began to think about processing and selling our surplus, for surplus there certainly was. And that is how Rowfoot Jerseys started.

Lady remained very much herd leader in spite of the arrival of younger, bigger cows. She had only to dip and sway her head menacingly – well, as menacing as an old Jersey can manage – for others to back off and behave. Over the years, she produced fine, healthy calves with equal ease to Limousin and Belgian Blue bulls with just one solitary heifer amongst them. She also fostered an Aberdeen Angus bull which we bought in a fit of pique at a piece of dismal steak. We thought it would be a wizard wheeze to rear our own which obviously, would taste so much better. When Angus was so big that he had to get down on his front knees to reach Lady's teats, we weaned him and grew him on. Then we lost our bottle and sold him, but that is another story. Lady went in to honourable retirement and finally went to that great pasture in the sky when she was well into her teens.

Within a frighteningly short space of time we had acquired six cows and sold cream, butter, cream cheeses and cheesecakes. In the summer we reared pigs. In the winter we fed the skim to calves, bought as tinies and sold on at the strong calf stage. Even when we went out of milk, the love affair with Jerseys continued. We were down to our last and fairly elderly cow when I had a call from Susan in Wales. Susan had decided to move to Ireland and whilst she was perfectly happy to sell her Friesians at a closing sale, the Jerseys were different. For Lady (Mark Two), Yelper and Caroline, money was not a consideration – a good home was. Time to go to Wales again.

The Jerseys were grazing in a field with 30 Friesian heifers. In a voice raised just enough to indicate that disobedience of any sort would not be sympathetically considered she called 'Lady, Yelper, Caroline, come here.' Now if that had been me, I would still be standing in that field in Wales trying to sort three from 30 but the Jerseys walked purposefully towards the gate and the Friesians stayed frozen, motionless. The gate opened, the Jerseys strolled through and that, really was that.

They loaded, without incident into the horsebox and we trundled back to Cumbria blissfully unaware of Rule

Number 352B (Paragraph 28, subsection iii) or something very like it, which stated that horned and polled cattle should never travel together. I suppose if you had been transporting a hundred youngsters with a variety of headgear then it could have been a problem but with three it was scarcely a consideration. Apart from the obvious lack of a beach ball to play with, they looked like nothing more than the Anchor cows all three facing sideways on one inspection, frontwards on the next. Needless to say, they arrived without incident and produced calves, milk, cheese and butter perfectly happily for several years.

We don't have cows any more, just a couple of signs proclaiming that This Dairy Uses the Simplex Hygienic Milking System. Which, of course, is a barefaced lie, these days.

Anyone who has a dog, cat or pet snaggletoothed fish will have talked to it at some time. It is better than talking to yourself and infinitely saner than conversing with a telephone answering machine. So don't worry about it. Enjoy the debate and rest assured it's one you'll always win . . .

It's Good to Talk

I've talked to them all, the dogs, the cows, the horses, not in a Doctor Dolittle sort of a way but as one might to a therapist. It is not deviant, it is not peculiar, it does not automatically mean I am certifiable. It's just normal, OK? It's because the English have 'relationships' with their animals. Entire televisual productions have been devoted to that between English women (it's always women, isn't it?) and their horses, their dogs. All right, an entire tele-vision series was also devoted to lavatories, but we'll leave that one for now.

Cat owners are the worst for talking to their animals. Eight out of ten have lengthy discussions about which variety, brand and format their pets prefer. Perhaps they should not bother with tins, pouches or packets at all and just settle for a nice fresh mouse instead.

Felines aside, the relationship rather depends on the creature. It is difficult to get up close and personal with a pig, relationships with pigs being essentially pragmatic and based on the idea that you feed them and just as they think they are getting the upper hand, you eat them. Sometimes, you go so far as to cure them – and they weren't even slightly unwell at the time. That's what I call really going the extra mile.

Loving relationships with goats are always impeded by

their horns. Sheep, I am sorry to tell you, just aren't bright enough to engage with man on an intellectual level. Mostly, sheep act on instinct rather than intelligence. Ask a sheep about the pros and cons of going into the Euro and I think you will be met with a blank stare but since blank stares seem the standard response to the Euro, maybe that's not so surprising after all.

We Brits have a funny relationship with dogs. This may be because they are, as my mum was always fond of pointing out, loyal. Though with Gyp and Tess, the focus of their loyalty is dictated by whoever is sitting nearest the biscuit tin at the time. Or it could just be that we identify with their imperfections. Only in Britain would a daily broadsheet devote three columns of bold type and a photographic portrait to the plight of an unquestionably ugly dog – great ears, shame about the teeth but I've been out with similar men – who had landed back at a rescue centre in Cornwall for the third time through no fault of his own and apparently was good natured, gentle and liked 'to play ball.' The next day, entirely predictably, the same newspaper reported that 700 people wanted to adopt him. At the other end of the scale are absolutely horrific stories of dogs thrown out on to motorways, grotesquely abused, mistreated and neglected. It's a bafflingly schizophrenic state of affairs.

As soon as relationships are mentioned, inevitably therapy follows. There's stress therapy, de-stress therapy, aromatherapy but have you come across Horse Therapy yet? In America (where else?) it is claimed that horses, with their sociable natures (I can think of one or two exceptions, but that is to be pernickety) and historic close association with human kind are ideally suited to a therapeutic role. A health farm in the Arizona desert claims that association with equines reflects and informs the way we form human relationships. Hmmm. Horse Therapy must be a bit like cognitive therapy but with a greater danger of having your toes squashed if you are shod in the wrong sort of boot.

The idea seems to be that you talk gently to your little horse, render unto him room service and personal care, clean out his feet and take him for a walk while the therapist assesses your communications skills. If anyone wants to try this but doesn't feel like tripping off to Arizona, give me a call and I'll let you come round and clean out as many horses' feet as you fancy. I am even willing – for a small additional charge – to develop the idea further and allow you to clean out two stables and tidy up a muck heap too while I settle back with a mug of coffee and assess away. It's a unique opportunity but make sure you come in winter when the horses are stabled to make it really worthwhile.

There's just one small quibble about this horse therapy and all its communication-reflection malarkey. I knew of one horse, imported from Belgium, who returned his new owner's instruction to 'walk on' with the same blank stare a sheep gives you if you ask it about the Euro. In other respects a tractable beast, he demonstrated the kind of selective hearing that children do when you tell them to wash their hands. There appeared no sensible explanation. Then the penny, or perhaps the franc, dropped. They spoke to him in Flemish and all was well. Moral: you may be clear, you may be assertive, but if it's in the wrong lingo, you're stuffed.

The connection between animals and man is nothing new. There's an old saying that there is no secret so close as that between a man and his horse. Centuries ago, ancient Arab warrior kings shared their tents with their mares and pretty honky and cramped it must have been, though no more of an antithesis to the horse's natural nomadic, browsing herd lifestyle than living alone in a stable, rugged-up and shod. It can hardly have been less odd for the sheik, though I suppose he and his filly could always curl up together and discuss their respective difficult childhoods between skirmishes with the enemy. Still, these days, any sheik who sidles up to a winsome filly is the victim of a red-top tabloid scam and reported to the authorities.

The Pat-a-Pet Scheme, where doggy visitors are taken hospital visiting was in its infancy when my Granny had broken her third leg (don't ask). Granny mistrusted the medical profession since they seemed hell bent on proscribing just about everything she enjoyed with the exception of watching cricket.

'Everything,' she would wail, 'is either illegal, immoral or fattening.' I never did understand why she bothered about the last as she was built like an undernourished whippet but I do know that she would much rather have woken up to a dog at her bedside than almost anything else, a bottle of Petrus being the only thing that might have given a mutt a run for its money. And did you know that stroking a dog lowers your blood pressure? Well, it does. Best check for fleas first, though.

There are many things I could do without in life – electricity bills, dried skimmed milk, almost everything in that mail order catalogue stuffed into the weekend colour supplements including such must haves as a pair of spiky sandals you run about in to aerate your lawn. However, I do need dogs – even dogs like Tess with her overactive idleness gland and her quarter past nine paws. I also need horses around much as other people need oxygen.

The more I know about people, the more I like my dogs. And horses, obviously. And nothing will prevent me from talking to them. I shall only worry if they start talking back.

When we still lived in suburbia and dreamed of country life, we indulged in some fairly extravagant fantasies, most of them inspired by John Seymour's estimable book, Self Sufficiency. It is a sort of 'How To' book of half-forgotten skills and crafts, from basket-weaving and brewing to tanning and curing. You have no idea how immensely satisfying it has been to turn such fantasies into reality and decorate the house with them.

Acid House

I have been busy curing. No, not the halt, the sick and the lame, the other sort – curing fleeces. Well, it seemed a shame to throw them away. This is (part of) the trouble with sheep. You start off with a whacking great animal which turns out to be comprised of a ridiculously small proportion of chops and joints, quite a bit of gubbins (I know that our future King has famously eaten sheep's head, but I just can't be persuaded to follow in his regal footsteps) and a monumentally vast fleece. At least there's some consolation in that our joints are bigger than those in the supermarkets as Small and Sidekick were shearlings rather than mere lambs. The size of the legs in the aisle-length freezers upsets me greatly; it strikes me as an act of cruelty to take the poor little mites away from their mothers at that arrested stage of development.

So to the fleeces. The first time I cured one was several years ago. We had bought a nice batch of Scottish Blackface lambs for overwintering, and they all looked healthy enough. To start with, anyway. Then one started to trail his back legs in a pretty alarming fashion. He was easy enough to catch; I had something of an unfair advantage. We had a Land Rover in those days, so we popped him in the back of it – he would have looked jolly silly sitting on the back seat of the Ford Mondeo we have now, but that's beside the point. The vet regarded him carefully and felt along his back in an unpropitious manner – for a sheep anyway. It looked uncannily like the way in which butchers at the mart feel the lambs they are thinking of bidding for.

'Well, if I were you,' spake the oracle. 'I would take him home and stick him in the freezer.'

It was one hell of a remedy for dodgy legs, I thought, but since it looked like he had trapped a nerve, the prognosis was iffy at best – and he was, as the vet so rightly pointed out, in prime condition.

I looked longingly at his luxurious tresses, and a plan began to form in my brain which, if detractors are to be believed, normally operates at a level somewhere just below that of the average amoeba, and I made a decision. I would take the sheep by the horns and get stuck into a bit of rug making. It was something I had often thought of having a go at and up until then the opportunity had eluded me.

To cut a long story short, he tasted wonderful – we invited the vet round for dinner to confirm the accuracy of his diagnosis – and after several complex and lengthy processes (see below for graphic details) the skin became a rug in the bedroom. And very nice it is too for feet on a cold winter's morning.

The recipe I had used so successfully on my Scottish Blackface skin contained concentrated sulphuric acid which, at that time, was readily obtainable from a decent chemist. Now, it ain't. I always run into this problem. When I was curing hams, and needed saltpetre, terrorists had found that this substance made bombs go off with even more devastating effect and used it extensively. Not surprisingly, chemists stopped selling saltpetre. Now I find it is impossible to get hold of sulphuric acid, since its properties have been exploited by such unpleasant characters as acid bath murderers. I did eventually run some to earth, but in dilute form and, no, it is nowhere near as effective, so next time I shall try a different cure, with alum. By then someone will probably have discovered a nefarious use for alum, so it will be banned too.

Sulphuric acid certainly is vicious stuff; even the curing instructions warned that the acid should be added to the water, and not the other way round, and I quote 'so that it doesn't splash into your eyes and spoil your beauty.' So don't try this at home, children. Before you get to the exciting bit of playing with acid, you have to trim the fleece – that is to say cut off all the gunky bits and wash it in brine. There is a suggestion that you can put it through a warm wash in your trusty twin tub with some borax, but since the prospect of clogging up the exit pipe with dirt is a real one, and the average call-out fee for a plumber is way in excess of the price of a ready made rug, that seems a bit of a non-starter to me. The fleece having been boraxed or brined, or both, and acid dipped, it then has to be dried and the membrane removed – a highly sophisticated operation involving the back of a chair (heirlooms and antiques are less than ideal for reasons which I am sure are self-evident) a lump of pumice stone and a liberal dose of elbow grease. Then you wash it again, brush it lovingly, and rub neatsfoot oil into the skin side. Voila. A sheepskin rug.

Now if you think all that sounds a right old fiddle just to avoid throwing it away, I would have to agree with you. But it is impossible to improve upon the righteous smugness of that 'with my own fair hands' feeling. Even if describing your hands as 'fair' by then is a travesty of the truth.

Somewhere in the midst of all the pickling and curing, I

thought I deserved a break and went off for a nice quiet Sunday afternoon ride. About half a mile from home, I caught sight of a herd of store cattle careering across the distant horizon, looking like a bunch of extras from a Spaghetti Western.

I've always had a soft spot for programmes like *Bonanza* and *Wagon Train*, which I watched as a child mainly because my cousin, who has a very unpleasant sadistic streak, used to tell me that if I opened the back of the tele I could get the horses out. I believed him, gullible little nit that I was. The only thing which prevented me from reaching for my father's toolbox and tampering with the back of the 16" black and white set was the prospect of the cattle coming out too, which I knew would displease my mother, who liked her carpets kept clean. The temptation was harder to resist in respect of the winner of the 2.30 at Kempton, but I have always been blessed with impeccable self-control (and a tendency to lie).

Farmer Eric's pursuit of his cattle could not be described as hot; it was more lukewarm, and his limbs were flailing like a human windmill in a hurricane. His efforts were having about as much effect as a bandage on a wooden leg, and the beasts disappeared from view. Then suddenly they appeared on the road in front of Ziggy and me. I don't know who was more surprised, them or us. They appeared to be playing a version of the game 'Last one to Armathwaite's a Cissy,' but faced with horse and rider they skidded to an uncertain halt.

Ziggy dodged left and right, impeding their progress and giving Eric time to scoot down the bank, hop over the wall and turn them round. Ziggy's future is once again uncertain; she might need a Western saddle after all.

About this time, we took the decision to leave commercial sheep to folk with commercial sized farms. Instead, we wanted, at the risk of sounding clichéd and corny, to do our bit for the planet and conservation, hence the Manx Loghtans. The Rare Breeds Survival Trust have one major sale a year and several smaller, affiliated ones; they are as different in character from the weekly Mart as it is possible to imagine. Except for the catering.

A Spent Force

I really hate buying stock. Arguably worse is selling because I feel unaccountably but quite horribly disloyal. I dislike both processes, not because of their financial implications but because of all the bother involved. As a way round this, I did actually consider the purchase of a 500 yard extension cable for the hover mower. You see my mum – whose grasp of matters agricultural was somewhat limited – used to believe that was how farmers kept the fields nice and tidy. She was outraged when she discovered the truth.

'What,' she snorted, 'you buy sheep, they keep the grass down for you and then you make a profit from selling them! No wonder farmers are rich.'

But let me go back to why I so hate buying stock. There are three basic ways of buying animals – privately, at dispersal sales or at auction. Opportunities to buy privately are few and far between, unless it's a pig, in which case it's dead simple. I ring Ivan up, tell him how many I need and wait for him to roll up with them, secure in the knowledge that my piglets will be squealing fit and priced sensibly. We can then settle down to the serious business of a good natter and a good dinner. Sadly, people like Ivan are even rarer than Manx Loghtans, so this sort of dealing is not something which happens all that often.

Then, of course, you can go to a farm sale or, slightly posher, a pedigree dispersal sale. Be warned, a farm sale is to a farmer what a testimonial year is to a county cricketer. Neighbours and the farther flung descend in droves, and ensure that the aspirant retiree is given a jolly good send off. It is perfectly usual for such workaday items as sheep troughs to make more than new ones would cost, and in the Small Items section, you can count on each box of miscellanea containing one useful item for every 43 rusty, useless ones. So unless you are a close personal friend or have recently inherited Great Aunt Maud's millions, farm sales have their drawbacks.

A day at a Pedigree Dispersal sale goes something like this. It will be raining, and there will be diversions on the motorway. It will take two hours and 56 minutes longer than you anticipated to get there and the farm will be situated at the end of a lane, which starts as tarmac, but quickly becomes single carriageway and then disintegrates into a dirt track with potholes the size of an average lunar crater. At the end of this you will find an auctioneer in a trilby, a camel hair coat and an unusually loud bow tie. Parking arrangements will be haphazard, and involve a lot of mud. If you have had the presence of mind to tow your trailer along with you, you can rely upon firstly, getting stuck and secondly not buying anything at all. You will need a tractor to pull you out, and the surly youth who effects this manoeuvre will demand a 'donation,' which will, he assures you, go to a local charity. Himself. The wagon parked next to you owes its continued mobility to the twin virtues of Sellotape and BluTack, and you will be moved to consider the previously unrelated issues of MOT tests and bribery.

The insanitary grotfest which constitute the loos at

some of these events is exceeded in awfulness only by the catering arrangements, which are of the Heart Attack on a Plate School of Gastronomy. You wait in a queue so long that by the time you are served, crimplene will have come back in fashion and the sum demanded for the refreshments will be roughly an amount of money normally associated with the losses of the more unfortunate syndicates at Lloyds. The chef and dispenser of this culinary catastrophe is of indeterminate gender, and more importantly, has omitted to scrub under its fingernails. There is no vegetarian option – the nearest you can expect is a hot dog without the dog, and the burgers are of dubious provenance. The onions are fried in oil so old that its first excursion into a kitchen was as velociraptor dripping and the bun encasing the oleaginous mass has the texture of a puffball mushroom and is only a little tastier. No matter, you progress to the drinks. Bovril, hot chocolate, tea and coffee all come from the same urn and taste strangely similar.

You reach into your pocket for the Mars Bar you brought with you, in expectation of an energy dip around l0.30am and peruse the catalogue. The cows you have marked off as potential purchases are not quite as you hoped. One is three-titted, another turns out not to be in-calf after all and the third has wild eyes and looks to be in the grips of a neurosis which only a trip to someone with a blue pyramid and a Greek surname could fix. You go home, beastless, bad tempered and bilious. Does this sound familiar?

Not to worry, there is always the Mart. Now Marts were invented by male farmers (you can obtain proof positive of this by examining the dimensions of the ladies' loos) partly to enable them to buy and sell stock, and partly as a haven from worm reps, wives and paperwork. At the mart, farmers can catch up on who is doing what with whom and how often. However, the catering is a distinct improvement on outdoor sales – at Borderway they serve shortbread 'biscuits' with circumferences equal to that of tractor tyres and, what's more, the ring is encircled by familiar faces.

'No,' farmers say when they get home, sated with shortbread biscuits and gossip, 'they were flying today, just not worth buying at that price.'

They then settle down in front of the fire, basking in the glow of a day well spent. Great places, marts.

The beef situation being what it is at present, worm farming looks a more attractive (and possibly more profitable) alternative though I concede that it must be pretty damned difficult to strike up a rewarding relationship with a worm, so I settled for yet more sheep in the end, sheep being ever so slightly more appealing than worms.

However, I thought rather than simply going and getting some more commercial sheep, it was time I did my bit for saving the planet and had a rare breed. Current top of the shopping list are some Manx Loghtans, because they have an assortment of extremely silly horns and look like out-of-work court jesters (no bells though, sadly) which appeals to my sense of humour.

More seriously, the Rare Breeds Survival Trust reckon that if a few planet-spirited individuals don't step in, the poor old Manx Loghtan will go the same way as the Dodo, instead of running about waggling its horns like a sawn-off moose. Besides, I like the weird, wonderful and exotic. I put this down to a reaction against having been brought up (or kicked in the bum and told to get up) in a tranche of suburbia so mundane it was twinned with Dullsville, and to never having had friends called Anouska or Sigourney.

Our Little Red Tractor was around long before it was adopted as a logo for food. A Massey 135 epitomised everything that is great about British engineering and it came to have a very special place in our affections, mainly due to the fact that it had the distinction of being the only vehicle we have ever owned which actually appreciated in value.

The Little Red Tractor

Winter has receded and I mourn its passing about as much as I would lament the cessation of a particularly rampant attack of toothache. I've been through the annual ritual – plugged in to 'Hugo's French in Three Months,' and packed the lot away again a fortnight later, realising that firstly, however belle France might be, you can't buy Marmite there and secondly I would be deprived of my nightly fix of *Neighbours*. I know some people regard slavish devotion to *Neighbours* as some sort of illness, on a par with chicken pox, but it is time to confess – I am a fan.

As the magnolia sprouts its gaudy buds and nature changes her winter coat of taupe (an inexplicably fashionable shade if ever there was one – it's more like the colour of dried dung) for one of proper juicy green, I begin to look forward to the arrival of our customary Cumbrian summer – temperatures soaring into the eighties and long, balmy (or should that be barmy) days of uninterrupted sunshine.

There are a few winter things I miss, of course, the metronomic cack-cack-cacking of the robin redbreast who has made it his business to act as foreman from a vantage point on the barn door each morning, overseeing my chores, for one. He and my mare Kareima reached an understanding which resulted, occasionally, in silence first thing in the morning outside. Usually, once Kareima sees the bathroom light go on, I have approximately ten minutes to get downstairs and get her fed before she starts to bang seven bells out of her stable door. I have tried to reason with her that she would not get faster service in a Michelin starred hotel and that ten minutes – for heaven's sake – is not long to get teeth cleaned, hair brushed, clothes and coffee on (a shot of caffeine being vital to kick start the body in my case), wellies de-spidered and a pleasantry or two exchanged with the collie dogs. But none of this cuts any ice with Kareima.

On the silent mornings she was motionless on account of the little robin perched high up on her rump, where he waited until she took her first mouthful of food. As she raised her head to chew, he dropped down into the feed bucket and helped himself to a bit of breakfast. He would then sit on the bucket rim, while she fed and then down he'd go again. This went on until the robin was full and Kareima never attempted to deny him his fill. She is a very polite horse.

He has never tried this with the goat, which suggests that robins are more intelligent than you might at first think. The goat recently attacked Gyp the collie dog with a degree of gratuitous violence usually associated with the more unpleasant cinematic offerings masquerading as 'art.' Millie bided her time, waiting until Gyp was standing with her tail goatwards, and then pounced, sending the dog into unexpected flight. She only just avoided a low-flying Biggles from Spadeadam but she has learned a valuable lesson – like cow pats and party political broadcasts, a wrathful goat is best avoided. It was then I had a blinding flash of sheer genius. We could disarm the entire planet, ditch all mines, munitions and militaria and replace them with legions of patriotic goats. Killing machines, goats. A potentially constructive use for the otherwise dubious science of cloning perhaps?

Millie Goat would have found herself on a one way trip in the direction of the freezer if it were not for the fact that the only recipe for goat which I possess goes like this. Step One – put the joint of goat into a pot and bring to the boil. Step Two – add a large stone and reduce to a simmer. Step Three – cook until the stone is tender. The goat is then ready to eat.

Now that the wind no longer lashes and whips in cold and vicious strikes I shall even miss my muck-spreading excursions, because last winter I was aboard a highly desirable, restored Fergie (the mechanical sort of Fergie, that is). My Massey Ferguson 135 spent much of last summer at the Newton Rigg Health Farm for Extremely Elderly Tractors. It provided the students with a very real challenge, because nothing much had been removed from it forcibly since Adam was a lad, whereas the ones they routinely take to bits and put back together again at college are dismantled so frequently that they come apart as easily as a kid's jigsaw puzzle. It went into the workshop with very poor eyesight (no electrics to speak of), an iffy exhaust which sounded rather as if it had eaten too many lentil stews and a distinctly unhealthy pallor. It emerged rejuvenated – fully operational lights, a husky, sexy even, voice, and Postman Pat red bodywork. Altogether a sight to gladden the heart.

What is more, it has benefited from Mr Clarke's ruling that vintage vehicles do not require road tax so I am no longer restricted to a maximum of six miles a week on public roads, in accordance with the terms of my Tax Exemption Certificate. Not that I ever did six miles, because with my sort of luck I would have met the only police patrol vehicle within a 50 mile radius and been instantly booked, given its condition. Naturally, I would have pleaded insanity.

Now that I can go where I like, I draw the line at day trips to Manchester. Penrith for the shopping is an attractive possibility on a fine day. At least a bright red tractor would stand out in the car park and I wouldn't have to spend ages looking for it like I do for my car.

The only snag with all this renovation is that it is far too smart to be doing a day's work. Which, if I may digress, is what I'm going to be in the next life. Too smart to work. I'm not going to be able to drive, cook, clean, grow anything other than older – disgracefully, and I'm certainly not going to work – because I've noticed, looking round, that if you are a bit helpless there's always someone daft enough to do it for you.

When the tractor first came home, I was told that it would benefit from a hard day's work, to get everything chugging around again. Things were quiet here at the time, so I offered two neighbours the rare privilege of disporting themselves upon my restored antique. This generous offer was accompanied by a single caveat – 'don't get it dirty.'

Finally, you will be glad to hear that Kareima's pregnancy is progressing apace. She bears a passing resemblance to Free Willy on stilts, and by the time this goes to press will probably need wheels surgically attached to her hooves to keep her mobile at all. We have already applied for planning permission and a lottery grant in order to implement a comprehensive door widening scheme, as she already has to square up to the opening and psyche herself up before negotiating the exit.

'Fools,' the saying goes, 'breed horses for wise men to ride.' Probably very true and this may well deter even the most determined would-be breeder. But then again ...

Extracting the Michael

We live in turbulent times. In recent weeks a man in a white suit has become an MP and MI5 are advertising for new recruits. Only the discovery that Jeremy Paxman was a closet Trekkie could upscuttle me more. Even so, nothing has had quite the impact upon me as did the arrival of Kareima's foal; as the due date drew nearer, my nerves were in the kind of shreds the Blessed Saint Delia suggests ideal for turning orange peel into the finest marmalade.

An old friend commented to me recently that having the stud owner as your next door neighbour represented the ultimate insurance policy. As it turned out, truer words were never spoken. Hazel, from Dolphaz Stud, informed me at about 8.30pm on Kareima's due date, that any expectations I had had of a decent night's sleep could be consigned to the NBC bin (No Bloody Chance, since you ask). She had noticed the tell-tale beads of wax on the teat ends, so there was an outside chance that tonight could be the night. That Thursday night I was up every two hours. Friday night, then Saturday night came and went in similar fashion.

On Sunday, my Goddaughter was to be christened at Brampton. By then my eyes were propped open with matchsticks and sellotaped into place, and bags the size of rucksacks drooped sadly beneath. In the photos, there is a baby (an extremely beautiful baby, I might add), three adults and a zombie whose appearance owed much to the twin virtues of Pan Stik and caffeine, hiding under a big hat. Meanwhile back at Rowfoot, Hazel – who I am recommending for canonisation, or at the very least an OBE – was maintaining discreet observation. Kareima was getting edgy, preoccupied and started to drip milk on Sunday afternoon, so we brought her in. She showed all the classic signs of starting the foaling process – digging the floor up (don't ask), prowling about the box and looking generally distracted. Then, quite abruptly, she stopped doing all this and went back to eating hay and looking positively seraphic.

Every two hours during Sunday night and Monday morning I looked at her and every two hours she looked back at me, with an 'oh, you again' expression. Hazel, unbeknown to me, had been up at 1am and 4am and by 6am we had both had enough and the vet was summoned to investigate. Mike pulled on plastic gloves, and we took a virtual walk into the pages of *All Creatures Great and Small* as he got stuck in up to his armpits. 'Hmm,' he said, 'I've got an ear.'

Now I do not know a great deal about the gynaecological and obstetrical niceties of the horse, but even I could work out that this was just slightly less than ideal. Not aerodynamic enough, you see, ears first.

Kareima was deeply unhappy by then and made a concerted effort to scale the stable wall, in spite of Hazel hanging on to the front end and Mike still being attached to the rear; he had located first one and then a second foot and manipulated them, spinning the foal around.

All this was to no avail as the mare's contractions were not strong enough and Mike gave her a drip of Oxysomethingorother to get them going. When he delved around inside, the foal was upside down again. Back to square one. Mike having relocated the oddly translucent little hooves, Kareima had the good sense to lie down and start pushing. Even so, it took the pulling power of three adults to persuade the foal into the world, while my husband stoically hung on to the headcollar and murmured soothing noises to Kareima. At first it seemed that we were just going to get a set of legs – endless, supermodel legs. The slimy mass wriggled promisingly; he snuffled, dislodging the mucus in his nose and mouth and looked around, bewildered. We must have seemed quite a reception committee, all four of us, now reduced to blood, sweat and tears – blood in quantities consistent with an appendectomy which had not gone quite to plan, sweat dripping from mare and humans alike, and my tear stained face looking like a poster promoting Agony Awareness week.

And what, at this moment of high drama did Kareima want? Food. She whiffled hungrily and dived in to a bucketful of Bob's Mix like some starving refugee. They really do behave very oddly at times, animals. Meanwhile her newly born son made wild, giraffe-like gyrations to get to his hooves; legs flayed in all directions and he staggered about a bit, fell over once or twice and then having got his legs organised went in search of a milky teat. Hazel, who knows about such things, opined that when he grows up he will have more front than Blackpool, such is the set of his wither. I just think he's a miracle.

I shot into Penrith to get some veterinary necessities – penicillin for Kareima, a sensible precaution considering the potential for infection caused by rummaging around amongst her innards, and tetanus and penicillin for Little Mickey. On seeing the sign 'Drugs' in the vet's surgery I asked for a bucket of Prozac as well as the horse stuff – I reckon I had earned it.

Having Mikolai is the last thing I ask Kareima to do. It's honourable retirement for her now. She has been the

most wonderful friend – I would not demean her by refer-
ring to her as a servant – and enabled me to achieve things
way beyond my own capability, just because of her hon-
esty and generosity. I used to ride the jump off courses
without walking them, in case I terrified myself witless,
and frequently needed a stiff gin before the competition.
When I started doing this at 10 in the morning it was
clearly time to give up. I look back on the glory days with
undiluted pleasure and recall long journeys in the lorry
enlivened only by the heady prospect of overtaking
Reliant Robins on the motorway (with a downhill slope
and a following wind) but much as I loved competing I
miss it not one jot.

Watching Mickey grow up is better than watching tele.
When he was two days old, he had his first excursion into
the great outdoors. First he discovered that he could do
something more exciting than walk – trot. Then canter.
He progressed to having a go at the land speed record,
and his latest trick is finding that he can execute a leap
four feet into the air with pike – something he practised to
good effect whilst in utero. After a foaling like this, the
'never again' syndrome sets in, but only for a day or so.
By the time Mikolai is ready to break in (that bit of Irish
Draught in him should endow him with some common
sense as I hack off into my dotage and perhaps he'll be
bored with vertical take-offs by then) Ziggy will be 10,
and if we are to breed something from her we shouldn't
leave it any later. And Fred (Flintstone) next door at
Dolphaz Stud is an unusually handsome chap.

Pigs are like Marmite, loved or loathed. Pigs might be pretty pre-historic in appearance but their meat is incredibly versatile. Mostly, we killed ours for pork but one year we were persuaded to run a couple on for bacon. Two Tamworths, fed on skimmed milk and left over jacket potatoes from one of those mobile catering units, grew to monstrous proportions. Hams were cured, sides rolled, everything but the squeak minced and made into sausage. You may be aware that pigs' intestines were used before the days of synthetic sausage skins, but did you know what else piggy intestines were used for? Contraceptives. Now you know.

An Awful Lot of Pigs

Have you noticed what I have noticed lately – that pigs are getting one hell of a big press? We appear to have been transformed into a nation of Pigophiles. However, there are exceptions to the rule, and farmers deep in the Romney Marshes are some of them. They have failed to succumb to the charm offensive of a number of escaped wild boar which are busily colonising a tranche of Kent chiefly because these beasts have been wreaking havoc on maize, hops, potatoes and just about anything else edible or careless enough to get within their line of vision.

Pigs are not fully paid up members of the Vegetarian Society – they are omnivores and will eat anything. And I really do mean anything, so the good burghers of the Marshes are understandably perturbed, although the situation has probably added a dimension to the discipline of minors on the Romney Marsh – 'behave yourself or I'll send you out to play with the pigs' – a dark threat which could be accompanied by demonic laughter for maximum effect. There are rumours of signs being erected too: 'Trespassers will be eaten.'

We are not talking an odd boar or two either; the creatures have been indulging in wild nights of torrid sexual excesses, resulting in an alarming rise in their population. The sows can manage two litters a year of up to ten piglets in each. I am no mathematician, but even I can work out that it doesn't take long for this to become an awful lot of pigs indeed. One farmer shot a huge boar which was the only porcine creature I have ever clapped eyes on which made the monsters we reared for bacon a few years back look like undernourished weaklings. It weighed as much as two fully grown men. I imagine that at the moment he looked down the barrel of his gun, the only place he would less liked to have been was in the front row of a Bay City Rollers concert and doubtless he took the precaution of taking aim from halfway up a tree because wild boar can travel at speeds of up to 25 mph. There is something vaguely ridiculous about the sight of a running pig – except if it is coming in your direction, in which case it is neither vague nor ridiculous, just an extremely potent incentive for getting smartly out of the way. Frankly, any attempt to escape on foot would be about as pointless as moving your deckchair from port to starboard on the Titanic.

Pictures in all the national dailies showed the dead boar strung up on the tractor front loader, trophy-like. If the farmer had been really smart, he would have asked Saint Delia for a few recipes – a carcass that size would have kept his entire family, including distant relatives in Australia, going for a year or two – though they'd probably all be heartily sick of it by the time it was finished. They could have run the full gamut of the culinary possibilities of the swine – braised pig, stewed pig, pig lasagne, pig pie, pig's trotters, pig's brains. All of which brings me neatly to another media appearance the pig has made recently.

I watched an entire TV programme devoted to pigs being taught to become more computer literate than I can ever aspire to be. The pig-besotted Professor Curtis, from the USA, showed us an impressive range of tasks which the pig was able to perform with consummate ease. If the Prof is to be believed, it can only be a matter of time before they take over the earth, or at least produce their own television programmes. Coming soon, to a screen near you – The Chopping Channel and the Pig Breakfast. Coronation Chicken Street will not be far behind. All of which leads me to conclude that George Orwell's allegorical *Animal Farm* might not have been so allegorical after all.

As one who experiences difficulty differentiating between a fax machine and a spaghetti dispenser, and who wrestles on a daily basis with the complexities of Windows, I take off my (pork pie) hat to any porker who can operate a computer. Until recently, Windows were something I looked out of, Fonts were things babies were christened in and Icons were biblical and nasty, especially false ones. My mastery of the computer extends only as far as the game of Solitaire. I realised what a sad nerd I was becoming when I found myself keeping a record of how many games I beat the infernal machine at. No pig would bother doing this – too intelligent, you see.

The only flaw I can find in Professor Curtis' otherwise persuasive argument is that completion of the so-called 'simple tasks' (one of which was operation of a computer joystick, which as you will already have guessed, baffles me comprehensively) rewarded the pig with food. In my experience if you show a pig food, it will do just about anything, including a short excerpt from *Riverdance* or a double back somersault, to get to the grub.

Many years ago, we decided to relawn and replant the garden. A small army of pigs was deployed as land clearance operatives; let's face it, a pig is the only plough you can eat, and plough they did, with considerable dedication to the task, though we were never successful in training them to go up and down in straight lines. Their favourite place for an afternoon siesta was in the greenhouse. One afternoon, they had slept on a bit and supper time came as a surprise. On seeing the bucket of delicacies – it was before all the tiresome regulations about swill, which nowadays is so bland and dull that Dickensian gruel looks a gastronomic treat by comparison – the most athletic of the group simply executed a perfect leap straight through the pane of greenhouse glass, scattering splinters in every direction but emerging without a single scratch on his body. OK, he got to the food first, but it did strike me as reckless behaviour for one possessed of extensive cranial attributes. Allegedly.

So, until I find a pig which can do joined up writing I shall remain unconvinced by all the speculation about pig intelligence. A pig will never walk out, willow in trotter, to open the batting on the hallowed turf of Lord's, a pig will never be the one asking the questions on Mastermind and a pig will never be a cultural attache. Not in my lifetime anyway. But I do see a meaningful role for the pig in modern society, as well as being the essential ingredient in a bacon sandwich. Pigs could become eco warriors. After all they shift more earth than Swampy (remember him?) and their tunnelling skills could be usefully employed when protesters are in urgent demand. The nice thing is, you could eat them afterwards.

Tess (on the left) and Gyp.

Millie Goat. The only female
I know with attractive facial hair.

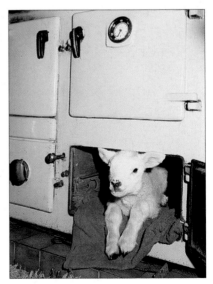

One lamb. One Rayburn. End
result: happiness. Who needs the
Great Outdoors?

Contemplating the imminent
arrival of the Euro. Who says Manx
Loghtans aren't deep thinkers?

This pig she would a wooing go.
Or something like that. Anyway
this is a Large Black sow.

The pin up girl. Lady, the perfect
island-bred cow.

Micky and Kareima. This is rare
photograph of Micky actually
wearing a head collar. He usually
managed to discard them.

A successful effort in the
showjumping at the
National Championships
at Malvern in 1992. It was
nothing to do with me,
I just tried to sit still and
let her get on with it.

RIGHT: Horny old devil.
Frederic from Tow Law.

LEFT: Big is beautiful.
Believe it or not there was
only one calf in Lady.
I was convinced that there
would be twins...if not
triplets. But then, what
do I know? JANE FAY

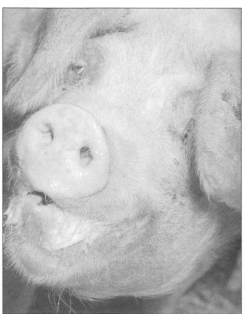

LEFT BOTTOM:
Give us a kiss!

RIGHT BOTTOM: Going
down to post for the 2.30
at Rowfoot. A Belgian
Blue Jersey cross lets rip a
little youthful exuberance.

Apocalypse in Eden. The smoke from a pyre engulfs a farm in the Eden Valley.

ABOVE: Not so happy days. Myself and Tess with an Eden Valley landscape bereft of animals during the height of the Foot and Mouth epidemic.

LEFT: Two sawn off dogs. Tess (left) and Gyp before they grew up! They were however already in training and attending classes on 'How to sit down and look very, very cute.' Needless to say they passed with distinction.

We live on goose juice for months after Christmas. Don't waste the fat by rubbing it on your chest – cook your spuds in it for the tastiest, crispiest roasties imaginable. Rub your chest with Vick, but whatever you do don't use Vick for your spuds. Some things, trust me, are just not interchangeable.

And a Merry EEC

Ah, Christmas. That orgy of over indulgence when we eat too much, drink too much and then try to convince ourselves, through the dyspepsia and the hangover, that we really have had an absolutely wonderful time. Wonderful, in spite of the furry mules from Auntie Gladys (when, for goodness sake, did you last see a peasant in furry mules?) and the dendrologically influenced Bulgarian Chardonnay brought by cost-conscious guests, for which we are expected to be exceedingly grateful.

Christmas always acts as a potent reminder to me that farming is about food. Turkeys do not materialise out of thin air, ready plucked and hermetically sealed; lambs which have an 'aaaah' factor of 12 on a scale of ten are destined to end up as platemates for mint sauce, even if the National Society for the Protection of Fluffy Cuddly Things would have us believe otherwise and geese, before they make contact with the family Wedgwood, are bad tempered birds which act as a better deterrent to intruders than the combined effects of burglar alarms and collie dogs.

We always have turkey on Christmas Day, chiefly because we'd need an entire skein of geese to satisfy the voracious appetites of numerous itinerants who descend for the festivities, claiming to be family. When they've all gone home, we have a goose for New Year. It is easily the most enjoyable feast of all.

I am always amused when people witter on about the problem of eating turkey leftovers for weeks. We never do. There's never anything left over. About the nearest I get to that is chucking a bucket of bones, an onion and a bendy carrot into the slow oven of the Rayburn and calling the resultant liquid soup. The only snag is that you have to remember to take it out and, by way of prompts, I leave myself little notes propped up on the breakfast bar. They say things like 'Puddings – ON!' and 'Soup, bottom' which could be misconstrued, I suppose. I do this because one year the soup sort of slipped my mind. For two days. I realised something was wrong when a curious odour began to permeate the kitchen, an amalgam of putrefying polecat and a sewerage works experiencing a technical problem. When the penny dropped, I pulled a pot from the bowels of the stove. Instead of a flavoursome marriage of turkey carcass wedded to toothsome veggies, it was a fetid, suppurating mass, bubbling menacingly and threatening imminent explosion. We didn't have any turkey soup that year.

Farming may be about food, yet it seems to me that the supermarkets do their level best to conceal the true origins of their edible wares and to distance the product on the shelf from the live creature, thus sanitising the product and protecting the sensibilities of the British shopper. Who would think, for example, that the vacuum wrapped splodge of amorphous gunge, squatting peaceably upon an azure blue polystyrene tray and helpfully labelled, is even a distant cousin of the wobbling muddy bulk that is pig?

The French have no such qualms. In France it is nothing to find a few stray, coarse hairs of the wild boar still attached to the skin, or signs proudly proclaiming the exact contents of the container – 'cerveau' sounds OK doesn't it, but when you realise that the tangled tubes on display beneath the picture of a smiley little calf are veal brains, you see what I mean.

Italians are not noticeably different. Some years ago, in Florence, I went to the food market. I would not like you to think I am a philistine, so rest assured, I went to the Uffizi too – but it was the market which fascinated. Great lengths of veal guts, not something you see too often in this country and whether sold by the metre or by the kilo I know not – were displayed in unrefrigerated cabinets. Fat ropes of salami hung from not especially clean rafters. Giovanni's fag hung decorously from his lips as he tossed scraplets of meat to a recently whelped bitch doing her begging rounds. She didn't need a sign saying '15 hungry pups to feed' – you could guess that was the case by the way her low slung teats made intermittent contact with the cobbled floor.

None of this worried me much. I have never suffered from Delhi belly, or any related complaint when abroad, a fact which I ascribe to years of drinking untreated milk which has promoted the existence of good bugs within my own personal eco-system. I am convinced that folk whose diet consists exclusively of homogenised pre-packed nosh simply lose all natural resistance to anything which is not completely sterile.

In the light of our European cousins' cavalier attitudes to food safety, it strikes me as more than slightly ironic that when we were selling cheese and cream, we had to comply with endless regulations, most peculiar of which was the Seamless Plastic Bucket Rule. The production of my first Jersey cow was prodigious. She never converted food into flesh and always looked like a walking hat rack, but boy, did she convert food into milk. By the time she produced in excess of five gallons a day my hands ached and my every waking moment was occupied with wondering what to do with all the surplus milk.

Money making scheme number 53B was born – buy a small legion of calves to drink the skim and sell the cream. Anxious that I should not be clapped into jail for transgression of some regulation or another contained within the small print of an EEC directive, I telephoned ADAS in Penrith and explained the situation.

'Well,' said a voice on the end of line, 'I don't know if you can do that. I'll have to ring Carlisle.'

Carlisle didn't know either. So the opinion of the Kendal oracle was sought. Kendal phoned me back to ask if I really milked the cow by hand, in tones which indicated that such an activity was considered somewhere between subversive and criminally lunatic. I confessed and awaited the arrival of a posse of psychiatric experts who would bear me away to a place of safety. They failed to appear but the 'phone rang again.

'It will be OK,' said a prissy voice, 'as long as you confine yourself to the use of a seamless plastic bucket.'

I tried hard, but I could not conjure up an image of an Italian or a Frenchman going to the local ironmongers and buying such a bucket. In fact, I reached the inescapable conclusion that as far as most EEC regulations are concerned, the French say 'pah,' the Italians ignore them and we in the UK set up a commission to examine them.

So enjoy your Christmas lunch, turkey, goose or whatever, secure in the knowledge that it complies with an extensive encyclopaedia of rules and regulations. This, I am sure, will do more for your digestive system than colonic irrigation could ever aspire to. And go easy on the Chardonnay. Cheers!

It may have escaped your notice but it is the males of the animal world who are routinely subjected to the most terrible of indignities. We castrate horses, cattle, pigs and sheep all in the name of 'easier management'. Hmm . . .

Nutcracker Suite

Mickey's status has changed. He is no longer man, but mouse. Or at least the vet says he will be in a few weeks when all that testosterone in his system has evaporated, because he has been subjected to the Unkindest Cut of All. Perhaps the glee with which I anticipated this was something to do with Girl Power, but I think it is more likely that I viewed the prospect of staring at his belly, through a fog of flailing hooves as he stood on his hind legs and waved at me, as less than pleasurable.

I was also tired of being used as a mobile teeth sharpener as his behaviour became increasingly colty. Aversion therapy resulted only in a slight modification of this tendency – he bit me, I smacked him, he bit me again, I smacked him again. Finally, the penny would drop and he would give up for a day or so – then we'd start the same tedious procedure all over again. Furthermore, his sexually deviant behaviour was becoming wearisome for his mother and I got to a stage where I thought that maybe we wouldn't need the vet to come and castrate Mickey after all, because one of her accurately aimed kicks at his vital regions would probably do the job perfectly adequately and a great deal more cheaply.

Of course, many of his funny little ways are endearing. Even though he has cost me dearly in lost and broken headcollars, his capacity to misplace or destroy them has been a source of perverse amusement. The first headcollar just disappeared.

He came in one night with a very smug expression, but no hat. I trailed about the field searching for it but to no avail, so I bought a garish blue one on the basis that when he took it off – as he surely would – I could at least find it easily. He broke that one. Then I put him in his first 'pony' sized headcollar, at which point I felt like a mother of a baby who had just got his first tooth through. He found out within 24 hours that he could remove this by judicious interaction with the water trough, with the added satisfaction of flooding the field. I gave up. I took it off altogether, fearful that he might hang himself, and now I catch him each night, put a headcollar on and lead him in.

By the time I came home from holiday, it was obvious that weaning and castration would have to be sooner rather than later. For every kilo Mickey put on, his poor old mum lost at least three. So, in spite of her noisy protestations, and feeling like a cross between Cruella de Ville and an axe murderer, I carted Kareima off to the other end of the village to stay with Claude and Polly, two mightily impressive coloured horses hairy of leg and fearsome of feature. Their combined weight is roughly equivalent to that of a small Royal Navy frigate; one does not mess with the likes of Claude and Polly.

Kareima's first instinct was to have a bite of succulent grass, then, suddenly she spied her new fieldmates, raised her head and took off, her tail held high and her neck proudly arched, in a ground devouring stride. In her showing days I called this her Big Trot, and it is such an extraordinary sight that it brought more than one event to a complete standstill. The optical illusion is that of a horse not touching the ground at all, but floating. She may be nearly 20 years old, but she still has incomparable style;

only someone with a soul of pure titanium could remain unmoved by such a wondrous sight.

Claude and Polly, whose acceleration from 0–60 is approximately two days, gazed on in awe, before coming down to make the acquaintance of this new, strange creature. An understanding was soon reached; Claude calls the shots. Well, it's his field, isn't it?

Mickey meanwhile, was only bothered about the whereabouts of his next feed, and was extremely grateful when he was released with his new friend Sherry, who is to disruptive foals what Nanny Smith is to mixed up infants. In fact, he was so laid back about the whole weaning thing that he was literally horizontal. One night I crept out to the stable to check on him and I found him fast asleep, stretched right out, and for all I know dreaming of nubile thoroughbred fillies. One ear twitched, silently acknowledging my presence, but he did not raise his head.

Next on Mickey's personal – highly personal – agenda, was the small matter of relieving him of a pair of circular appendages. I was reliably informed that this dual amputation would result in noticeable improvements in his temperament. He would become more tractable and docile, less aggressive and less likely to bite. With such numerous and far reaching benefits, why stop at horses?

Just to lay a major guilt trip on me, Mickey suddenly mended his anti-social ways. He stopped nipping, stood like a lamb to be caught and gave up barging through me as if I were invisible. I still called the vet. (Ratbag, I hear you cry. Yes, that's me.)

Euan gave him the first injection and his eyes glazed over. That's the foal's eyes, not Euan's, of course. His eyes looked fine throughout, perfectly focused and aided by a headlamp clamped to his forehead, cyclops-like, the better to oversee the delicate procedures with the scalpel. After

151

the second jab Mickey swayed drunkenly. The third knocked him out and the operation was completed without incident, Euan's dexterity with a needle causing me to wonder whether he might be a member of the Royal College of Needlework as well as the Royal College of Veterinary Surgeons.

I could not watch. Having spent a holiday amongst a contingent of ageing Americans whose fondness for facelifts resulted in several having the appearance of superannuated Barbie dolls with more tucks than the average Victorian nightdress, I was right off surgery. I contented myself with sitting at the head end, listening to the ominous crunch of apparatus which appropriately enough resembled a set of giant nutcrackers.

Mickey came round quickly, with an expression of 'great trip man' on his woozy features and then he was back on his feet and whinnying – admittedly a few octaves higher than previously – within minutes. Euan, who speaks fluent Horse, translated the last whinny as a term of abuse, casting doubt on the legitimacy of our respective births.

Four hours later, Mickey had recovered to the extent that he was demanding to be let out. He walked off into the gloom of a winter afternoon, slightly bewildered that part of his undercarriage had unaccountably gone missing, but apparently undisturbed by this realisation.

At least he'll never know what he missed.

There are those who might say that staring out of the window as much as I do is a total waste of time but I never cease to be fascinated as well as baffled by animal communication. Sam, our porky little driving cob and Mickey play fight like a couple of naughty boys; they bite and nip without ever apparently sinking their teeth into each other's flesh, rear up on their hind legs and chase each other. Why?

Not Such a Silly Old Moo After All

'There are more things in heaven and earth, Horatio, Than are dreamt of in your philosophy' – Hamlet.

What with the ghost and the onset of an Oedipus complex, poor old Hamlet had quite enough to get himself into a right stew, but I think he could have been suggesting that all sorts of things were beyond our collective ken, not just apparitions and peculiar relatives. Amongst these, I would venture to suggest that we do not know much about animal behaviour and communication. By animals, I do not mean the bunch of House of Commons lemmings, whose headlong rush towards political correctness recently has been enough to induce madness amongst the farming community on an unprecedented scale.

We almost reached a pitch whereby Granny's mild dyspepsia inspired a nationwide ban on everything she had eaten within the last 24 years and probably her denture fixative as well.

No, I'm talking real animals here. And Hamlet was

right, because although we have managed to put a man on the moon and be absolutely whizz at nuclear physics, where animal communication is concerned we are only just past first base.

Take cows for a start; they are anything but silly moos. Very sensitive moos indeed, if my heifer Fluff was anything to go by. She had been reared as one of a group and when we bought Dove, who had been another of that number, they greeted each other like old girls at a school reunion. Thereafter they went everywhere together, grazed the same tuft of grass whenever possible, sat chewing their cud muzzle to muzzle like a pair of bookends and lived side by side in the byre, rubbing along in mutual contentment. Poor Dove fell victim to an injury and had to be put down; she was a delightful cow and a superb milker and I missed her, but nothing like as much as Fluff missed her. Fluff grieved. She would walk in to the byre and moo forlornly at the empty space where Dove had lived. Please don't try to tell me that I imagined it all because Fluff's coat lost its lustre, her milk all but dried up and she went off her food. Oh, yes, time healed but it seemed to take ages and in between, poor Fluff was a sad sight to behold.

Cows also have a fascinating system of babysitting arrangements. Many a time, you will notice the dams off grazing while the calves are obediently clustered around one matriarch. Look again, a little while later, and you will notice another cow in charge of the babies; responsibility for childminding is rotated amongst the group. I have absolutely no idea how they arrive at such a sophisticated procedure. All I know is that it happens.

Even a cow's tone of voice alters according to the circumstances. The noise a cow makes at the time of calving is a gentle and rhythmic lowing; there is no mistaking the naughty nature of her desires when she is bulling, nor the desolation of her call to an errant calf which has temporarily absented itself. Dumb animals? I don't think so.

Horses too, are big on communication. When Ziggy was weaned, we barred up the hole above the bottom stable door with an arrangement of chicken wire in a wooden frame and the obligatory half metre of baler twine, so that she could still see out but not climb out. Horses do funny things at weaning time, and door mountaineering is close to the top of the list of deviant behaviour. Old Rajah, in the stable opposite, always had a curiously high pitched whinny for such a big horse – rather like Brian Blessed talking with Julian Clary's voice. As soon as Ziggy was alone, Rajah's whinny took on an unexpectedly low tone, as if to reassure the young foal by imitating her mother's deeper call. Strange, huh?

Later, when Ziggy was going through her rebellious teenager phase, desperate measures were called for and I turned her out with Rajah, who then struck a pose consistent with his previous career in the police force. No quarter was given; he flattened his ears against the back of his head, bared his tombstone-like teeth and narrowed his eyes. Then he swung his sumo-style backside round and indicated that any minor transgression would result in her being kicked into the middle of next week. Momentarily his murderous appearance made Hannibal Lechter look like a reasonable guy with a catholic appetite. No words needed to be spoken; it was unambiguous communication of the highest order. Ziggy's manners improved from that day forward.

Maybe that is where we humans go wrong. Instead of indulging the anti-social mores of the little darlings we should pack them off to some feisty maiden aunt with a temper as hot as a chicken vindaloo and a graduate of the same school of nursery management as Rajah. I don't suppose there is much difference in hooliganism whether it is in horses or people – it is just that we are on our hind legs all the time rather than just some of it.

Lambs are great communicators. OK, they haven't appeared in inane adverts bleating on about how good it is to 'tawk' but they never lose their mothers in a crowd, like kids do with predictable frequency at agricultural shows throughout the summer. A ewe has no such problems; her bleat is unique so only her own offspring respond. Ewes and lambs may get separated at feeding time, yet within seconds of the last grain of feed being cleared from the trough, they are noisily mothering up again. Occasionally, a greedy opportunist lamb might sidle up to a neighbouring mum who looks like a bit of a soft touch and attempt to sneak extra rations, but such temerity is usually met with a deft kick, followed by the ovine variation on tossing the caber, hurling the hapless lamb high into the air and landing it, painfully, some distance away. It's communication, all right – I never said that sheep were subtle.

People do say, though, that they are stupid. I was once misguided enough to volunteer this opinion (in the days before I knew any better) to a neighbour of mine and do you know what he replied? Peering into the murky depths of his ale he said: 'Aye, Jackie, but stupidity is a shocking common affliction in people too you know.'

To which there was absolutely no answer.

Before you dismiss me as a complete loony and this as a load of anthropomorphic tosh, go and have a look at the birds in your garden. You will see that they have an equally mysterious means of establishing, quite literally, a pecking order. Like people in a queue for a hamburger at a fast food van they wait their turn for a meal at the hanging containers of nuts and seeds. I have noticed, incidentally, that sparrows queue politely but blue tits can be extremely impatient.

Something should be done about blue tits' manners.

Manx sheep are not just multi-horned, they're multi-purpose too. You can eat them, wear them, wipe your feet on them and make fancy crooks from their headgear. A very useful sheep indeed. Add to this litany of virtues the fact that they are also decorative and I can't help but wonder how they ever got to be 'rare' in the first place.

Golden Fleece

The Manxes have arrived. I know this sounds like some sort of armed invasion, but it really is not quite so alarming as all that. It's just my new flock of sheep. I use the word 'flock' loosely, since they number only ten in total; well, it seemed only decent to get into double figures. In acquiring Manx Loghtans I am trying to do my bit for conservation. At the risk of sounding more boring than a Black and Decker drill bit, I shall just leap briefly upon my soapbox and deliver a short homily.

If we are not very careful, our living heritage – a number of breeds of cattle, sheep, pigs and horses, not to mention poultry and the odd goat – are in danger of disappearing down the toilet bowl of commercialism. It may be that none of them are fantastically profitable in their own right – perhaps they yield carcasses too small for the late 20th century marketplace, or they may thrive best in wild tracts of land, which themselves are disappearing at a rate which ought to alarm us, or maybe they are not prolific enough to be viable.

For whatever reason, they have declined in this wonderful world of ours, obsessed as it is with the pursuit of ever higher yields and bigger profit margins. But I'll tell you this much for nothing – they are every bit as important to the history of our land as any listed building and just as deserving of preservation as any work of art. To stand by and watch them die out would be an act of the worst sort of apathy.

I trust you will be delighted to learn that during the last 25 years the number of breeds of farm livestock lost to extinction in Britain has been halted. Why? Because of the commitment of the RBST – the Rare Breeds Survival Trust, which not at all coincidentally, was formed a quarter of a century ago. Indeed the Trust has ensured that many breeds have increased quite dramatically in numbers; Irish Moiled and Longhorn cattle, for example, and of course, the Tamworth pig. Just think, but for the efforts of the RBST the antics of the Tamworth Two may never have lightened up the life of Britain during the dark days of winter. To be absolutely accurate, only 50% of the blood flowing in the veins of Butch and Sundance – for such was the nomenclature they acquired during their 15 minutes (and the rest) of mostly tabloid fame, was pure unadulterated Tamworth, but Tamworths are currently on Priority List One with the RBST, which means they are in 'Critical' danger of disappearing. Yes, OK, Butch and Sundance only disappeared temporarily, and subsequently languished in quite absurd luxury at some Pig Health Farm or other, but you know what I am driving at.

You may never have had the pleasure of making the acquaintance of a Tamworth pig and may consider the presence of Irish Moiled cattle on the planet as not being exactly pivotal to your personal happiness, but hold on a minute and consider this unpalatable fact. Suffolk horses – those whoppers who pull ploughs, or at least they used to before East Anglia was turned into one huge great prairie devoted to filling Euro-silos with grain we largely don't need and can't sell – are also on the 'critical' list of RBST priority. Saddleback and Gloucester Old Spot pigs are 'endangered,' Dales and Fell ponies are both 'vulnerable' and my Manxes have only recently been promoted from vulnerable status to the marginally more assured 'at risk.' Isn't it a good thing that a band of enthusiasts, who were probably classified as somewhere between 'barking' and 'eccentric' when they kicked off 25 years ago, are doing something about the situation?

The Trust is not a bunch of other-worldly dreaming idealists; it inhabits neither Disneyland nor the moral high ground of the contra-carnivores. It recognises that rare breeds cannot survive without some commercial appeal so it runs a meat marketing scheme promoting meat from extensively reared rare breed sheep, cattle and pigs, through accredited butchers and encourages the usage of wool from rare breed sheep. All in all, the RBST is doing sterling work to ensure that our living heritage stays just that – living.

I'll abandon the soap box now and introduce you to my sheep who all have names like your favourite auntie. There's Pat – she's perfectly proportioned and a quite exquisite example – and her pals Petunia, Patsy, Priscilla, Peggy, Petra, Paula and Pastal, together with two matriarchal figures, whose presence is an essential calming influence. Manx sheep can scale walls at a rate which would absent them from any high security prison in a matter of minutes, and possess jumping ability of which an event horse would be proud, so I thought that discouraging these natural, if undesirable tendencies could be best achieved by a couple of older girls whose high-jumping days were over.

Officially designated as 'primitive' sheep, Manx Loghtans originally hail from the Isle of Man, although I am sure you will be relieved to learn that they have a full complement of four legs, not three as you might have expected, given their provenance. They can have up to four horns, which means that the outside of their heads can get a bit crowded, whilst the inside is teeming with wild thoughts – mostly hatching elaborate escape plans. They are dinky in size, being slightly larger than an average Labrador and coffee, or loghtan coloured. And here's today's completely useless nugget of information – the word 'loghtan' derives from the Manx for 'mouse brown.' (It is odd that the mice I catch in traps, in various stages of development from infants right through to parents, grandparents and second cousins twice removed are grey, not brown at all, but I shan't get all pedantic about detail.)

As Manx fleeces are this arrestingly alluring shade of mouse, I am exploring the possibility of having the wool spun and knitted up. This will result in possibly the most expensive sweater in the North of England but there will be a certain satisfaction from being the only person in the village wearing my own sheep.

Sad to say, I am not up to the knit-one-purl-one bit in spite of the fact that my mother was a highly accomplished knitter. Of string dishcloths, mostly. Following in the family tradition I once knitted a shawl on needles as big as pokers. Swathed in this garment (groovy, heh?) I lurked in dark corners at parties fancying myself as a bit of a hippie. It went some way to compensating for my lack of the very apogee of hippie heaven, an Afghan coat. These conveniently doubled as housing estates for displaced fleas and many hippies had to have them surgically removed at the end of the decade. But the cool garment for the 21st century is definitely a mousy cardie. You read it here first.

I have a confession to make. The guy who lived next door loathed my boss almost as much as I did and we conspired together to humiliate him. One night, we drove to his Swedish girlfriend's house where, as we had expected, the Boss, a man who really should have stayed in his crypt, had left his car in the driveway with the keys still in the ignition. We locked the car and went home with the keys in our possession and a sense of natural justice in our hearts. I don't believe the Boss ever suspected me, or indeed my accomplice. Wicked? Yes, of course it was but it felt very, very sweet.

Memories are Made of This . . .

Do you believe that nostalgia ain't what it used to be or do you, like me, quite like sifting through the bran tub of your personal history? Occasionally amongst the retrospective bric-a-brac I uncover some sparkling gem of light relief, but more usually I recall the awful, the dismal and the depressing. Why? Because unlike most normal people I do not dodge the potholes of memory lane, rather I dwell on them, recalling misery with all the clarity of a pane of glass freshly polished with Windowlene.

Take the events of my 'gap year,' except I'm too old to have had one of those – instead I had an 'I Don't Know What To Do Next So I'll Do Anything Rather Than Grow Up For A Year' year. This necessarily involved animals, farms and the great outdoors. There was also a hideously unsuitable boyfriend somewhere in the equation, with whom the parents were underwhelmed, but they acquiesced to my plans on the basis that it would get both animals and him out of my system. The parents were right on one score – he went, but wrong on the other because the animals didn't.

First I worked for a retired Brigadier, and his completely dotty Master of Foxhounds wife. They were a pair of Great British Eccentrics, with whom, you may not be surprised to learn, I felt entirely at home. Occasionally, I strayed from my usual milieu of the calf pens into a milking parlour of gentle, strawberry pink Dairy Shorthorns. It was a carefree, Anne of Green Gables, existence.

But I was young and exceptionally daft, so lured by the prospect of one or two exciting horses to ride (headcases, in hindsight) I moved on to haymaking, pigs and yet more calves, on another farm, which at first sight appeared to have escaped from the pages of a 'Property For Sale Colour Supplement.' But all was not as it seemed. The authentic timbering owed less to the Tudors than to the ministrations of Bodger and Codger (builders – we dare if you care, or some such equally risible pledge) and although there was a pond it was filled with stagnant gunk not trout. The swimming pool, instead of being a worthy addition to a small country estate, had accumulated a dense alluvial silt which supported so startling a variety of aquatic life forms that it was surprising no marine biologists were encamped on the adjacent lawns.

It was a funny farm, in more ways than one. None of the gates worked, but that was of little consequence because the stock could get through any of the dykes. Inevitably, catastrophes ensued; Friesian bulls took themselves off for unaccompanied early morning walks with such frequency that the simple act of taking the dog out first thing carried with it a level of risk normally associated with bungee jumping in a high wind. On one such occasion, the cowman emerged from the farmyard and hollered 'go back yer bugger,' to the bull. If I had not seen it with my own eyes, I should be inclined to disbelief rather than the other option, but turn the beast did, and obediently retraced its steps. Relief? It felt more like divine deliverance.

The inadequacy of the fencing also meant that nocturnal marauding cattle were commonplace much to the consternation of nocturnal marauding motorists. The farm boss, one of the latter, was conducting a-not-very-discreet affair with a comely Swede in the next village. Now, I sleep the sleep of the just and the knackered; I am the only person I know who needs to set an alarm clock surrounded by coins on a tin tray to be sure of waking up, but even I could not sleep through a hullabaloo so tumultuous that the detonation of an entire barrel-load of gelignite would have seemed a minor distraction by comparison.

In amidst it, curiously, was a splash. A very loud splash. I could, I suppose, have stuck my head back under the covers and ignored it, but instead I poked my head out of the caravan window to investigate. Predictably, the boss, full of the milk of human kindness and fresh from one of his assignations, fired a volley of abuse, which he followed up with an exhortation to get outside and do something useful. Call me an old defeatist if you like, but it was difficult to think what I, a scantily clad 17 year old female, could possibly do about a Hereford bullock snorkelling in the murky depths of the pool, while a number of his companions looked on in awe. Well, I presumed he was snorkelling because it was before synchronised swimming was invented, and anyway, being solo he had no one to synchronise with.

The remaining events of that night are thankfully a hazy

memory, but the swimming pool was decommissioned from that night forward, though the surrounding lawns carried the pock marks of cloven hooves for months to come. It looked as if the Devil himself had been partying. The squalid caravan I lived in was so cold that the only way to get dressed without suffering frostbite was to undertake the operation beneath the duvet and then emerge into the outside world fully clothed. I swear that even the rats whose bewhiskered noses I grew accustomed to seeing peeping from gaps in their twilight world twixt floor and wall, wore mufflers and mittens. But at least the van was a sanctuary from the battle zone of the boss and his wife who spat bile at one another from sunrise to sunset – and often beyond.

The van was marooned in the farmyard, which meant that each time I had been out at night, I had to park my mini as close to the back door as possible and then climb over the gear stick – an act of supreme delicacy in itself – and let myself out of the passenger's door. I was then obliged to run the gauntlet of the boss' geese. They caught me once, and inflicted a painful peck on my hindquarters. Riding out three racehorses each morning with a very sore bum was ample justification for bearing them a king-sized grudge so I was tickled pink when the boss' wife decided both to divorce her husband and to rid the farm of his wretched geese.

The geese were despatched with the minimum of fuss, but the boss himself was harder to displace. Come to think of it, he was the first genuinely psychotic personality I ever met. When the divorce papers arrived, he lobbed a chair in the general direction of his wife; it ricocheted off the Kenwood Chef sending a spume of partially pulverised gazpacho ceilingwards. When I saw the farm advertised in a glossy national publication 20 years on, I wondered if the gazpacho blobs, which had dried to the exact colour of a flying ant swatted with a rolled up copy of the *Racing Post*, persisted as a reminder of that cataclysmic September day.

All things considered, I wasn't sorry to leave. Now do you see what I mean about maudlin memories?

I am just beginning to get to grips with the Manxes, now. Though they still have the advantage, obviously.

Counting Sheep

I have been watching my flock, not exactly by night in the Biblical fashion, but watching them nevertheless. And I am utterly bewitched by the hierarchical system and normal behavioural patterns of my little group of Manx Loghtans. I rather like this phrase 'normal behavioural pattern.' I first came across it when I was languishing in a hospital bed watching a chap on breakfast TV banging on about farming methods. Farmed animals should, he asserted quite rightly in my view, be able to act out their normal behavioural pattern – that is to say, pigs ought to have the freedom to root, cattle to graze, and presumably, sheep to die at will and without serving notice to quit.

Incidentally, I was only in hospital a week but when I was told that full recovery would take six weeks, I did one of those things they do in 19th century novels – a sardonic smile. Ha! Six weeks of 1) Watching the racing in the afternoon, and conveniently the National Hunt season was just warming up nicely; 2) Reading thick books; 3) Having an afternoon snooze. I began to wonder if a relapse might be in order. Needless to say, after five days I was bored witless and took to haunting the byre in a pink fluffy dressing gown to ensure that my cows were being properly milked. Inertia and indolence are not my scene. So, watching my rare breed sheep is a nice peaceful activity, but in small doses.

I used to think that only terribly posh people kept Rare Breeds – the sort of folk who anoint their chips (or perhaps that should be pommes frites) with balsamic vinegar and feed their houseplants mineral water. This is probably quite wrong but clearly, some of the potential flock owners are unsuspecting shepherds, if the Manx Breeders' Group leaflets are anything to go by. I quote for the benefit of those who do not believe me: 'Sheep spend most of their time either grazing, walking or resting. When a sheep lifts its head from grazing it will usually face the direction in which it intends to walk.' Does this come as any surprise to you? No, I thought not. It didn't to me either. However imbecilic a sheep may be it does at least look where it is going and doesn't do a Mr Bean on the nearest fence post. There's a bit on mating too, but let's face it, that's the same the world over, whether you're a sheep, a human or a snapping terrapin.

I suppose I have spent more time amongst these beguiling little creatures than the commercial sheep I have had in the past. Possibly because of their feral background, they were more than a little wild when they arrived. Initially they regarded me in an Orwellian four-legs-good-two-legs-bad sort of fashion. Rather than get down on all fours – though, truly, I did not dismiss this out of hand – I resorted to simple bribery and plied them with Bob's Mix, a confection so delicious that I've been elevated to the status of bestest pal. Now they trot towards me each morning, going 'bleh, bleh, bleh' and sounding just like Prime Minister's Question Time.

I could set my watch by them. 8.00 they are down the bottom of the field, by 8.30 they are milling about around the trough, and if – heaven forbid – I'm late, they nick off about ten minutes later. They return once they spy me and my little blue bucket, but they give me as filthy a look as a sheep can muster to convey their displeasure at being kept waiting.

One is quite obviously the leader of the flock. She is one

of the younger ewes, so there seems no obvious deference to age. On behalf of her mates, she keeps alert (surely this country's got enough lerts, perhaps she should be a loof instead?) head up, ears twitching at intervals, nostrils aquiver. If she detects anything unfamiliar, she sticks her head high in the air, the better to read the signals borne on the wind.

She asserts her inalienable right to feed first with force if necessary. In a daily ritual a second sheep – always the same one – challenges for the privilege; they confront each other and lock horns with an earsplitting clack. Then they scowl at one another and retreat to opposite ends of the trough to eat, each pausing occasionally to check the whereabouts of the other. And by the way, a Manx tup (ram) has a very clear idea of his place in the scheme of things. First. He has four horns each up to 2 feet long and if you quarrel with him he'll poke you in the eye.

Breakfast time apart, they take their rest below the top of the hill well out of the wind and snuggle up tightly, so tightly that I sometimes wonder if they are playing a special sheep game – how many sheep can you get on how small a tussock of grass.

I have a theory that the more primitive the species, the more ingrained are their instincts. We can learn much from these old breeds, with their complex yet intuitive behaviour, and I shall continue to watch them. So be assured that if you catch me leaning on a gate, my body may be idle, but my brain is doing a moonwalk.

Possessed of a pioneer spirit noticeably absent in my Manxes – about a third of which have no sense of adventure and remain on their Isle of Man homeland – a few weeks ago I ventured beyond the county boundary into Northumberland. (I had my passport with me, just in case.) The purpose of this foray was to see the unique Chillingham Wild White Cattle which have roamed the area for about 700 years, untouched by human hand. Indeed, on the rare occasion human hand has touched, other members of the herd have responded by killing the contaminated one. They eat only grass and meadow hay, eschewing even straw unless in extremis, and reject concentrates even then. The King Bull fights for supremacy of the herd and the cows creep off to calve in privacy, later introducing their calves to the herd in a complicated admission ceremony. The system of communication between them can only be guessed at and I came away with enormous respect for these wild and magnificent beasts. Their herd behaviour might be anathema to pacifists, but there is no denying that it is highly sophisticated.

We could do worse than to learn one thing from the Chillingham Cattle, as we walk the footpaths of Cumbria especially if we have a doggy companion (and frankly I feel a bit of a spare part walking sans dog). The Chillingham cattle stampede when agitated, agitation which often stems from a perceived threat to their calves. Whilst the potential danger of getting into an argument with a bull is well known, we fail, all too frequently to accord the suckling cow, be she Wild White or Furious Friesian, the respect she deserves. We may know that Rover is too old/daft/uninterested, but Daisy doesn't and she will metamorphose into an enraged beast if her calf is imperilled. Or more importantly, if she thinks it is. Sadly, the failure to appreciate this situation has had particularly tragic consequences for a handful of walkers.

Warehouses full of agricultural accessories are filled with the same temptations as any other retail outlet. There is a very real danger that by the time you leave you will have convinced yourself that your life will not be complete until you have bought a goodly proportion of the goods. You may return home with supplies of pig wormer (in spite of not having any pigs), elbow length rubber gauntlets (for which you will surely find a use), yellow sheep marker (slightly out of date and a real bargain) and a box of bolts. But leave that calving machine behind. You really do not need it.

Calving Time

I am not a natural born shopper. I just never have the time. You see, on dry days there is a horse to ride and on wet ones a shed to divest of cobwebs. In the house, I do not use the offensive term 'cobweb,' I call them spider sanctuaries and stress the environmental good sense of not disturbing them. It is an excuse which has served me well down the years.

As far as supermarket shopping is concerned I have lists, and neither dither, explore nor browse. Purveyors of 'new improved' products stand no chance with me; I buy the same stuff I did 15 years ago with clinical simplicity – I get what is on my list and then I go home. If I go without a list I am adrift on a sea of indecision, unable to make up my pathetic little mind whether to have own brand coffee (this usually turns out to be a mistake because it generally tastes like sewage effluent spiked with pulverised Feed and Weed granules, but that's another matter) or to live expensively on my favourite Arabica. I indulge in few luxury items, and coffee is one of them.

In my days of cow keeping, I used to have an early morning cappucino, before anyone this side of Milan had heard of the stuff – I made a cup of good ground coffee, took it down the yard and held it six inches below Lady's teat, she being the most tolerant, and gave a goodly squirt. Worked a treat. Nowadays, I have a machine which produces nearly as good a cappuccino to a sound-track of hissing and spluttering, and doesn't need cattle fodder.

The only shop which is my natural milieu is the agricultural merchants, and I anticipate the weekly trip there with a frisson of enthusiasm. I have always rubbed along nicely with the chaps in the Penrith branch of Carr's who, over the years, have good naturedly relieved me of a small fortune.

When Carr's outgrew its quaint pigeonnier at the top of Castlegate they moved into a building with all the charm of an aircraft hangar on an industrial estate. What it lacks in architectural merit it makes up for with capaciousness and stocks everything the most avaricious peasant could desire – tractor parts and spreader chains, shafts for gripes and clothes for rain, feed for everything which breathes from camelid to cow (but no Pot Noodle), sprays, dips, lotions and potions the like of which would cause even the witches in Macbeth to stop stirring their cauldrons, and heaven knows what else. For those who prefer the homeopathic approach, I expect they can probably get eye of newt and toe of frog – but not from stock of course, just to order.

The other week I was visiting Carr's, my mission to acquire one of those wildly expensive licks which my Manx sheep like to snack on – a gastronomic affectation totally out of kilter with their native Manx diet of rough moorland grass and the occasional kipper.

Closeted amongst the gizmos and gadgets there was a

fellow examining a piece of apparatus which looked like a catapult the mother of the Cerne Abbas Giant might have bought him for his fifth birthday. 'Go on out and play, Cerne and don't annoy the Stegosauri from number 25.' But this was no giant's catapult. It was a calving machine. I have very delicate sensibilities where such things are involved, and if I were Daisy, one look at that contraption and I would no doubt produce quads, pronto. But the gentleman fondling its extremities with reverence assured me that it 'saves a lot of effort.' Hmmm.

Perhaps I should have had one of these when I had the Jerseys because my own memories of calvings are of intense physical effort and a facility with rope tricks which would put the average Indian to shame.

The first cow I bought did not even provide an adequate dress rehearsal for what lay ahead. I acquired her three weeks before she was due to calve and I resisted – with no little difficulty – the temptation to leave her where she was until after parturition. The night before her due date, I tucked her up in a deep bed of fragrant straw and by morning there were two. This calving lark seemed like a licence to print money, because in less than three weeks her sturdy Limousin cross bull calf featured prominently in the list of top prices at the mart and effectively redeemed about a third of his mother's purchase price. It was enough to rekindle my faith in the tooth fairy.

Needless to say, this happy state of affairs did not last for long.

Contrary to received wisdom it is possible for Jerseys to produce extremely decent beef crosses, particularly when put to Belgian Blue bulls. And mine never had any problems calving them – child bearing hips, you see. But for some inexplicable reason I had dreadful problems with pure bred calves, chiefly that they were all the wrong sex.

175

I spent hours pouring over articles, and Herd Books; I sought advice as to whether New Zealand or Danish bulls were best, whether a reintroduction of some Island blood might improve my stock or whether to just take the Lucky Dip Bull of the Day.

And do you know what – all the pure Jerseys, with one exception, were bulls. Consequently, we lived almost exclusively on veal. My fried calves' liver in lime butter narrowly escaped the attentions of a TV chef, and my Osso Buco became a legend in its own lunchtime, but numerically, if not emotionally, my herd of Jerseys remained stable.

Dove's calf was that exception – a heifer and a Jersey. Which was a mite unfortunate really because Dove herself was not the prettiest cow. She wore an expression of permanent, fixed horror, had flat feet and a hairy spike of punky fur running along the top of her neck. As her calving date approached, I watched her hawkily. She had been fidgeting away for an hour or so, but seemed to be making little headway beyond getting more and more agitated and fretful. Eventually, we attached ropes and hauled at the emergent but stubbornly wedged feet. Reinforcements were summoned and Tom, our neighbour, stood thoughtfully in the shed doorway.

'I'll fetch the tractor,' he muttered, turning on his heel. That was enough for Dove. She gave a mighty heave and propelled a weedy heifer calf into the dank December afternoon. Considering her part of the bargain well and truly kept, Dove refused to have anything further to do with the calf, which I christened Rosebud, although looking at her spindly legs, Twiggy might have been more fitting.

Against all the odds she pulled through. In time, she had calves of her own and thankfully, was a better mother than her own.

But with the benefit of the greatest calving tool of all – hindsight – I think the gentleman in Carr's was right. At the time of Rosebud's birth one of those machines would indeed have saved a great deal of effort. Mine.

People say collies make lousy pets. People say that collies need to work. What happened to my two, then? What they regard as the essentials of life are, in no particular order: a cuddle; a Manx Loghtan rug to sleep on; a fire in front of which to set the Manx Loghtan rug; no noisy housework to be done during daylight hours; digestive biscuits on demand. Oh, and another cuddle would be nice.

Dogs are Hard Work

'The idea,' opined my neighbour, who had missed his true vocation as a Wise Man and fetched up in the Eden Valley in the 20th century instead, 'is not that you keep sheep, but that they keep you.'

Nineteen ninety eight was the year which changed all that. Shepherds' purses emptied and you counted yourself lucky if your sheep kept you awake, never mind in business, with prices slumping lower than a snake's belly button. Still, lambing time will cheer us all up – won't it?

Lambing is when we really notice sheep, rather than just thinking of them as illustrations on the rural wallpaper. During the rest of the year they punctuate the landscape like so many commas on a page; come Spring they achieve headline status. Extroverts stand on their mothers' backs, king-of-the-castle style, whilst gangs gambol up and down dykes with all the restraint of children in supermarket aisles.

But there is more, much, much more to keeping sheep than just lambing. The rest of the year is an unrelenting daily round of dosing, worming, trimming, scanning, injecting, clipping and dipping. Thankfully, sheep do not have to be dipped as often as they used to. Only a few years back, in accordance with edicts from the Ministry, sheep spent nearly as much time under water as Jacques Cousteau. Now there is even a preparation which obviates the need to dip altogether, which is an absolute godsend for keepers of small flocks such as my Manxes.

Of all the tasks which fall to even the shepherd, none is more fraught with hazard than foot dressing and last summer, due to extremely wet conditions, my sheep suffered from maggots in their feet, an affliction I am happy never to have come across before. But who would have thought that dressing sheep's feet could seriously damage your complexion? Freddie, my Chief of Staff in a vigorous maggot eradication campaign, will testify that it was so. There we were one minute, merrily exterminating maggots to our hearts' content and the next minute we were in the realms of You-Couldn't-Do-It-If-You-Tried farce.

The foot trimmers took on a life of their own and orbited into a spin so elegant, so elaborate that it reminded me of Peter Mandelson at the zenith of his powers. They landed, scoring a direct hit on the canister of violet foot spray, which emitted a colourful shower of liquid in a gracious arc, covering Freddie from cap to wellies. He returned home an alien vision in pointillist purple. I am only grateful, if slightly surprised, that he has been allowed to come and play at Rowfoot since.

Of course, there is one logistical obstacle in expediting any one of these tasks of basic stockmanship. You have to move the sheep first. You can do this one of three ways. The first is to train your flock to recognise a bucket of feed – and this is the crucial bit – follow it. Efficacy rating – six out of ten, except on a windy day, when they are easily distracted and go off in as many different directions as there are sheep.

The second method involves enlisting the assistance of

a small army of helpers, working on the premise that the combined effort of six humans is roughly comparable to that of half a dog, however incompetent. Efficacy rating – zero. And, a word of advice here – be sure to select people whose friendship you do not value too highly because it is axiomatic that you will fall out during the operation. So, if your sheep need shifting just before Christmas, or around the time of your birthday if you have a twin, you can expect to make significant savings on gifts. Equally, if you are seeking incontrovertible grounds on which to obtain a divorce, then be sure to include your partner. Only a boating holiday in the South of France carries a higher rating on the Divorceometer. Believe me.

Thirdly, use a dog. Efficacy rating – depends on dog, but however useless, he has twice as many legs as you and ten times as much influence over sheep. One hopeless, cretinous dog is better than any number of humans, and I speak from experience as I've got two. In the time which a good dog would have saved me I am reasonably confident that I could have studied for a degree in anthropology, perfected my origami and learnt the xylophone.

Dog number one, Gyp, has an overactive initiative gland and suffers from acute selective deafness when faced with a small flock of sheep. On a good day, I can at least stop her in her tracks and make her sit, but on a bad day – and yesterday is as good an example of a thoroughly bad day as I can think of – I can make her do nothing at all, in spite of finishing up with a sore throat from screaming at her, and threatening to tie her to the washing machine for time immemorial. Considering that Gyp hates the washing machine, issuing such a threat was a despicable tactic.

Number Two dog, TV (I'd rather be watching the racing from Haydock) Tess, tried, for the first time in living memory to be half useful. A real change of heart, there.

Intermittently, she threw me a 'Confused of Tunbridge Wells' look, wondering if she, or her sister were the target for my highly vocal terms of disparagement, insult and exasperation.

I had not intended to bring all the sheep in as it was only my magnificent borrowed tup, Pretty Boy, who needed a foot inspection. The maggots of summer have gone, but a wet autumn and even wetter winter have meant more, but different, foot problems.

I had caught him easily enough the day before at the trough, but he is far too bright to let that happen a second time and took off at full tilt. Did you know that God only gave the sheep four legs for reasons of aesthetic symmetry? They certainly don't need all four judging by the speed Pretty Boy could travel at on three. So there was nothing for it but to gather them all up and pounce on him in the pen – as much as it is possible to pounce on anything with horns his size.

Dogs notwithstanding, the sheep were secured eventually and the Boy upended for his emergency pedicure. And the purple stuff went in roughly the right direction, too. Oh, happy day.

So now you know all about the hazards of dressing feet, you may want to put that plan for a few sheep on hold. Still, they say goldfish can be very rewarding.

Agas and Rayburns epitomise the country kitchen in a way no other appliance does. It might be an exaggeration to say that I couldn't live without mine but I would certainly rather not have to try. It's not just the cooking, either. When a tree falls down in the next village and cuts off all the power, you will have to run about in the dark, your gas central heating loses the will to live but your Rayburn will keep you toastily warm. If you can get near it for collie dogs, that is.

Great Balls of Fire

When I say 'farm machinery' what do you think of? Tractors, muck spreaders, flails, combine harvesters, variable chamber roller balers – well, yes, but let's not get too carried away. All of those are farm machinery in the conventional sense, but there is one piece of equipment which most farmers would be loath to part with, especially in Spring and it lives indoors.

More correctly, it rules the kitchen with an unspoken tyranny which makes Herod look like a kind-hearted King. It is the Aga. Or in my case, the Rayburn – a poor man's Aga; Agas star in rustic sagas whereas humble Rayburns are just domestic bit part players. Nevertheless the Rowfoot Rayburn is a vital, if not actually decorative (mine is municipal lavatory tile blue) weapon in the farmer's armoury against cold thighs, dead lambs and wet clothes.

When we first came to Rowfoot, we wreaked a fair bit of structural havoc, which meant that for some time I had no other means of cooking than the blue beast itself. This did not disturb me unduly; I had spent some time living on a farm where the Aga was – and probably still is – the one and only means of cooking, heating water and thawing out anything which drew breath, so I just stood in front of my Rayburn and addressed it as one would a haggis on Burns night, although in more informal terms.

I think I said, 'it's you and me now, mate.' It belched a bit of soot at me and our friendship was sealed. In the early days it became rather over-excited about heating water. As the tank approached maximum temperature, indoor thunder resonated throughout the house; everything shuddered in an architectural fit, pictures swayed on the walls and light fixtures trembled. By diverting some of the hot water into radiators, Ray's rampant tendencies were pacified a little, but cooking was quite another matter.

Regrettably, I have inherited all my mother's culinary skills. She had many remarkable qualities, my mum, but cooking was not one of them; she was the only person I have come across who could burn boiled eggs. Nor did I improve at school. It was called 'domestic science' then, and indeed, many of my efforts resembled chemical experiments more closely than anything edible. My recollections of the first few weeks haunt me with a clarity I can only describe as being every bit as electric as the cooker. The first week, we were charged with cooking breakfast, which involved some milk boiling over on to some incinerated remains of toast beneath – this was in the days of eye level grills, but only if you knelt down. The second week, we made gingerbread and mine was OKish, except that I had forgotten to put the ginger in. The third week, I assembled an apple crumble and neglected to light the oven.

The fourth week, the teacher, Mrs Evans, whose diminutive stature concealed a Herculean personality, met me at the door of her hallowed domain and instructed me not to go in, not to pass go and not even to think about £200.

'Go away and do your Latin 'omework,' she said in her measured Welsh lilt, 'and don't, for God's sake ever come back.'

There was menace in them there words, so I went, gratefully chanting 'ambulo, ambulas ambulat.' To my knowledge I have neither poisoned nor inflicted untreatable gastro damage on anyone, so Mrs Evans would be proud of me now, especially since I have progressed to doing that very 'country' thing of making bread. Although my first loaves were more like offensive weapons than anything fit for human consumption – the dogs wouldn't touch them and even the garden birds left the crumbs, no doubt mistaking them for lead shot – I have improved a bit since. Honestly.

But it is in the Spring when the Rayburn really comes into its own. Many a hypothermic lamb has been popped into the reviving warmth of the bottom oven, in which, under normal circumstances, I cook stews overnight. (I have always felt on safe ground with a good stew.) A hastily scrawled note reading 'lamb in bottom oven' could be dangerously ambiguous; there could either be a tasty casserole coming to optimum toothsomeness, on the other hand the oven could be serving as a temporary refuge for a small cloven hoofed occupant with incipient rigor mortis. The Patient Roll of Honour is impressive: 'Small' – half dead Mule/Suffolk cross, a rejected triplet – cured (that is 'cured' as in 'got better' not pickled, dried, preserved). 'Fluffy' – fully three quarters dead, and dangerously premature judging by his fleece, which was devoid of lifesaving tightness and density – cured. 'Droopy' a saggy-eared sad runt, hypothermic – cured. 'Rabbit-hole,' named because that's where he took shelter from a marauding jet several hours before I found his tail sticking limply out of a hole – cured.

Of course, there is a price to pay. Rayburns are filthy

things, and for the duration of the winter everything is covered in a light film of coal dust. The chimney has to be swept a couple of times a year, and in the intervening periods, needs a bit of attention from the DIY Flue Doctor, and as I'm Jackie of All Trades here, that's me. It is messy and tiresome but I just regard it as a premature excursion into second childhood, and as I liked mud and puddles in my first one, it is no great hardship.

In fact, it is a matchless joy to wiggle a length of bendy wire topped out with pointy black fibres, like a sewer rat plugged into the mains, up the chimney and there are few things quite so satisfying as several kilos of soot, little sticky bits of tar and the odd cremated bird slipping down your arm. Oh yes, you're a real country dweller with a Rayburn.

Rustic wannabes imprisoned in urban enclaves dress in Barbour jackets, fit bull bars to their four wheel drives (and wonderfully efficacious they are too, because the last time I was in the King's Road I saw not a single Simmental) and install Agas in Kensington flats to lend substance to their fantasies, but I think this is missing the point. After all, if you live in Chelsea, of course you might prefer to dry your best La Senza knickers on an overhead airer, but you hardly need to desiccate a freshly cured fleece, boil barley for the elderly mare's supper, bake bread, resuscitate an orphan lamb, heat the water for your bath, warm your collie dog and get chilblains on your thighs, all at the same time do you?

Now, if you'll excuse me I'm off to investigate the contents of the bottom oven.

I do go back to London occasionally but there has to be a reason. Once, I left Carlisle early in the morning, in bright sunshine. I arrived in London in pouring rain and trekked – unsuitably dressed – down to Barnes to see Granny. Soaked, tired and terminally fed up, I arrived at the hospital. She peeped out from under the covers, muttered 'bugger orf,' and pulled the covers over her head. She didn't mean it. Or at least, I don't think she did, but with a reception like that it is hardly surprising that I don't make the journey too often.

Homeward Bound

Yesterday, I noticed a pair of buzzards riding the thermals above Hangingbrow Wood. The presence of a covey of partridge in the wood struck me as comparable, on a calibrated scale of Utter Wondrousness, to Messrs Armstrong and Aldrin's presence on the lunar surface in 1969. The soft toot-tooting of an evening owl fracturing the fragile evening quiet moved me quite ridiculously and I noticed afresh how voluptuously the fields roll in this part of Eden. Why all this sudden sensitivity? Because, dear reader, I have been in London, that's why.

My exposure to the concrete megalith factory-fantasy that is Milton Keynes started it off. Incidentally, when the train stopped there I noticed a poster bearing the legend: 'In 1880 the average speed of a horse drawn carriage in London was 15 mph. In 1997 the average speed of a car in London was 15 mph.' To affirm the reliability of this information, the source was quoted as the Government Traffic Census. Now, as far as the modern world goes, I know that I am as out of step as a line dancer with hiccups, but

187

it did make me wonder – is that really the best we can do for progress over 100 years?

No matter. The Branson Wagon rattled on into the great metropolis, and for the first time in five years I went back to re-une, which is, I suppose what one does at reunions, with old colleagues. One, whose physiognomy now sports as many lines as a piece of screwed up graph paper, contrives to keep body and soul together by selling advertising space on refrigerators and washing machines. Another now writes serious columns for newspapers and claims to be paid £1 per word. Whether he earns as much for conjunctions as for adverbs and what cost he puts on commas, remains a mystery but preposterous pay slips aside, I count myself far richer because my attempts to thwart ovine mass suicides are set in far better scenery than his urban scribblings.

It was a good party, but I don't really subscribe to all that 'tired of London, tired of life' stuff. Beyond a deliriously successful mooch around the art galleries I find that being stuck in the city, where the only wildlife you come across are grey tree-going rats (quite unequal to our cute Cumbrian reds) and the occasional ornamental pelican, is not much to my liking. Like a fish on an omnibus, I am out of my natural habitat.

Below the eyrie of our Portman Square hotel room, evening traffic screeched and hooted in raucously un-owly tones. Feeling absurdly homesick, I took myself on an imaginary perambulation around the fields of home, wandering through the gate and on to the hill to look at the wood. This little wood is our legacy to posterity and I trust that posterity will be suitably grateful for it.

The trees are more than saplings now, though not yet grown up. They are teenage trees, leggily immature and gangly, with unreliable inclinations and prone, if not to acne, then certainly to swaggering bouts of rebelliousness.

Tubes and stakes are gradually becoming superfluous as the treelets within become self-supporting; great grassy tussocks grow beneath them as shaggy as Sixties hairstyles and gradually a habitat which only a few years ago looked as likely to tumble into the abyss of extinction as the woolly mammoth, is regenerating. Only the speed of this process has surprised. Partridge have moved in with the haste of a bunch of squatters and their presence gruntles me greatly. There is another flock of small, brownish unidentified flying objects too.

It is my intention that in the fullness of time I shall be planted in the wood too, though when I tell anyone this they give me one of those looks normally reserved for three legged lurchers – tolerant, pitying even, yet tempered with a modicum of affection. I begin to be taken seriously when I explain that I have a deep-seated distaste for expensive firewood in the shape of a fancy sarcophagus and that cardboard biodegradable coffins start at £49.50 plus VAT.

One might be fun, but in the eyes of the Local Planning Authority, it is also the limit on the quotient of people you can plant without permission for Change of Use. You might, of course, consider that even a single corpse is one too many, taking into account the adverse effect exercising this privilege might have on the value of your house, not to mention the potentially catastrophic consequences on your summer bedding plants. It also raises one worrying question. Namely, if you fail to get permission for Change of Use, do the Chief Planning Officer and the Grim Reaper come to exhume you, and charge you posthumously with breach of Planning Law?

Anyhow, now that I have examined my little wood, in my virtual peregrinations I amble on to the top pasture and look down across the fields where a haytime long ago a plaintive cry sang out from the lips of an innocent: 'Uncle Jim, you've baled half a rabbit.'

I remember an occasion when the whole of the sheep field seemed to take on a lunar appearance itself (perhaps I should have phoned Buzz and Neil to see if they wanted to come round to play) covered, as it was one autumn, with a million mushrooms. I stroll back along the hedge-line, watching for weasels, spotting sloes, and climb the stile, concluding my boundary tramp not with a customary warm glow, but a bump back to a real world of traffic din and needle-thin rods of evening rain bulleting down on sullen grey pavements.

So it felt good to be, in Mr Garfunkel's words, Homeward Bound, with some nicely loony travelling companions bound for a post-nuptial Bad Taste party at Dalston. Although whether Dalston was ready for a fella clad in a silver lamé catsuit, with multi-coloured feather boa, was a matter for speculation. As the train took the strain through a cleavage in the hills, I became newly aware of just how stunningly beautiful and blessed is this corner of England. Is there, perhaps, a sustainable argument for padlocking anyone who disagrees with this contention to a lamp post in central London and leaving them there for, say, three days or until they beg for release, a condition of which would be renunciation of Full Moaning Rights.

I think so, don't you?

A brief but thoroughly comprehensive gallop through two whole millennia of Cumbrian agricultural history. And yes, the phraseology in the opening sentence is quite deliberate.

1066 And All That

The new millennium, up with which we are all fed, is upon us. As far as I can see, much of the significance has been obscured by arguments about domes, ferris wheels, rotundas and pyramids. Cuboid and spheroid structures aside, I suppose that at such times, we can be forgiven for going all reflective and ruminative, a bit like my old goat, Millie, who gives not a tinker's cuss about the millennium as long as she gets her ration of hay, a dried up bit of toast and three strands of pampas grass a day (I know, it must be like chewing razor blades, but who am I to quibble with a goat with such eclectic taste?)

With the new millennium came arguably the greatest challenges since the immediate post-war period to an industry under siege from rising costs and falling prices, from BSE and a poor public image: just as well that none of us knew how much worse it was going to get as Foot and Mouth lay in wait for us a year hence. It seemed quite bad enough at the time that alongside farming, traditional rural leisure pursuits were also under threat as pro and anti hunting factions bickered over exclusive rights to lofty principles of justice, freedom and conservation. Up there on the moral high ground it was, to coin a phrase, getting a bit crowded.

Not that life was any more peaceful at the start of the last millennium when – and this might have a familiar ring to it – we were engaged in some fearful squabbles with the

191

French. So serious did things become that some of the English (who were runners-up in the Hastings fixture of 1066) renounced Golden Delicious apples altogether. And if you happened to be a beef farmer in AD 2000 the passage of nearly a thousand years was obviously far too short a time to make the Entente any more Cordiale.

Further back still, in the first Millennium the poor old Celts who bestowed the name 'Cumbria' upon this favoured land, were getting to grips with the everyday problem of counting sheep. Perhaps they didn't sleep too well, the Celts. Their legacy, a supremely distinctive method of enumerating sheep – yan, tan, tethera, methera, remarkably survives to this day.

After the Celts, Cumbria was dominated by the Romans who landed in Kent in AD 43, probably nipping through the Nothing To Declare (except perhaps an insatiable desire to rule) channel at Dover. As one disembarked, he was heard to utter the words 'Sic transit gloria' meaning 'we had a rough crossing, but felt fine afterwards.' (He didn't really. I made that bit up. It's really to do with transitory human vanity, which frankly, is far less silly but also far less fun.)

Inexorably, the Romans made their way northwards, raping and pillaging as they went. In spite of their best efforts, and Hadrian making a thorough nuisance of himself a century or so later, nothing shifted the Brigantes, who farmed and fished in and around Cumbria, before, during and after the advent of the Romans. I'd say that even the combined effects of BSE, a strong pound, enough red tape to strangle a woolly mammoth, avaricious supermarkets, an urbanised population, and an upsurge in vegetarianism are small beer compared to the might of the Roman Empire. So, there would appear to be a minimal long-term threat to the survival of Cumbrian farmers who trace back to the Brigantes.

For those with an unbroken line to the Neanderthals, though, and there are a few, I am afraid there is no hope. The Romans established Emperor's Estates (which sounds like a property agency with rather dubious credentials) villa estates, which they worked with slave labour (little change there then) and coloniae, farms occupied by retired soldiers to keep them amused without falling back into their old habits of raping and pillaging. They relied not on the combined wisdom of Newton Rigg, the National Farmers' Union and the Min of Ag and Fish (as was), but on Vergil's Georgics for advice on stock and land management.

A good bloke, and clever with it, Vergil reckoned that Crop Rotation was a Good Idea, noting that wheat grows best after beans, vetches and lupins. He advocated rigorous stock and seed selection, and believed passionately in the practice of straw burning, advancing the little known theory that fire helped to dry the soil and open its pores (a nice image, even though I don't suppose many modern day farmers would take the same view for the same reason).

I have to take issue with him on one point though, and it is this – chuck out, he said, though obviously in Latin, the rams with dark tongues lest the fleeces of their progeny be flecked with grey. Well, Vergil, old son where does that leave my Manxes?

Still, he was back on surer ground with his recommendations on horse-whispering, advising 'pat your colts on the neck and murmur flattering words of praise.' Goats, he suggested, benefited from zero grazing rather than browsing free range, and should be taken bundles of lucerne, trefoil and salt-sprinkled herbs. That's Vergil for you, eloquent as well as practical. Nothing about pampas grass, though. I am not making this bit up. Truly.

What else did the Romans leave behind? Cherries,

pears, apples, plums, walnut and chestnut trees, the scythe and the measurement of the acre, which represented the standard day's work for a two-ox plough and would still be with us as a unit of agricultural measurement but for the EEC which appears just as keen as the Romans on rape and pillage though it employs marginally more subtle methods.

After the Romans had gone, Our Friends in the Norse visited and may have brought with them the ancestors of the Herdwick sheep we now claim as Cumbrian. Some folklorists argue that Herdwicks descend from sheep which swam ashore from the wrecked ships of the Spanish Armada, but I don't buy this. In the absence of hard evidence – and I have yet to see a sheep with a convincingly Latin moustache, wearing a wetsuit or doing a passable backstroke in the local municipal pool, I support the theory that Herdwicks came with the Norsemen. They have that cool, detached Scandinavian, Mika Haakinen look, don't they, Herdwicks?

So there you have it, a brief but thoroughly comprehensive gallop through two whole millennia of Cumbrian agricultural history in less time than it takes to deliver unto a goat a respectable portion of herbs and trefoil. You can go off and party with a clear conscience now.

The thing I remember most about this wet day was the exceptionally fine bags of chips we bought on the way home. And I don't even like chips, but they were hot which was more than the occupants of one Ford Maverick were that Sunday morning.

Frederic, frae Tow Law

I rather like this time of year. Between Autumn tupping and its Springtime harvest, in the silent, foetal world much is happening. Lambs swell their mothers' bellies and slow their progress, but outside the world lacks any sense of urgency. A few spindly tendrils of grass emerge from subterranean seclusion, experimentally, as if pausing to consider the wisdom of advancing further and as the mornings become ever lighter, birdsong crescendos melodically. I can once again perch on the dyke now that the risk of rising damp in the rump region is receding and watch the flock secure in the knowledge that the wonderful annual renaissance we call Springtime is comfortingly close.

Unhurriedly, I holler my familiar feed time call to arms. 'Sheep, sheeeeeep!' And they stream over the brow of the hill, this funny little flock of mine, primitive, robust, resourceful, different altogether from fleshy modern day commercial sheep. One or two ewes leap dementedly. Barren, empty, I think gloomily. Then I remember that Manx are very surprising sheep indeed and reassess – twins, probably. Each.

Frederic, as usual, leads the way to the trough, his antlers arranged upon his dark brown head as if in a vaguely obscene gesture. I shall miss Frederic when he returns to his owners, Paul and Louisa, in Tow Law, after his winter sojourn at Rowfoot.

On the day we set out to collect him, it had been a clear and sunny November morning in Ainstable. It was not a clear and sunny morning in Tow Law, but in Ainstable we didn't know that. Up towards Alston, conditions deteriorated. We plunged in and out of murk. The poet in me says it wasn't murk at all, but a dewy-droplet haze, like giant's breath exhaled into a chilly dawn, casting a gauzy curtain across the Pennine vastness. The realist in me knows it was thick, dense and moodily impenetrable gloom.

Many miles later, in Tow Law, it was raining with Swithinesque persistence but meteorological considerations are secondary to the pursuit of the perfect sheep. Even if perfect sheep do turn out to be three fields away. Half way across the first field, a spectre complete with devilish horns began to materialise in the mist. A Minotaur perhaps, reincarnated in all his bestial Cretan horror, in Co Durham? No. A buffalo then, a bison or even an Auroch? No again. This, in fact, was a bull, a diabolical Dexter called Lawson – after Chancellor Nigel in his fat days, before he discovered the Hay diet, or more likely the silage diet – and he was looking faintly murderous, the Dexter that is, not the former Chancellor. Marginally encouraged by the fact that he was mounted on sawn-off legs, which might minimise his athletic ability, I reckoned I should be able to cross the field faster than he could, although Wellington boots did nothing to encourage prospects of optimum velocity. The eponymous Duke, of Wellies fame, doubtless highly skilled in the noble military art of delegation, had whole battalions to scamper through the clart on his behalf so, as far as portents go, he hardly counts.

What is more, athletes, you will have noticed, have been

somewhat tardy, commercially at any rate, to endorse Hunter or Nora whilst falling over themselves to promote brands like Nike and Adidas. That I was pondering such details, with a large black bull poised menacingly due South of me, beggars belief, particularly as now it was raining . . . ice-cold drizzle settling on my neck and tracing a steely rivulet down my spine.

'He's fine, aren't you Lawson?' enthused Paul, scratching the Dexter's patent leather nose. Thinking bulls are 'fine' is slightly less sensible than believing in fairies at the bottom of the garden. Like the male of any specie, Lawson had the potential to be unpredicta-bull, irasci-bull or just plain untrustworthy. I am amongst lunatics, I thought.

There were three tup lambs to choose from, Frederic, Ethelred and Fubar. FUBAR? Yes, it means Fouled Up (or something very like it) Beyond All Recognition. Paul said it was a geological term, but frankly it sounded pretty basic Anglo Saxon to me. And anyway, we had to catch them first.

As we circuited the field for the umpteenth time, in pursuit of these three and with the eye in the back of my head working overtime to chart Lawson's progress or lack of it, I ceased to care which one we managed to lasso as a prospective spouse for the Rowfoot girls.

Particularly as it was still raining. The dog had taken unilateral industrial action and buggered off home (wise dog, I thought) and Plans A, B and C all failed miserably. Eventually, employing an elaborate subterfuge involving decoys and buckets of grub we eventually penned the wayward triumvirate of tups into a corner and got down to finer points of selection. I had already rejected FUBAR – I could never take an animal called FUBAR seriously, I am afraid, so would it be Ethelred or Frederic? Ethelred might be ready for anything, but his horn placement was not quite spot on, so we turned to Frederic.

'Clean legged, excellent fleece, better horns but a slightly furry tail,' said Louisa. Frederic clenched his buttocks in a vain attempt to conceal the offending item.

Furry tail or not, Frederic got the nod. Later, I joined him in the trailer, took off all my clothes and wrung them out, which unusual turn of events Frederic took in his stride.

Over time, he has been generous enough to overlook my little naturist lapse and we have become friends. I can sit on my favourite dyke – from which I can spy the spiny treetops of Combs Wood and saddle peaked Blencathra further away and daydream most satisfactorily – and stretch out a handful of Bob's Mix to him.

Frederic's chocolate hued head reaches forward, brushes my palm with his rubbery lips and, Barbie-pink tongue darting in and out, he nibbles thoughtfully, preoccupied with problems of his sheepy universe.

I shall miss him when he goes home to Tow Law.

*Don't get me wrong, here. I am not disputing that cleanliness is
next to Godliness; it's just that I would rather not get too close
to my Maker for a little while yet, if it's all the same to you.*

Squeaky Clean

Hygiene is a dirty word. Bugs and bacteria are crawl-
ing about British farms in covert posses, concealing
themselves in fur, feather and fleece if popular mythology
is to be believed. Is it really like that? Are farms really
getting dirtier, or has our environment become so shrink-
wrapped, double glazed and air conditioned that our
resistance is diminishing, because it has to be one or the
other really, doesn't it?

A funny thing occurred to me this morning while I was
shifting some ess-aitch-one-tee, muck by any other name.
And it was this . . . humans are the only specie to have
evolved hand washing as a necessary preliminary to
eating. Dogs not only don't bother, they continue to eat
square meals or any other shaped sort, without due regard
for where their tongues have been. Which just goes to
show that very few dogs are influenced by scaremonger-
ing in the newspapers.

New research suggests that the increase in childhood
allergies like asthma may, in part, be due to a lack of
'good bugs'; a theory which would neatly explain why,
unlike the overwhelming majority of my fellow travellers
in China, I escaped the Tiananmen Trots. I, a raw milk
drinking, home killed meat eating, fully paid up dung
bunger, had sufficient good little bugs galloping about my
system to fend off Far Eastern nasties. Even the over zeal-
ous (or perhaps that should be paranoid) couple who

religiously bought bottled water for cleaning their teeth, suffered horribly.

Of course not all farms are clean enough. Some, I grant, have approach roads which look like the aftermath of a mud slide following a volcanic eruption, yards which double up as machinery graveyards, and more plastic than Barclaycard knocking about the place, but they are unlikely to be establishments open to the public.

And all this obsessing over cleanliness is nothing new; it is just that recently it has turned into an art form. In the days when we sold cream, cream cheese, cheesecakes and butter direct to the public from the farm gate, or to hotels locally, the Ministry inspected us, our premises and our cows with quite frightening vigilance and frequency. The Ministry vet arrived bearing those twin talismans of officialdom – a clipboard and a smarmy grin – and inspected away while I filled out forms and Lady the cow struggled, often expending considerable effort, to describe a perfect arc in mixed media of liquid dung and air.

These congenial interludes ceased when the EEC decided that in order to protect the health of the nation – or Ainstable and its environs, anyway – it would need tiles (white, preferably) here, stainless steel there, twice yearly inspections at a cost of £90 a time, and probably wholesale modification of Lady's agitated bowel movements too. It was all too much – about £4,000 too much to be precise and we threw in the towel and sold the milk quota.

The cows went on a Suckler Cow Retraining Scheme (sadly not funded by any European money box) and I learned one very salutary lesson – cows are much better at rearing calves than humans, with the possible exception of Colin Harrington at Mounsey Bank whose expertise in these matters is second to none.

Of course, farmers would find all this easier to take if we all played on that figment of the politician's fantasies, the level playing field. But it seems a bit rich that we can watch food programmes on the BBC in which the presenter engages a gnarled Frenchman in some jolly conversation. Monsieur, bonce adorned in Gallic beret at perilous angle, explains happily that oui, oui, he conjured up his Soupe de Poisson Formidable in that shed there – the one at the back of his house, with rusting hinges and a door with all the qualities of a prospective mystery item on Going for a Song. And were there any tiles – white or otherwise? There were most assuredly not. No stainless steel either. Far less any rubber gloves, signs saying 'wash your hands,' regulation washbasins, or white hats in sight.

Only once have I been blighted by infection caused by animal contact, and that was when I caught Orf from a sheep. Orf is a nasty, scabby, affliction and although unpleasant isn't actually life threatening, although one accident I witnessed was – a brief but bloody encounter with a butching knife. The consequent visit to casualty involved a wait so long that the victim was in grave danger of death by boredom or worse, over-exposure to women's magazines.

So I suppose I've been lucky really. My own immune system must be pretty robust, mainly because my youth was a Dettox-free zone. I confess, though, that I drank a whole bottle of bleach when I was four – it was an attention thing, and I was held upside down and shaken vigorously for several minutes afterwards. (No, don't mutter 'well that explains it then.') My mum might have been fanatical about Spring cleaning, and its seasonal pals, Summer cleaning, Autumn cleaning and Winter cleaning, but she had no scruples whatsoever about a devilish little practice she called Dog Owners'

201

Revenge, visited upon my father when he transgressed.

I suspect I was also a victim of this ritual which went as follows: pick the 'peeps' (doggy sleep) from the dog's eyes, then season lightly and stir, with secret ceremony into father's dinner. And serve. It was always doomed to be an empty gesture, this attempt to challenge the physiology of a soldier who had dined on rat (a bit like chicken, but the tastier for not having been battery reared, he said), when supplies failed to materialise on the North West Frontier. I expect mum felt natural justice to have been honoured at the time. He suffered some terrible health, my dad, but most of it was consequent upon having jumped out of far more aeroplanes than is strictly advisable for any earthling and nothing to do with hygiene sabotage.

So your home can be just as fraught with danger as any farm. It will, I know, cheer you enormously to learn that as well as dust which lurks unseen, you can catch toxoplasmosis from a domestic cat, psittacosis from a budgie, and the family dog might, for all you know, be giving free lifts to fleas.

Extra on-farm risks pale in comparison with this lot, even if they do include ringworm – itchy and it makes your hair fall out – which you can catch from affected horses and cattle. If you were really unlucky you might pick up Lyme disease from a sheep. But do not fret, it is very rare, not serious and can be treated with antibiotics.

The proprietors of farms open to the public are unusually meticulous and intrepid folk, only trying to raise an honest buck, although any rise in their agricultural income is likely to have had all the celerity of a lame tortoise and been outstripped by a far steeper rise in accompanying stress levels.

Buoyed up by the knowledge that you are statistically less likely to catch a deadly disease from a cow pat than you are to trip over and break your leg on one, grab any chance you can to give children a chance for a bit of hands-on (though make sure they wash them, we humans need to) contact with farm animals.

After all, this is Cumbria, not the Amerindian jungle.

The cottage has been a great success. We moved down there our-
selves, to test drive it over Christmas. Won't it be nice, said my
husband, for the family to all be together in the house. What he
really meant, of course, was won't it be nice for us and the dogs
to get a decent night's kip while the house is swarming with
toddlers . . .

The Old Dairy Cottage

I rang a Helpline the other day. I am not teetering on the edge of a breakdown – well not imminently anyway – but as page two of my Saturday newspaper had spookily anticipated that my copy of the free Road Atlas supplement would be missing and provided a Helpline number to call in just such an eventuality, that is what I did.

I got through to a prepubescent imbecile who spoke fluent Estuary and greeted me with ''ello, may name's Nigew, how may ay hewp yoo?'

I asked Nigel to send me my missing map PDQ or as fast as snail mail could manage. We navigated my name and rank fairly seamlessly, but Rowfoot's lack of a number baffled Nige, and by the postcode stage, our tele-phonic communication was under some strain so I spelt it out for him.

'Charlie Alpha Four, Nine Papa Zulu.'

Nigel regained composure to the point of animation.

'Carlisle, ooh that's Scotland innit? Wossit like – aw fiewds n'stuff?' I took a very deep breath, resisted the temptation to tell him that this far north we still daubed ourselves with woad and couldn't get BBC2 and explained that yes, sheep we had, and fields aplenty. It is precisely that profusion of fields, sheep and bucolic bliss that lures hordes of holidaymakers to Cumbria and if latest projections are to be believed, the popularity of this corner of England is poised to increase still further. Even so, I still expect Helplines to outstrip farm tourism in the league table of growth industries, appearing as they do on every product from limescale loo cleaner to dried pig's-ear dog chews.

Since the departure of the soft-eyed, gentle Jerseys, the old byre and dairy had been cowless and redundant, a temporary repository for junk in transit to its final resting place, nothing more. What is more, a moo-less byre is not just alarmingly unproductive; it soon becomes a mirthless, melancholic place. Something had to be done with it or to it, that much was certain. And as Saint Tony of Islington reminded us, in his inexplicably upbeat sermon to the rural throng recently, Diversification is the Way, the Truth and no Strife.

We had explored the possibility of conversion before but shelved the project for a variety of reasons. This time we had clearer ideas and opted for early consultation with the district council planning department and county council highways in an effort to avoid playground politics later on. Without exception, local government officers were helpful and practical. We had passed 'go.'

Next stop Farm Tourism. The official's eyes glazed over as he fantasised about the future of Rowfoot's several other barns, sheds and stables.

'You could convert this, this and this,' he reckoned, his upturned palm cutting a swathe through the morning air, at a stroke mentally evicting horses, goat, and fodder and mentally replacing the lot with a holiday complex. It will not happen, trust me. The builders moved in – Eric and his brother David. There is something of the Scarlet Pimpernel about Eric. He's there one minute and evaporates into the ether the next, with an elusiveness as natural as his ability to mix cement. Bit by bit, the cobbly floors came out, and a concrete one went in, the roof came off providing probably the most expensive firewood this side of the national dateline and creating a major homelessness crisis in the woodworm world. Walls sprouted up and we had two bonfires which would have delighted even the most ambitious pyromaniac.

I answered lots of tricky questions about window heights and beam siting, and now I'm getting to the ones I can do – curtain colour and kitchen units. I saw some units in 'distressed cherry' the other day, which struck me as rather sad. Perhaps the cherry would like to talk about it. And now I have to decide what to call the little dwelling. I think it will probably be The Old Dairy Cottage, for the very good reason that that is what it is, but 'Midden View' was tantalising too, because that is what it is too – although once I have galloped a couple of laps clinging to the handles of a runaway rotovator, the justification for that particular nomenclature might be harder to divine.

I have retained, restored even – if restoration can be something as low key as a scrub with a potato brush and a lick of yacht varnish – the 'Simplex Milking System' sign on one of the beams for the sake of authenticity. The trouble with authenticity is that rather like double banoffee cheesecake you can have too much of it. So the small nuggets of desiccated cow dung and the extravagantly swagged and tailed cobweb curtains have been ruthlessly excised.

There is one problem with this diversification lark, though, which seems to have been entirely overlooked by Our Leader. Diversification demands more than manual dexterity with a gripe and a yard broom and skills other than stockmanship. For a start, it helps to know how to drive a computer. Until a short while ago, I thought that macs were something you put on to keep the rain out, that a mouse could be caught with a bit of cheese and that to get into a discussion about Stuffit Expanders or Excite might be very unwise indeed.

Salvation arrived in the shape of a beast called the Computer Bus, which comes to a halt in the pub car park on a Friday morning and hooks up to a three pin plug, via the window of the gents' loo and provides IT Training to rural communities. Oh, there is one highly technical requirement – it needs a level surface to park on otherwise we all slide down one end.

My own computer has not yet crashed head on but has survived one bothersome shunt; since when I have received emails from ex-colleagues scattered about the globe, some of whom I truly thought were dead. That's progress. Whether the same can be said for doing away with the stalls where Daisy and Fluff chewed cud and produced sufficient quantities of methane to power half of the Furness peninsular remains to be seen.

We have a new sewerage plant in Ainstable. Recently installed, highly efficient and an all round good thing. Trouble is, we're not linked to it.

The End Game

A rural existence involves rigorous adherence to many customs and rituals, some odder than others. One develops a familiarity with neighbours' vehicles, which are acknowledged by anything from a brief twitch of the right hand index finger to a passage of the upraised palm through a full 180 degrees, depending on A) how intimate is your acquaintance with the oncoming driver and B) whether your personal preference is for discretion or downright exhibitionism.

There is widespread havoc when anyone changes vehicles of course, but time is a great healer; the certainty that the world has chosen to ignore you may inspire an irrational desire to drive headlong into the path of passing tractors, trailers or other heavy traffic in a terminal display of Munchausen disorder, but do not fret as this will normally abate within a fortnight – the world will recognise your pistachio coloured mini-moke by then.

And then there's sewage. Sewage is Nature's little joke, just to ensure that country life does not topple into an abyss of self satisfaction.

There is not one farmer amongst those I know who enjoys the luxury of the Flush It And Forget It lavatorial arrangements of the urbanite. As a hick in the sticks, without access to an anonymous metropolitan sewerage system, you never, ever, get to enjoy a passing relationship with your sewage. In fact you spend a disproportionate number of your waking hours planning its future.

When we first came to Rowfoot, the vestiges of an earlier system were still in place if not (sadly) still in use. I am ashamed to say that I neglected – it must have slipped my mind – to tell my mother that we did have the flushing sort too, on the first of her visits. Instead, I introduced her to the single seater in the garden and presented her with a rather fine porcelain gasunder (its goes under the bed, see) for night time. She made urgent enquiries about the times of trains back to civilisation, traffic noise, street lights, proper pavements and Marks and Spencer food halls within walking distance.

She stayed, but as I have already mentioned only after I was shamed into explaining the true circumstances to her. I recall my crest being slightly fallen by this ignominious process, you will be pleased to hear.

Like many farms, we have a domestic septic tank. Most of the time, we hardly know it is there – it just does its own dirty work. But come the day it needs emptying, and it suddenly assumes all the temperamental unpredictability of a nervy racehorse. There are two ways in which to persuade it to yield up its subterranean cargo. You can employ a firm to do it – big tanker, big bucks – or you can, believe it or not, do it yourself.

But you will need a tractor, a slurry spreader and a whole raft of understanding neighbours or a ticket to Aruba where you will spend a month languishing under palm trees while you dream groundless dreams that during your absence your neighbours might forgive the olfactory assault you have delivered unto them.

Let me tell you the Tale of the Tank. It may or may not be called Thomas. Real names have been changed in order to protect the innocent, but similarity to any person living or dead is entirely deliberate. And if you recognise yourself I hope you have the grace to be severely embarrassed.

And if, after reading this tale of sewage and its disposal, you still fancy moving out of town, you are obviously determined and all I can do is suggest that you contact a good estate agent. Just don't say you weren't warned.

It is a calm summer morning. The sun is high in a cloudless sky. You are living the good life, in a world where grass is something you cut and make into hay, not something criminals do, nor something you smoke either, even in Glastonbury week. God's in his Heaven and all's right with the world. There is just one incipient blot on the horizon – the septic tank needs emptying and this could be just the day to do it.

You've contacted the waste people and – oh! Horror! – it is going to cost 25 quid. You can't have that so you'll do it yourself. You locate a slurry spreader and successfully negotiate borrowing it for the day. You sweet-talk the tractor driver and send him off to do the deed. He inspects the chamber.

'It needs a l'aal bit of a stir,' he says, being wise in the ways of such things. And he blows a draught of air into the pit. It bubbles and froths most obligingly.

'A l'aal bit mair,' he says.

You trust him, he's a sound fellow. More air is introduced. And it is at this precise moment that things take a turn clearly signposted 'Worsewards.' The concrete lid on the pit takes on a life of its own and makes a bid for freedom, in a perfect perpendicular trajectory propelled by a plume of poo with all the force of an emission from a well-endowed sperm whale. You have heard the phrase 'frozen with terror' no doubt. That tractor driver was it. Happily, the moment passes, the lid crashes back into place and the spreader sucks in its grisly cargo with indecent gluttony. Whither to spread it?

'I'll keep it well back from the road,' says the tractor driver, helpfully. But this intercession on behalf of the family living nearby falls on stony ground and the farmer decrees that the fertiliser's final resting place should be in uncomfortable proximity to their dwelling. Now, wasn't he a naughty pixie? And if, as suggested, the muck spreading was related to an earlier altercation – a ticklish little matter of some bullocks, a newly laid lawn and an open gate then I'm a banana. So, as they say, think on . . .

Sewage disposal has been a major factor in our recent byre conversion. We have had to pump the stuff uphill, so a socking great pit (it would have been neat if I could have told you that it was dug by a builder called Cecil Pitt, known as Cess to his mates, but sadly this is not the case and no amount of artistic licence will make it so), pump and pipe had to be installed and once again, I am only recognisable by the sight of my generously proportioned bottom sticking up in the air as I crawl about re-cobbling the yard.

I confess, I am experiencing problems with this; I am not entirely convinced that it was necessary to number all the cobbles consecutively and for Eric to insist – perfectionist though he is – that they be relaid exactly in the same order. Anyway, I am engaged on this task now that I have finished grouting the bathroom and the loo, rather skilfully although I say so myself.

There we are again. You see what I mean about sewage being a preoccupation?

Those who remember the atmosphere which used to prevail at Test Matches at Lord's – quietly rippling applause, civilised comment and murmurs of approval – will feel completely at home at a dog trial. Add some sunshine, a picnic and a bottle of chilled Chablis and you have the absolutely perfect day out.

Guilty as Charged

Last week I dreamt that I had a ferret called Irene. Perhaps it is time to call in the Dream Doctor and while they are illuminating my inexplicable nocturnal fantasies, they can shed a little light on whatever it is which induces twitching paws, quivering whiskers and low whimperings in my dogs' slumbers too.

A mere mortal can but guess at what lies behind such canine crinkum-crankum but I should think that a starring role in a One Man and His Dog Christmas Special is the stuff of the ultimate doggy dream. This year, Rowfoot collies Gyp and Tess will settle down to view this festive treat with particular interest. You see, they are personally acquainted with two of the participants.

Bill and Jaff, who lodged with us for the duration of the recent International Sheepdog Trials (and don't fret, I'm not going to make any cheap jokes about how many were found guilty) represented Scotland in the Brace (pairs) class. As they live at Ollaberry in Shetland after which one falls off into the freezing confluence of the Norwegian Sea and the North Atlantic Ocean, Bill and Jaff travelled to the mainland aboard a ferry. A very nice ferry, but a ferry nonetheless and in a crate in the bowels of the thing. Happily, neither was seasick.

After a long car journey they had a short sleep in

Kareima's stable, renamed the Rowfoot Canine Suite and lavishly refurbished with a straw bed, a bowl of water each (this was a refit of the no expense spared variety) and a hook on the wall, before departing for a quick revisionary workout with my Mad Manxes. Frederic reportedly waggled his antlers once or twice but couldn't remember what to do next and recognising the superior authority of the Shetlanders, gave up and behaved impeccably thereafter. A wise move, on the whole.

Bill and Jaff set off in the middle of the night (6.45am) for the Trials course with their handler, Andrew, who had read the rules, memorised the course, walked it, had nightmares (some, but not necessarily all of which feature ferrets called Irene) and wrestled with a multiplicity of doubts about his ability to complete it within the time limit.

The Trial starts with the outrun. The dog goes to 'lift' with the minimum of theatricality and palaver. The sheep should then flock together and trot towards the handler, negotiating obstacles – gates – sited randomly, even pointlessly from a doggy perspective, on the journey. They should stay in one cohesive group, not splinter into microflocks and the dog is penalised if they pause to graze, answer a call of nature or admire the view. Although of course, any ovine producing documentary evidence of having broken stride to produce a lengthy, well argued polemic on 'Declining Standards in Modern Public Service Broadcasting' (with particular reference to the excision of One Man and His Dog from Winter scheduling) will, naturally, accrue bonus points.

After wiggling them about through yet more gates the dog brings them into the shedding ring, where he has to separate some wearing red collars from others with none. The dog, not having read the rules, hasn't a clue about the collars' significance, red or otherwise. The sheep are similarly baffled. 'Red, red,' one ewe was heard to bleat to another. 'Red – so, so 1980s.'

During the shedding a great deal of stick waving goes on. There should, however, be no swearing, cursing or psychotic behaviour from any of the participants, but as anyone who has ever tried to move sheep anywhere on this planet or, I daresay, on any other will tell you, while such control is essential in competition, it is only rarely practised at home. Especially the swearing bit.

Then comes the drive. Handlers of both sexes will assert that collies are very intelligent dogs, even if quadratic equations and Platonic translations are beyond them. Male handlers will add that unlike women, collies are proficient drivers, having an acutely developed sense of direction and being able to differentiate between left and right. Lady handlers will tell you that collies are also clever enough to recognise when they are totally lost and will pause to seek further directions. In the interests of equality, I accept both opinions unreservedly.

The climax of the perfect trial is penning. The shepherd, by now at the end of his own tether and that attached to the gate, waves his stick about again. The dog, creeping lower than a politician's morals, darts hither and thither until the sheep are secured in the pen. The gate clatters shut and ideally, the shepherd remembers to undo it again and release the sheep before heading towards the beer tent at a brisk trot.

No provocation is sufficient to justify the dog ever biting the sheep, nor should it bite its handler and under no circumstances must the handler bite the dog. If the dog loses its temper, its rag or its way and nips the heel of an errant sheep it is penalised. All of which seems harsh really, because the dog is simply manifesting its frustration at the uniquely sheepy shortcoming of having been born fairly intelligent and becoming progressively more stupid with the progression of time.

There is no pugilistic air-punching frenzy at the cessation of hostilities between handler, dog and sheep, no cacophonous cheering, just enthusiastic, appreciative applause from the ringside assembly. It would be all rather British, except that it is so international – standing at the packed ringside I heard guttural German, impenetrable if not actually double Dutch, every burr, brogue and inflexion of English, Scots, Irish, Gaelic and Welsh. And American, which is a completely foreign language to everyone.

What of our heroes Bill and Jaff then? Sad to relate, they did not cover themselves in glory, but I am certain this can be attributed to one thing – trees. Shetland (rural) has none. Nor is it especially well-endowed in the lamp post department and gate stoops lack both the proportions and that perpendicularity so alluring to male dogs. Finding themselves suddenly surrounded by trees in glorious profusion had such a deleterious impact on their psyche that they temporarily lost concentration altogether.

Gyp and Tess will still be barking for them at Christmas. G and T, of course, have never done an honest day's work in their lives, adopting a brilliant and highly efficacious strategy of affecting extreme stupidity. In short, they make the term 'sheep dog' appear oxymoronic. No, make that just moronic.

Rowfoot looks a big house from the outside, but you have to remember that much of it is wall, since each is about three feet thick. Never does this become more apparent than when you decide that the only way of accommodating the grand piano/new bath/hot water downpipe, is to take down a wall. The hole you require may be two and a half feet wide but the one you end up with, having removed boulders which have been in place for 300 years, will be nearer double that. Carrying them downstairs means you do not need to lift weights at the gym that week.

Rowfoot Revisited

'People,' said our visitor sagely, 'must have died here.' It is true that Rowfoot's wonky walls must have witnessed several passings from temporal to spiritual life, but I remain reassured by the fact that this affliction visited each individual only once. The ghosts of farmers past and I rub along well enough together, indeed one or two of my predecessors I regard as the nearest thing I've found to ancestry, since a preliminary rummage amongst my own family history revealed an Irish rogue and a couple who were to marital harmony what Captain Bligh was to team building.

My paternal grandfather, the Irish roguish one, reportedly traded in three legged donkeys which he sold with assurances of success in the Grand National to his more gullible countrymen. Had disaffected clients not pursued him with such assiduity he might well have carried on bog trotting to the strains of Danny Boy, but not being one for confrontation he fled to England. A wise career move, grandfather, all things considered.

On the distaff side, I have absolutely no idea what my maternal grandfather looked like as dear grandmama, a demon with a Stanley knife, excised the fella's head with worrying precision from every single family photograph. The Headless Man originated from Jersey suggesting that my affection for Channel Island cattle could perhaps be attributed to genetic predisposition.

Cumbria, or more accurately Cumberland then, looked terra altogether a great deal firma on which to connect with history. In the mysterious east of the county at Rowfoot, John Brown paid the Lord of the Manor of Armathwaite the princely rent of sixpence ha'penny (that, for the benefit of post-decimalisation babies, is almost three pence) rent for Rowfoot in the year 1787. By the 1820s John Brown's body had attained the elevated status of Yeoman Farmer, so the lad had, in modern parlance, done good.

Yeoman John's daughter, Elizabeth, married a Joseph Goulding from Lazonby and in 1841 they were farming at Rowfoot. And here's a thing – Elizabeth was born in Oxford Street, London. Why? What on earth were her parents, farmers in the northernmost reaches of the kingdom, doing in Oxford Street of all places? They had hardly jumped on a Virgin Supersaver Special and gone to check out Marks and Spencer's flagship store for the weekend had they? History is extremely unsatisfactory when it raises unanswerable questions instead of doing its job properly and providing definitive answers. Still, as one of my teachers used to say: 'History teaches us that nothing is often a clever thing to do and always a clever thing to say.'

She also told us that Frederick the Great's father, in a last ditch effort to toughen up his unfortunate son, made the poor lad kneel on dried peas, that King Charles stammered and that King James was more than likely gay. I do not know whether such a woman should have been trusted.

Back in the real world of 1851, Joseph and Elizabeth had 61 acres at Rowfoot. Their son John, a butcher, married Mary Leach of nearby Broadbeck Mill, but Mary along with several other members of the family perished in 1865 for reasons unexplained. There's another snippet of highly unsatisfactory history for you. John expanded the holding still further to 230 acres, mind bogglingly vast for the time, and apparently carried on butching. A butching ring to secure stock while the deed was done remains to this day in the shed at the top of the yard.

The farm's burgeoning fortunes were probably linked with the necessity to provide fodder for the influx of Irish navvies engaged on the construction of the Carlisle to Settle railway and records show that Mary Lightfoot of Rowfoot delivered joints of meat wrapped in white cotton to Carlisle by pony and trap. The gig in which Mary undertook her weekly excursions was almost certainly kept exactly where we now keep our modest chariot and even if she wore smocks and skirts not jeans and sweat-shirts and used rather less Anglo Saxon vernacular in the encouragement of her beastie than we employ to roust Sam along, it still constitutes a discovery of neat symmetry.

We have no immediate plans, though, in these post-diluvian times to emulate Mary's method of crossing the Eden by fording it at Holmwrangle. It would mean buy-ing two sets of flippers for Sam, you see, and funds are a trifle stretched so soon after Christmas.

Rowfoot's fortunes declined in the 1880s. There is no further mention of Mary, pony or trap, but John held a closing down sale and, incredibly, followed his son Joseph to the Yukon, where they staked and worked a claim. If Oxford Street had been distant, then heading off for the

Yukon must have been like embarking on an intergalactic mission. In a boat.

In the farm's heyday – or hayday even – cows were tethered flank to flank in a byre heavy with air of cud-chewed milky sweetness, their calves asleep in wooden pens, high sided for warmth, long before poor ventilation was regarded as the root cause of pneumonia and cross-infection an omnipresent risk.

This shed, which once housed half a dozen bovine families, is now the spacious retirement quarters of my old mare, Kareima. Now her family history I do know about and it is a great deal less murky and more aristocratic than my own. She descends from Arab horses imported to England from the desert by a family called Blunt in the 1870s and the entire dynasty lived in bucolic splendour at Crabbet Park in Sussex. It's good to know but it's not quite the same as finding out you are related to Mary Queen of Scots, is it?

In wild West Cumberland my husband's antecedents, all of whom originate from within the county boundary, were thoroughly reliable folk not a bunch of peripatetic nutters like mine. The Moffat womenfolk did all the things Cumbrian women were expected to do, making butter and sewing samplers, and a few completely unexpected ones too – farming on their own account and breeding Clydesdale horses. We are a bit hazy about the men, but we do know that Uncle Joe, the albescence of whose upper forehead owed much to the angle at which he wore his hat, bred shorthorn cattle.

So, in many ways, Uncle Joe is very like Fred the Great because in the case of both men it is the little, seemingly unimportant facts we know about them which illuminate our understanding of the bigger picture. Probably insufficient to claim aristocratic connections though, as only the horse of the family can.

School dentists have much to answer for. To get me to the dentist for the first time in 38 years, I needed valium. It was not enough; I was still panic stricken and I assure you, that is not a term I use loosely. The second dose was, in the words of a member of the Royal College of Nursing, 'enough to deck a donkey.' That I now manage to go without the aid of mind-altering substances says much for modern dentistry, compassion and Charlie Ross.

Gnashing of Teeth

Animals, you will have noticed, are different from humans. They do not possess the same unattractive propensity to disappoint that humans do, they do not fail to display parking discs and rarely default on bills. One characteristic they do share with the human race, though, is that almost invariably, they possess a set of teeth.

Teeth are my current fixation, mainly because the greater part of my life has been spent in the grip of an acute dental phobia. As each milestone birthday approached, 20, 30, 40, I have wondered whether I would make the next before a visit to a dentist was necessary. At the very mention of dentists I become as highly strung as a shrimping net, a paranoia which traces back to a childhood incident involving a drill which first saw service on a construction site, lots of blood, and the unsteady hand of a psychotic harridan trained at Smithfield. Am I making myself clear?

If such a thing occurred today the dentist would probably have been struck off, I would have been vigorously counselled and awarded zillions of sue-age dosh. But none of that happened and thereafter panic, untrammelled by logic, progress or understanding, set in every time a dentist hove into view.

At the age of eight, I determined never to visit a dentist unless half dead with toothache. At the age of 46, I was half dead with toothache. At the point where enduring the agony became marginally less attractive than sorting it, I reached for Yellow Pages which in my pain-addled state seemed sensible enough. One enticingly claimed to cope with phobics and lo, its website was designed by Stephen Caudel whom I had interviewed for *Cumbria and Lake District Life* magazine some time back. It might not have been the most scientific method of selecting a dentist but as it has turned out to be uncatastrophic too I am not complaining.

We have reached an unlikely but successful accommodation. I keep my eyes wide shut (a visor has not been totally ruled out) plug in my walkman and practice self-hypnosis. Add to this barrowloads of understanding from Charlie Ross who possesses neither horns nor any obviously manic tendencies and has not, thus far, called me a prat, a pillock or a coward although all of these monikers are justified and a kind hygienist called Gemma who doubles as a sound technician for the volume control when necessary. I have now made sufficient progress that I have put away the prayer mat and taken off the stabilisers. I would be lying if I told you that I had never had more fun but now an appointment at Aglionby Street Dental Practice, Carlisle, induces nothing more than mild trepidation.

The funny thing is, however negligent I have been of my own laughing gear, I have always religiously attended to that of my horses', mindful that a horse would look silly with a tumbler full of dentures by its hayrack. Anyone brave enough to look a horse – gift, or any other variety

– in the mouth will find incontrovertible evidence that all equines have an 80 a day Gauloises habit. Their teeth encompass the entire exciting spectrum of brown, from bilious ecru through to charred mahogany, shot through with an occasional lively jaundice seam. Not a pretty sight maybe, but an important one as teeth provide a reliable age-indicator up until about the age of ten or 12 after which the process becomes less and less accurate. If a horse for sale has dental appendages like shovels and is described as 'bombproof' it is probably best to check whether this means 'very safe' or 'born during Second World War.'

Equine dentistry is becoming ever more specialised but remains a component part of mainstream veterinary practice. The annual scale and polish ritual for a horse involves a sort of crow bar with a rasp at its extremity, the sight of which is enough to horizontalise a dental phobic and extractions are another matter altogether as horses' teeth are like the iceberg which was the nemesis of the Titanic – only a fraction of the total is visible above the surface.

Paul May, our vet, was summoned when my elderly mare needed to have a loose and rotting tooth removed and administered general anaesthetic. Quite attractive too, I thought, all that oblivion, but its allure began to diminish significantly after watching two and a half hours of Paul's bodily contortions in an effort to wrest the offending molar from its home of the past 22 years. It finally yielded and its opposite number on the other jaw popped out obligingly to keep it company – a perfectly matched pair, each about four inches long. I thought of fashioning them into earrings – stylish in an ethnic, lost African tribe sort of way – but dismissed this idea on account of their weight, the prospect of my earlobes and my armpits operating at the same latitude having little to commend it.

I have never quite got to the point of brushing my dogs' teeth – although perhaps I should have done as Gyp, possibly the lickiest Collie in all Cumbria, has dog breath best described as the ultimate person repellent. And it is time to admit that the farm cat is not called Smoky, in spite of that being my assertion on a survey confirming that she enjoyed her free sample of Kittimix. She is called Fang. Why? Because where other felines have a pair of canine teeth, she has just one totemic spike. I do not know what happened to the other one, she probably left it behind in a rat or a starling somewhere.

Cattle burp and belch their way through life. I had two calves called Ethane and Methane which emitted breath containing combustible gases roughly equal to the total output of Sizewell B, and frankly anyone getting near a dairy cow's mouth with a lighted fag was always living dangerously. But cattle are just martyrs to their intestinal ruminations rather than dental defectives.

Sheep, however, are a different matter. If an auctioneer pronounces a ewe presented for sale 'correct above and below' then the prospective purchaser can be assured that she has a full set of chomping machinery – the better to eat into the profits – and that both teats are in working order. Sheep neatly sidestep the dental realities of life by meeting their Maker long before their teeth wear out. Very occasionally an elderly ewe's plans for an early demise are thwarted by superhuman shepherding, and she finds herself with an empty mouth save for one wobbly spike, sticking up like a lonely monolith. A quick twist, a sharp pull and hey, you've just qualified for a diploma in ovine dentistry. She will never bite you again when you are dosing her with wormer, but she'll give you a nasty suck.

Like horses, sheep's teeth determine their age. In the case of the shepherd, though, exercise extreme caution and trust only the documentary evidence on his birth certificate. His teeth might be plastic, or made of Blackpool rock. Can you really trust a man who claims to have had 200 per cent lambing figures for the last five years, consistently? Then, of course, there's hen's teeth . . . but we all know about those don't we?

A personal memoir of the hideous Foot and Mouth pandemic. This piece first appeared as the lead article in Cumbria and Lake District Life *and provoked an overwhelming response, a huge wave of compassion, much from total strangers.*

Apocalypse in Eden

It is preternaturally quiet; silence the most eloquent voice of tragedy. In the distance smoke signals of despair – an inky plume spiralling skywards from the pyres below. All around, fields are bare, shocking and inescapable monuments to the ravages of foot and mouth. No new lambs play, noisily demanding milk from their mothers. Parlours which once hummed with machinery as gentle cows yielded up their milky harvest stand awfully, dreadfully silent.

Tractors which plied the roads, ferrying ewe nuts and silage have been replaced with monstrous wagons, their grisly cargoes sheeted in red plastic. Low loaders carry diggers, lifting gear and plant whose terrible task is palpably clear; others bear coal, pallets, sleepers for the pyres.

With speed which made wildfire look leaden-legged, the virus discovered in Essex was traced to Northumberland and imperilled wild moors and fells as far apart as Dartmoor and Lakeland. It has now decimated the Cumbrian livestock population in a way that floods, climate changes, recessions and world wars never quite managed.

At my farm, Rowfoot, there is a gap on the kitchen window sill where the goat bucket used to be. No need for it now. No bags of Bob's mix in the feed shed. Millie Goat and the Manxes are gone. Application could, theoretically, be made by owners of rare breeds for exemption but consider for a moment the implied moral dilemma. I had 32 sheep which I enjoyed keeping. But unlike the beef and dairy herds nearby I had not invested a life's work in them, nor was I reliant on them for my sole income, nor did others depend on them for employment.

The loss of my Manx Loghtans is of a rather different complexion, as it reduces the numbers of an already rare and primitive breed still further but their Isle of Man homeland, at least, remains clear at the time of writing. It was anyway, no time for self-interest. Driven more by hope than science, one by one farmers in Ainstable reached the same decision – the sheep must go if the remaining cattle were to have any chance. It was a sacrifice of almost Biblical proportions. And calamitously, it has failed. They are building the pyre for one herd now. The others can only do what we have all become so skilled at these past weeks – wait. And hope.

Confusion reigned absolute. It was impossible to get accurate details from MAFF (Ministry of Agriculture, Fisheries and Food) about the proposed cull – the status of which altered during the space of one chaotic morning from 'voluntary' to 'illegal' to 'compulsory' before finally reverting to 'voluntary.' Throughout the crisis, information from MAFF was unobtainable, incomplete, conflicting or quite simply wrong. In a moment of black farce, I tried to access the MAFF website. What did I get? Not a list of infected premises, but the home page of the Michigan Association of Fire Fighters, a fine body of men doubtless baffled by the recent number of hits they have recorded.

The first of many body blows came with the news that Les Armstrong's Kirkoswald farm had succumbed to the virus. Les, a fine farmer and natural diplomat has found himself an unwitting celebrity as a powerful spokesman for agriculture in his National Farmers' Union role. Les –

it just seemed impossible. After that, they fell like so many skittles – stockmen, showmen, internationally renowned breeders, neighbours and friends. Each familiar name on the MAFF website brought a fresh wave of despair. Sometimes I simply put my head in my hands and wept.

We all began to refer to the virus as if it were a sentient being – it's creeping down the valley, it's jumping, it's no respecter of reputation. Shepherding, that usually peaceful task, became a penance suffused with dread. Searching, searching for traces of an invisible enemy. I stood and stared at their mouths, their feet, their faces and then back at their feet again. Nothing. Increasingly, I wondered whether primitive breeds enjoy enhanced resistance to viral infections. Some day, it would be nice to know.

If Louisa and Paul's Rentapeasant outfit, from whom I borrow a tup each year, continues to escape we quite definitely need to know as their rare breeds holding remains unscathed but surrounded by infection in Tow Law; rather like St Paul's in the blitz. Louisa's response to my urgent email about Monty, this year's tup, was unequivocal – do what you have to do.

It was not as easy to betray Millie our elderly pet goat. The nice valuer looked at her and asked her, very politely, what she was worth. She gazed back at him from golden, glass-marble eyes and said nothing at all but thoughtfully began to eat the MAFF paperwork. Consigning healthy animals to a pointless death is only slightly less appalling than the disease itself, so that walk across the fields on a sunny Spring morning, the air heavy with dew and irony – it was perfect lambing weather – was long and agonising. Millie Goat, whose only crime was to have cloven hooves, trotted companionably alongside. The sheep were already loaded. Among their number just Unihorn looked round at me, her head cocked quizzically to one side as usual. Feisty little Unihorn, the only one I called by name, survived blow-fly strike as a lamb, lost one eye to infection in spite of penicillin and then pulled one horn out in a bloody conflict with a fence post. If ever a sheep deserved a better end than a captive bullet and a burial pit on a disused airfield, it was she. The walk back was endless, silent but for the goat chain clanking like a convict's in my wake.

Meanwhile those unaffected were experiencing other difficulties. Movement Restrictions. 'Finished' stock – those ready for market – stayed at home instead, at best eating into profit and dwindling supplies of hay and at worst, going beyond optimum condition and in the case of cattle, beyond the crucial age of 30 months and ending up virtually worthless. Out in the fields, sheep brought down from the high fells to more clement conditions in the valleys for Winter overstayed their welcome on land for Summer hay, ewes close to lambing were trapped on inhospitable terrain away from expert shepherds and as Spring drew ever closer, the innate wanderlust of upland sheep brought threats of fines, or worse.

Farmers in cull zones overwintering stock for absent owners less understanding than our Rentapeasant friends, faced other challenges. Far removed from the horrors of immediacy, such owners reacted in one of two ways. They either wanted their sheep culled, fearful of assisting the passage of infection to 'clean' areas or they stuck it out, insisting that as long as they remained uninfected, they wanted them spared. Those in situ just sweated. And waited. And then waited some more.

Horror stories proliferated. Cows shot in sheds and left so long that they quite literally blew up, cattle shot in fragile pens stampeded taking gates, foot and mouth with them. A wailing lone lamb adrift on a sea of slaughtered carcasses, healthy stock killed after misdiagnosis, allegations of profiteering on coal and pallets. An endless, fathomless, pointless litany of tragedy. Others, though, told positive tales of transporters and slaughtermen dealing with their hideous tasks with compassion and sensitivity. Any which way, it was akin to living in a war zone.

I am not just upset on behalf of those hard working farmers whose loss is absolute. I am angry. Very, very angry, because the outbreak spiralled out of control due to paralysis and indecision at the start when a swift cull might have contained it. And that is not hindsight – that is the lesson which has not been learned from the 1967 outbreak and assuredly ought to have been. Cumbrian voices warning of agricultural meltdown were ignored even as outbreak became epidemic and then Agriculture Minister Nick Brown's mantra of 'it's under control' began to sound increasingly like Corporal Jones' in Dad's Army. 'Don't panic Mr Mainwairing, don't panic . . .'

And for the distraught farmers who had to spend days imprisoned in their homes, tortured by the sight of obscenely heaped carcasses and inhaling the foul stench of their putrefaction, I did not feel just anger, but an odd combination of vicarious blind rage, indignation and enormous sympathy. None of which was of the slightest use, of course.

Questions too. Why the delays in diagnosis, slaughter and disposal? Why were the Army not deployed sooner? What of the strange enquiries made about timber procurement at the end of 2000? Why, exactly, was it so difficult to get substantive information from MAFF? Did anyone, anywhere, look out the 1969 Report on the 1967 outbreak? Does burning carcasses actually spread the disease as that Report suggested? And what the hell was going on at the end of 2000 in Northumberland between MAFF and the apparent source of the outbreak at Heddon on the Wall?

To these and countless other questions, Cumbria and indeed, the rest of England, deserves proper answers. Not weaselly spin, but answers as direct, as honest as those Brigadier Birtwistle, in charge of the grim operations at Great Orton gives when he is questioned. Now there's a man who made life under a military junta look a positively attractive option.

The future looks no clearer. Valuation cheques, more compulsory purchase than compensation, may or may not be sufficient to finance restocking, whenever that may be – no-one seems clear on that either. In the interim, there's no redundancy payout, no unemployment benefit for the self-employed and short time or lay-off for workers. All routine has disappeared. Those pegs on which stockmen hang their daily round are gone – no bedding down or scraping out, no feeding time, no milking time. Even the seasons will cease, temporarily, to have much meaning, all synchronicity with the natural world gone up in acrid smoke.

Isolation in the immediate aftermath of disease presented its own problems as freedom was curtailed and life became a complex round of passes and permissions. Men never knowingly in touch with their emotions before, were suddenly overwhelmed by them. Different people found different solutions. Les Armstrong flung himself into yet another round of negotiations; some assuaged grief by helping neighbours, enduring repeatedly what most would shrink from facing once, others translated helplessness into vociferous campaigning zeal. A few, understandably, locked their doors and grieved in private.

Those directly unaffected by loss themselves buoyed up those crushed by it. Kindness rose from chaos like a phoenix from ashes – a bag of carrots left hanging on the gate 'to cheer the horses up,' bunches of flowers, plants, phone calls, cards and endless emails some from the other side of the world. Talk to anyone afflicted by the apocalyptic events of the last few weeks and they will tell a similar story of sustaining, vital support. Some, like the Carlisle florist who delivered flowers just as she had done in the past, became unwittingly embroiled in the catastrophe.

'Where's your goat?' she asked, having formed a special friendship with the unique Millie on previous visits to Rowfoot. The explanation was as difficult to deliver as it was to hear. I have revised my oft-moaned assessment that human nature stinks. It doesn't. Generous spirits still flourish.

The industry must use this interval wisely; a thorough reappraisal is long overdue and now is as good a time as any. Meaningful contingency plans must be designed to protect our agricultural heritage from future disaster, with proper funding for research, a thorough exploration of all the issues surrounding vaccination, establishment of a nucleus of genetic material and reserve flocks of the Herdwicks and Roughs unique to Lakeland.

At Springtime the countryside should sing with new life. Instead, there is an empty Eden. Yet Cumbrian farmers and stockmen are renowned for their resilience and for many, attentions are already turning to restocking, restarting. For others, the memory of relentless shooting, pyres, pits and silence is too raw and it is too early to think of a future.

There will be Manxes again at Rowfoot. But never another Millie Goat.

234

FMD had this county in a stranglehold. We were all angry, all hurting, all completely perplexed by politicking. But elsewhere there seemed little understanding of the restrictions on our everyday lives and the continuing refusal to acknowledge the depth of the crisis.

Experts Set the World on Fire

I think I must be getting old. Old, jaded and very, very cynical. Because, lately, when I hear any statement preceded by the words that it is 'in the opinion of Government, Ministry' or even worse 'acknowledged experts,' I groan first and then instinctively reach for the zapper to switch the sound off. Sometimes, I get this bit wrong, and reach for my mobile phone instead. Later, stabbing irascibly at the handset, I wonder why the little gizmo which has just increased the volume on the low-fi (it's an old machine) refuses to summon up some distant pal equally satisfactorily. That it sometimes takes several minutes for me to work out exactly why, gives a clue as to just how easy it is to get me totally banjaxed these days.

Events of recent weeks have certainly led me to conclude that 'experts' are a pretty rum lot, whatever their currency. Nutritional experts are benign if aggravating, peddling their sophisticated form of recycling – it's just a matter of waiting for the wheel of fashion to rotate in your favour. Look what happened to milk. It used to be Great Stuff, shovelled remorselessly down the gullets of unwilling infants at a time when olive oil was something you got from the chemist in artfully shaped bottles, poured on to cotton wool and poked into the same unfortunate's ears. Then milk morphed into Bad Stuff – a fat laden heart hazard. Now, coincidentally at the very time of dismal farm gate prices, milk is hailed as Good Stuff again, full of calcium, fresh, good for you.

At least there's a little more consensus amongst safety experts. They agree that, in the interests of preserving your corporeal completeness, it is probably inadvisable to leave the tractor chugging along in second gear while you jump off and adjust the turnip chopper on the back. Especially if you are on a slope.

It's the foot and mouth experts you really have to watch out for, every one of them armed with ample empirical or epidemiological evidence and keen to carpe their particular diem. Self-styled wizards relying on a bit of good old hocus pocus were just as assertive, just as convincing and at least had the virtue of being entertaining. The pointy heads patrolling MAFF's (Ministry or Agriculture, Fisheries and Food, later to become DEFRA) corridors of power must be just about the oddest collection since the Muppets. Their assiduous extermination policy ought to have ensured self-induced obsolescence as so few farm animals survive north of Shap that financing an entire Ministry to oversee their welfare seems a profligate use of public monies. Still, no argument on the 'Fish' front – formulation of Ministry policy throughout the crisis consistently exhibited all the reasoning ability of a moderately bright halibut.

I am no scientist. In spite of the tutelage of a scholarly lady who looked like a walking twiglet with a hairstyle attributable to a complicated chemical experiment involving axle grease and curtains, I retained a spectacular stupidity around Bunsen burners and copper sulphate.

But, three months into the outbreak, even I got a bit of

a rattle when I heard a 'top government expert' proclaiming with some authority that the cull was probably pointless and that the virus was unlikely to be airborne. Culling, he seemed to be suggesting, was based on nothing more scientifically sustainable than the premise of chopping off your head to obviate a bad migraine next Tuesday – effective, yes, but also terminal and pretty daft. If he'd come out of hibernation earlier, there might have been some point to this observation. As it was, I just wished he'd piped up sooner. Asleep alongside him in the woodwork were the boffins from the local health authority. Two months down the line, they were moved to acknowledge that the pyres might, just possibly, have implications for public health. Somehow, I would have been just a little surprised if emissions saturated with diesel, disease and carcinogens didn't.

I am still perplexed though by other, earlier experts who said that this virus was rather like an It Girl – it could only survive without a host for about a fortnight. So, why is it going to take until the Autumn to cleanse most buildings, dismantle some and destroy others completely? And here's another thing. If, as yet more experts told us at the start, heat and sunshine kills the virus, how come that it is endemic in Africa which I had always thought of as a pretty warm and sunny sort of a place? But as I said, I'm no scientist and very easily confused. Just look at the trouble I have with zappers and mobile phones.

Mindful of the need to clear up these little misunderstandings I have prepared a little multiple-choice Tripos for Senior MAFFmeticians. And here it is.

QUESTION ONE:
When will my Compensation cheque be coming?
A) This year.
B) Next year.

C) When the sun is over the yardarm, Jupiter aligns with Mars and the area of the triangle on the hypotenuse becomes unequal to the sum of the triangle on the other two sides.

D) Ask the halibut.

QUESTION TWO:
What should I do with my left over silage now that I have no cattle?

A) Remove the exterior 12" and spray the rest with an approved solution to render it safe for future use.

B) Burn it.

C) Leave it as it is and hope for the best.

And that, sad to relate, is based on a true story of an exchange between a farmer on an infected premises and a posse of hooded figures in papal white, canvassed at different times. The first thought that the answer to Question Two was definitely A. But our hero was distrustful of a substantive answer from MAFF, and sought a second opinion. See answer B. To try to clear the thing up once and for all he asked a third space-suited alien who came up with answer C. Inconsistency? Ignorance? Incompetence? You choose. All I know is that people have been tarred and feathered for less. And meanwhile, of course, the microbes were still partying on the silage.

QUESTION THREE:
Has anyone located the phial of Foot and Mouth virus missing from Porton Down? More importantly, is anyone looking? Oh, and for this question a straight 'Yes' or 'No' will not just suffice, it would actually be preferable.

NOTE TO CANDIDATES:

Write only on one side of the paper at any one time. If you would like to apply for the post of Minister of Agriculture, include you Wellington Boot size. If different from you IQ rating, please specify. Misuse of the apostrophe carries the death penalty. Cross no Ts dot no Is and make it up as you go along. Manipulate what figures you like. Well, why change now?

Cynical? Yes, perhaps. But as the poet said, all is changed, changed utterly. The land I love is still a kaleidoscope of dappled green, pleated and folded, rolling ever onwards to a distant union with a lustrous sky. Visible scars of the plague are mostly buried or burnt now and Eden's timeless beauty remains perversely intact though oddly lifeless; no sign yet of its unravelled fabric knitting seamlessly together again. The people and their invisible scars? They are quite anther story.

To rub salt into the wound, I have received correspondence from MAFF to the effect that I will now have to use a licensed shearer when next I decide to shear my sheep. This does present something of a problem. MAFF have already slaughtered all of my sheep and my pet goat Millie. There is nothing left to shear, by anyone with a licence or otherwise. Perhaps MAFF might just have been aware of this.

We swapped the climate of madness at home for one of calm and sunshine in Northern Cyprus. This country is perhaps more remarkable for the things it lacks – nightlife, golf courses, high rise hotels – than for those qualities it does possess: peace, natural beauty, hospitable people. Don't go if you expect slick efficiency. They don't do slick or efficient much.

Running Away to the Sun

When the going gets tough, the tough get going. Trouble is, toughness is not among my attributes, so I got out instead. I ran away for a week and allowed rest and sunshine, the oldest, surest anti-depressant known to man, to do its work in Northern Cyprus. Not to be confused with the other bit of Cyprus famed for Ayia 'Slapper' Napa and local difficulties at Akrotiri, Northern Cyprus is a bite-sized piece of paradise floating in the Med, unrecognised by anyone except the Turks and largely unnoticed by the rest of the planet. There are no lager louts, just Saga louts reliving the island's colonial past supping Brandy Sours. Only one real danger exists – that of being hit on the head by a ripe avocado.

You can plop into a crystalline ocean to look for turtles and float when you tire of swimming; watch birds and spot wildflowers. My only reservation about the wildlife was the entry in the guidebook which read 'most of the snakes in Northern Cyprus are fairly harmless.' It was the 'most' and the 'fairly' I didn't much care for. And as everything operates on Turkish Time which is just before you get to 'stop' altogether, the miseries back at home soon seemed a lifetime away.

Mad dogs and Englishmen might venture out in the midday Mediterranean sun but Cypriot sheep, who can't slap on Squillion Factor sunscreen, have far more sense. They languish under eucalyptus trees in flimsy corrals while old fashioned, short legged Friesians swish a tail – when they can summon up sufficient energy – at the midges. Goats with glossy coats the colour of Bournville chocolate, hang dog expressions and ears with malfunctioning springs, browse the inland plain under the watchful gaze of a bronzed and ancient shepherd who will either be shuffling desultorily in their wake on his own two legs or travelling Biblical style astride a donkey with a languorous gait.

An obscure but ancient edict demands that all shepherds in Northern Cyprus must possess no front teeth at all. Whether the shepherd is of the perambulatory or the mounted variety this is adhered to rigidly. Beyond that, there are few rules in the Turkish Republic of Northern Cyprus although Turkey thinks it might quite like to join the European Union, so that could all change. If that happens, Northern Cyprus can kiss goodbye to sweet, salty sheep cheese fashioned by horny-handed, sweaty-palmed peasants, and orange juice pulped in two-roomed roadside shacks by families scratching half a living from a citrus grove. It is unlikely that the EU would much like the entrepreneurial initiative of the vendor with a melon stall on the dual carriageway, just at the start of the diversion bit, either, but hey, you take the rough with the smooth.

But do you know what the really bestest thing about Northern Cyprus was, for that glorious, gilded week? No tele, and no daily ritual visitation of the MAFF (they're DEFRA now, of course) website and no swathes of green lifelessness. And very little mention of Foot and Mouth beyond a few southern Brits who were touchingly sympathetic and distressed to hear that no, actually, it wasn't all but over.

Reality kicked in again on the homeward flight when we were told that to comply with MAFF/DEFRA directives the plane had to be disinfected before landing. Do you know what happened next? A charming air hostess with plaits the like of which boys in my primary school class used to tie to chairs, walked the length of the aircraft, rather too briskly for my liking after a week on Turkish Time, and anointed the central aisle with a couple of squirts from an aerosol. And that was it. Done. Cleansed. Safe. Call me an old sceptic, but I was not even mildly reassured. Still, if ever the air hostess felt like a career change, she and her squirty stuff could be pressed into action on any farm in Cumbria, where the job is taking altogether longer and proving just slightly more complex. Or at least it was until DEFRA decided to move the goalposts just as effectively as MAFF had done before it (could the two by any chance be related?) and at the time of writing it was difficult to sort out the clean from the unclean. Although the dirty issue of money and costs was at the heart of the issue, just as it was probably the root cause of the epidemic in the first place.

I had left England as gloomy as an Aussie bowler up against I.T. Botham at the crease in 1981. I returned buoyant, rested, sunned and impatient to get back to work but having lost more sheep than Bo-Peep could shake a crook at, I find myself at an unseasonable loose end. So I have painted all the shed doors, the front gate and railings, rotovated the vegetable patch and sown lettuce, onions, organic and perpetual Popeye fuel. The stables are scrubbed, swept and ready for whitewashing. I am now stripping wallpaper on the landing, planning a coat of paint for the dining room and working out the colour scheme for the study. What then, I ask myself? I don't reply because, let's face it, talking to yourself is not just pointless, it may, indeed, ensure that the future is seen from the comfort of a padded cell. But I gave it a bit of consideration, anyway. Silently, naturally.

I could perhaps revive my political career which came to an abrupt halt when the Monster Raving Loony Party refused my application for membership. After all, I was once – and this is true – on a debating team with Janet Ellis. We were both, in those days, J Ellis. Easily differentiated, though, as Janet was destined to be filmed in bed with John Thaw (*The Sweeney*, circa 1975) give out Blue Peter badges and be the mother of Sophie Ellis-Bextor. Sophie is very, very famous and although I am not so cool that I know the words of all her songs, I do know this: she can tie a knot in a cherry stalk with her tongue. And very few people can do that, even fewer than those who got a Blue Peter badge. I was not one of those either.

Better leave politics alone then. I could go back to selling ladies' knickers, as I did during my gap year although my enthusiasm for returning to this employ is diminished by a vivid recollection that some of the customers were even more difficult than Manx sheep. One demanded to be telephoned the instant her cerise jersey camiknickers came into stock.

'Here's my number,' she boomed, apparently convinced that anyone working in a shop possessed the intelligence of a subnormal gnat, 'and if ai'm not in, I shell be ite.' My heart was never in camiknickers after that.

I could be a painter perhaps. The Dulux sort, obviously, though I feel that my real vocation lies in grouting. I became pretty dextrous at grouting when the Old Dairy Cottage was undergoing its transformation. It is an oddly satisfying occupation, though tough on the fingers for those who eschew the neat little plastic spatulas provided for the purpose. So, until I can restock with sheep there's only one thing to do. Devote my waking hours to dreaming up unlikely acronyms for DEFRA. Don't Even Fink of Restocking with Animals, perhaps . . .

Christmas is always a time for reflection, isn't it? This year, the recollections of Christmases past – whether filled with childish nostalgia or grown-up workaday memories, seemed especially poignant.

Chestnuts Roasting on an Open Fire

I never really bought that whole Santa Claus myth, even as a child. No-one, you see, ever managed to provide a satisfactory explanation for how my 1959 present, a hand made farm yard complete with little plastic animals (about as many Friesian cows as today would constitute Sentinel Restocking, a couple of Large White pigs, a goat, a donkey and six mule ewes, since you ask) arrived on Christmas Day. How did Santa, a generously proportioned old codger, get it or him down our chimney? Surely the dimensions of both his girth and my farmyard exceeded even the widest point of the chimney breast.

Most of all I distrusted Santa because of his appalling dress sense – a man who thought that an outfit inspired by a 1950s knitting pattern and executed in Massey Ferguson (Series 2) red was a good idea was simply not credible. The model farmyard raised further questions. Father had blocked up the original Edwardian fireplace with a fetching white-glossed hardboard fixture, mainly because mother regarded as 'a pesky dust harbourer' anything deserving of the derisory epithets 'original' and 'Edwardian.' This was 1959, remember.

If – and it was a big 'if' – Santa was real and intended to continue abseiling up and down chimneys for a living, he would have to deal with the hardboard, then run the risk of melting his boots and possibly scarring the soles of his feet on the electric fire, though this was unlikely as it was hardly ever lit. Such was our state of semi-permanent refrigeration in South West London that the possibility of twinning with a home in South West Murmansk was a constant source of lively debate.

More than the presents (with the notable exception of the farmyard), the thing I really looked forward to at Christmas was pulling the wishbone of some undernourished poultry specimen after its seasonal ritual dismembering. And what was that all about – the bit with the extra shard of bone being lucky? Anyway, if I got it, I gestured it first dangerously into space then at a parent and wished heartbreakingly hard, year after year, first for a dog and then a pony. Mother remained implacable on the dog front. She hadn't liked dogs since my father returned from India accompanied by one. More specifically, he returned with a one-eyed bulldog on a lead in one hand and a mongoose in the other. Mother issued an ultimatum of the they-go-or-I-go variety. The length of time father took to reach a decision on this one did little to enhance marital bliss, or mother's affection for imported livestock.

Father defended the engaging little creature mother unkindly referred to as The Rodent, arguing reasonably enough, that in India a pet mongoose was excellent insurance against snakes. Mother equally reasonably, argued that there weren't all that many snakes roaming around South West 13. No-one asked me, and anyway, I'd have still preferred a dog or a pony.

The dog happened eventually. Puffin wasn't just for Christmas, she was for life, mainly because she was so ugly that nobody else would have wanted her. The result of an illicit liaison between a Jack Russell terrier fully conversant with the Kama Sutra and a Dalmatian bitch distractedly staking out the local postie from a vantage point on the stairs at the time of the rape, Puffin had four legs, an abundance of spots and a tail that wagged. And that was enough for me.

The pony remained a childhood pipedream, though, so when I look out of the window now at my 'boys' Sam, the driving cob who has had so much grass this year that we have sometimes had to wait for him to breathe in to get him between the shafts at all and Mickey, the youngster, I feel absurdly grateful. Not just to have them but to have something – anything – live and running about. Especially this Christmas as they will be the only livestock at Rowfoot.

Over the past 19 years, we have had cows to milk, or sheep to feed or pigs to fatten 365 days of every year. I have never thought of stock as a 'tie' at Christmas, rather, a welcome respite from mind-numbing domesticity (I mean, does anyone like peeling potatoes?) and shamefully, a justifiable reason to escape visitors too. There are, after all, only so many times you can listen to 'Chestnuts Roasting on an Open Fire' without wishing to lash the chanteuse to the nearest telegraph pole with electrical tape and fire pellets of cranberry jelly at them from a specially modified water pistol.

You can do many things from the comfort of your fireside these days from ordering a pepperoni pizza (easy on the capers, because anything that's nice with capers is even better without them) to text messaging friends in Patagonia. What you cannot do though is feed sheep. You have to go outside. I have always found it useful to deter wannabe companions by muttering something doom laden.

'I may be some time,' delivered in sonorous tone, is a useful one and usually ensures a solitary reverie – well, solitary except for a couple of dozen sheep, two collie dogs and a partridge which may or may not be in a pear tree, but you get my drift. Last year, I wandered out to feed the Manxes their Christmas dinner – no different from dinner any other day of the year, but you'll find that sheep rarely quibble over minutiae like that. Their dark legs were concealed in a thin, low lying mist while their bodies seemed to hover just above the ground like sheepy-shaped clouds, their almost but not quite noiseless munching broken only by a cackling and rattling in a far off copse. It might have been a banshee playing on a set of spectral maracas but more likely it was a pheasant. Then, an unearthly rasping sliced through the silence, probably a chain saw or a quad bike but in the eerie chill it had all the menace of a sound straight from Satan's toolbox. This year, if the stillness is broken I shan't be out there to hear it, whatever it is. I shall be listening to the umpteenth rendition of 'Chestnuts Roasting on an Open Fire' instead.

And finally, there was something else special about a recent Christmas and it was this – No 7 in the Hardback Fiction list was Second Wind by Dick Francis while its opposite number in the Paperback Non Fiction sales was The Little Book of Farting. That's what I call really neat juxtaposition.

250

As a rule, reading a diary is compellingly voyeuristic. Still, for every rule there is an exception and this may well be it since it is neither compelling nor voyeuristic. Just daft, really ... like its author.

Diary of a Lottery Winner

Noddy Holder has yelped his last 'Isschristmuss' for another year and that, at least, is something to be grateful for. It's New Year's resolution time again and mine is the same as usual: I shall keep a diary recording my innermost thoughts (and details of overdrafts). Mine, unlike Bridget Jones's (v daft), won't be made into a film, makes no attempt to emulate Sam Pepys' erudition and will not be illustrated by any Edwardian Lady's water-colour wildflowers, just possibly some doodles.

Most importantly, I shall not be Pooteresequely painting the inside of my bath red because that might be a step too far down the stony path of eccentricity, even for me. I've been having a bit of a trial run, and here it is, an unexpurgated excerpt:

THURSDAY: Downstairs lights fuse. Husband repairs fuse. Lights fuse again. Husband repairs fuse, muttering darkly, but lights go out again. Ring electrician and run about (v carefully) in the dark for rest of day.

FRIDAY: Jane (old school friend) arrives for weekend. Recognise her instantly. She's the one who gets off the train with a notice hanging round her neck where her specs ought to be. Notice reads: 'Wake Me Up At Penrith.' Wonder if husband's purchase of new set of earplugs on way home might in any way be associated with Jane's arrival. Assure Jane that despite indications to the contrary we have paid the electricity bill and that tomorrow house will be extravagantly illuminated. She gives me a pitying look, the sort that people reserve for elderly, deaf cats.

SATURDAY: Electrician arrives. Carpets, floorboards and tempers are raised as house is systematically dismantled. Evidence suggests that mice have been dining royally on electricity cable amuse-geules, before progressing to an eclectic fusion of grey polystyrene insulation and green wadding hors d'oeuvres. Why, I want to know, are there no electrocuted mice, lying on their back with their feet in the air? Husband, having briefly discarded earplugs, suggests that resident rodents prepare for orgy of cable-chewing by swopping their little hobnailed boots for little rubber ones. How does he know that mice wear hobnailed boots? Well, he says, the one performing the opening sequence from *Riverdance* on the bedroom ceiling at 2.46 this morning was quite definitely wearing that sort.

SUNDAY: Out for a drive with Sam and the trap. Jane thinks that the Arse and Cart would be a good name for a pub in the London suburbs, ideally sandwiched between The Ferret and Firkin and The Possum and Skateboard. I am not too sure.

MONDAY: Buy 3kg pot of mouse poison from Carr's and wonder whether to get all Ronseal about it and do what it says on the tin (which will undoubtedly result in rodents decomposing en masse within 3 foot thick stone walls and infusing entire house with execrable pong) or just drop it on their tiny little heads from great height and cremate them in the Rayburn.

TUESDAY: A firebrick falls out of the Rayburn. They don't warn you about this in the adverts do they? Scrub Mass Mouse Cremation option and buy 3kg pot of fire cement. Speculate on uses for empty 3kg pots, of which I seem to be acquiring an impressive collection.

WEDNESDAY: Oh joy. The highlight of the week, a mailing from my new best pen pal DEFRA, who have now outstripped even the *Reader's Digest* in their desire to correspond with me. I have worked out why I have always failed to win the *Reader's Digest*'s swag, by the way – it's because there's no bank in Ainstable. They kept offering to deposit my winnings 'in the bank in Ainstable' you see, but as there isn't one they couldn't. Simple, really.

So what are DEFRA telling me today? Well, that new regulations mean that if I wanted to move stock I could. Possibly. If I applied for a licence. And if the animals already lived on an unrestricted farm in Cumbria, not one on Form D premises nor on the Penrith Spur obviously. And if no animals had been moved onto those premises within the previous 21 days. And then a lot of stuff about biosecurity and serological testing which brings my own blood, bile and several other bodily fluids to a jaunty simmer. All this strikes me as a bit like cleaning the skirting behind the fridge (do you know anyone who does that? So do I, but they do have a tendency towards clinical paranoia), this activity being theoretically feasible, but ultimately pointless. Similarly with this DEFRA mailing, reading it from cover to cover including the date is a waste of time as our new sheep will have to come from outside the county, and by the time that's allowed different regulations altogether will be in place.

THURSDAY: Sign petition lobbying Government for Public Enquiry into foot and mouth. Normally regard petitions as last refuge of the illiterate, dreamed up by cretins in possession of even fewer grey cells than facts but make exception in this case.

FRIDAY: These sheepless times have been tough on ticks too; they are reduced to travelling second class, by dog and one has hitched a ride home on Tess, finding itself at Rowfoot when it really wanted to get to Armathwaite for a spot of shopping or a pub lunch. Daub parasite in Festering Banana coloured nail polish and pray for its peaceful overnight suffocation.

MONDAY: Buy new Lottery ticket. Decide that if I win, will go to Corsica (five numbers) Machu Picchu (five numbers plus the bonus) and with all six, will buy a Hebride and sit on it.

WEDNESDAY: Spend some time gazing idly out of window. Wagons are rolling again, as some farmers tentatively restock. You don't need to be one of those guys who talks about Mars messing about in Jupiter to predict that in the post-restocking weeks, whisky sales will rise, sleep patterns will be erratic and there will be much breath-holding and silent prayers. It's cattle mostly. Some say we should let the cattle establish first, others don't seem to agree. Time will tell.

THURSDAY: Two feathered friends visit Rowfoot. First, a sparrowhawk nips round for a breakfast meeting on the lawn. With a blue tit, sadly. Then a portly pheasant swaggers up the middle of the road. With all these wagons and the way some locals drive, he will be paté by tonight. Last year, if I waited quietly, I would see the Partridge Families creep out from the wood and finish off the leftovers from the sheep troughs. Make mental note to lurk about near the wood at dusk, risking prosecution and possibly frostbite in interests of conservation.

THURSDAY: (two weeks later). Realise I do not have sufficient discipline for this diary keeping lark. Still, it shouldn't be long before I can get back to sheep keeping. Where's that number for DEFRA?

It is time to look forward. It is also time to reflect on how much, or more importantly, how little has changed. Whilst the country-side is getting back to normal and farms are restocking, amazingly, there are still no contingency plans for any (heaven forbid) future outbreaks. And people thought I was joking when I used to say my goat could do as good a job of running the country as most politicians . . .

One Year on After Foot and Mouth

We had that utterly ludicrous conversation that you always have in a doctor's waiting room. You know the one. It starts 'how are you?' and the other person says 'fine, how are you?' and you say 'fine.' It is at this point that I expect the doctor to leap out from behind the patient calming device – usually a fish tank full of colour-ful specimens circuiting aimlessly – and scream: 'Well if you're both fine what the hell are you doing cluttering up my surgery?'

He never does of course, demonic behaviour being con-trary to the Hippocratic oath. My interlocutor – we'll call him Norbert since no one anywhere is called Norbert except a trucking bloke in France surnamed Dentressangle who ought to be commercially twinned with our own Eddie Stobart – and I progressed to the subject which has dominated lives and headlines for about a year now, and his little face lit up like a stray Swan Vesta.

'We're getting cows tomorrow.' His glee might surprise some. After all, this means a return to working more than 70 hours a week, piddling little milk cheques and trails of mud through the house again but he was truly happy. Because at last there is a feeling that, at long last, life is beginning to get back to normal. It is the same, that feeling, at Rowfoot too.

Although we have not restocked yet at least we can let our holiday cottage again. In a normal year, letting a quaint little place with more exposed beams than a sawmill and interesting exposed stonework (what is particularly interesting is how the window stays in place at all as there is no discernible keystone, but no matter) would be fairly straightforward but this was hardly a normal year.

Perhaps our guardian angel was on his lunch break when we decided to diversify into tourism and while I'm thinking about it, what an opaque term 'diversification' is. The Royal Hospital for Incurable Optimists has a special side ward for aspirant diversifiers. They share the facility with would be parents since both groups possess only vague credentials for their respective jobs – lots of enthusiasm but an absolute dearth of previous experience, qualifications and contingency plans.

The challenging circumstances of the F&M year notwithstanding, we had some nice visitors amongst whom were one couple who were married but probably not to each other, and another pair (married, these) neither of whom drove but who travelled just as far and as fast on racing bikes. They had a specially modified trailer complete with border collie pennant attached to the lady's wheels for their dog.

'He barks when he goes downhill,' they said when they booked. Moss returned to Leeds as barked-out as a dog can reasonably expect to be.

Around us, too, there are signs of regeneration and as Spring comes, the seasons will begin to have meaning again, the days structure and the weeks shape. And once we get sheep again, this dog walking nonsense will have to stop. They've gone a bit soft in this hiatus, have G&T. Tess not only quivers pathetically in a light frost, she has decided that in the rain the coal shed is a better place to pee than anywhere exposed to the elements. Like the vast open wastes of the garden for instance. Last night we walked past a field of next door's newest acquisitions, fat bottomed bullocks with sweet breath and inquisitive dispositions. A group of them thundered across the field, skidded to a halt perilously close to the wall, stared and picked their noses in that thoughtful way that cattle do and toddlers simply cannot manage, with their long pink tongues. Were they pleased to see me? Oh yes, judging by the startled expression on the face of the leader, every bit as pleased as a lobster might be to spy a pan of boiling water. This menacing beast peered at me from deep brown eyes, perhaps aware of quite how deeply ridiculous he looked with two bright yellow EEC-approved pendulous plastic tags attached to his elephantine lugs and exhaled, sending a sweet, methane-drenched cloud to evaporate into the cool evening air. His mates hung around behind him until they all concluded that a swaddled female and two collie dogs posed no threat that their collective hulk could not deal with and trod closer.

Damp hung in the air like a disaffected teenager, the kind of damp that works through your jacket and comes to rest in your bone marrow, pervasive damp. It was quiet, but silent no longer. Little sounds made life-affirming notches on the quiet – a distant tractor firing up, a quad bike rattling into life, sheep grazing, an oddly familiar muffled tearing, ripping of grass, a sound none of us really ever noticed before the silent months. An old ewe coughed asthmatically, a rasping, hacking cough. She should give up the Woodbines. I leant on the gate for quite a while in the crepuscular quiet, listening to nothing in particular.

That is what we have all missed.

By next morning I had shaken off this contemplative mood and filled with constructional zeal attributable to the success of the patio I laid in the cottage garden last year, set to work on a short stretch of dry stone wall. Had the patio been laid by a 'professional' I suppose the epithet 'bandit' might spring to mind, but since my efforts resulted in a surface no more hazardous than the average municipal pavement, I was reasonably pleased. It may be perversely praiseworthy to build a wall without anything to hold it together but the process satisfies two entrenched Cumbrian principles.

Firstly, it is fun to cock a snook at nature if you get the chance because she makes life so damned difficult so much of the time, and secondly, why pay anything if you don't strictly need to? Just a few words of advice about dry stone walling – wear stout boots with tough toecaps because the Laws of Gravity and Sod suggest that you will drop the biggest stone on your foot; wear gloves and do not bother getting your nails French polished in the week prior to your labours, and finally, and most importantly, wear big pants. Those thongy things masquerading as knickers will not do. Too much bending, you see. If you are good at jigsaws without the benefit of a pattern on the box, then you have a future as a dry stone waller because you need an eye for what fits where. Freddie, my walling mentor, says that a good waller never picks up the same stone twice though this might be because the Good Waller simply chucks away the wrong stone in a hissy fit rather than put it down and pick it up again but I suspect this was not really the inference to be drawn. On a pleasant day, with the sun on your back, walling has no peer on the job satisfaction scale.

So, on with the boots and on with the song: Hi ho, hi ho, it's off to work we go, with a bucket and spade and a hand grenade, hi ho . . .

Percy did not much care for 'hexperts,' they had a nasty habit of sending him bills in the aftermath of their visits and his preferred currency was a bit of pig or a pheasant rather than the shillings and pence variety.

Percy's Progress

My uncle was a countryman. Words like solstice and Michaelmas and fallow were part of his everyday lexicon, though silage clamp and 8-furrow reversible plough with auto-reset and variwidth were not. With endless patience and pride he trained his own gundog which trotted at heel, attached by an invisible thread of devotion. He fished, tying flies with mesmerising dexterity in spite of having fists like bunches of Fyffes.

He could name obscure varieties of tree at one hundred paces and spent hours watching birds. Not bird watching, which is something quite different, but watching birds, enthralled by their movements, their songs, their habits. Those in his garden he regarded as close personal friends and the occupants of the vast swaying walnut tree were especial favourites, though he was not beyond shooting magpies for the greater good. He was a man who lived in harmony with the natural world and its creatures and encouraged me to do the same. So, whenever I have been complimented on any of my stock I have hoped his ghost was eavesdropping.

Although he gave me away when I married, he was not really an uncle at all, just one of my Granny's coterie of eccentric friends. Granny – and this may come as a surprise – was just slightly eccentric herself. She smoked ciggies from long and ineffably elegant holders, took me to Lord's to watch cricket and taught me to drink gin. When I was six.

Back then, we lived in penury. Only we called it London, Ess Double Ewe Thirteen (SW13). Some kids from my school had family holidays in exotic locations – Branscombe in Devon and the Isle of Man – not overseas exactly, but over some sea at least. Such destinations were luxurious beyond both my imagination and my family's financial reach and I was parcelled up, put in the care of the guard and sent to stay with Granny's friends, who were all quite dotty.

They were an elite group, my uncle, aunt, James and most memorably, Percy and Lucy, who led a fabulously bohemian lifestyle scandalising local polite society, living together but never quite getting around to marrying. Not that bachelor farmers find it any less tricky now, identifying that elusive little window between lambing and first cut silage, hay and harvest but there was not quite the same excuse in the Sixties as no-one made silage then. Still, that is to be pernickety and though Percy and Lucy didn't marry, they did lots of other things. Percy mainly sowed wild oats and then offered up impassioned prayers for crop failure, the lady Lucy having proved deft and accurate with forks of both toasting and pitch varieties. He rode a one-eyed horse, a pastime which promised to end in tears or an unscheduled visit to casualty but happily did neither, drove another and bet enthusiastically on other people's. If he won the Pools he would buy a racehorse, he said, but this was always unlikely as he never completed a coupon, much less an Agricultural Census form.

Theirs was a very old and very pink house with drunken timbers and wonky floors, the rooms liberally hung with cobwebs so ancient that it was entirely possible that they were the subject of preservation orders. It limped from one decade to the next under a regime of genteel neglect, none of its previous incumbents having the proletarian obsession with housework which afflicted my mother in Ess Double Ewe Thirteen. All around were perfect, endless hay meadows permanently gilded by a low and fervent sun. It was a place where anything was possible. Indeed likely.

The Marquis of Hastings is recorded as having breakfasted on Claret and Mackerel cooked in gin (I think it is probably safe to assume that he discarded the piscatorial constituent of the dish) but Percy's tipple was Chisky – roughly equal quantities of whisky and cherry brandy – with peerless horizontalising qualities. In the twilight hours unpolluted by Chisky, Percy was not much given to palely loitering; he liked activity. Poaching, mostly. Nothing intentionally criminal, you understand, he just subscribed to the socialist ethic of wealth redistribution, yet the local constabulary rarely troubled him. Some say that this immunity was in some way connected with the excellence of his home made sausage, crafted from the succulent flesh of Saddleback pigs which rooty-tooted about free range. There was one story involving Percy, my uncle's garden shed, an illicit still, and a policeman being delivered home in a wheelbarrow. But I am sure it was apocryphal.

The total acreage of Percy's holding hovered just under the 100 threshold. It was not so much a mixed farm, as a mixed up one – a dozen or so Hereford cattle, a flock of sheep of indeterminate lineage, sows, piglets and porkers (numbers of which varied on a daily basis), four ponies, one broken down ex-racehorse (we were touchingly encouraged to believe that it would win a race, one day – given a year or so to mend its legs, improve its wind and perhaps even get the hair to grow over the bald patches left by ringworm), two dogs, an assortment of wildish cats and some poultry with plumage as colourful as Percy's own personality.

Percy was more Red Baron (his permanent rosy glow owing much to the Chisky) than Grain Baron. His land valiantly struggled to disprove the old adage that weeds and wheat do not grow together, but then, in those halcyon days, East Anglia was not a vast prairie sprayed with chemicals from a helicopter. There was little machinery, save a reliable grey tractor and an unreliable red baler which sat quiescently in a barn for 10 months of the year and spluttered into violent rages for the remaining two at which times Percy quelled its wrath by poking bits of wire, stick and God only knows what else into its temperamental innards. Eventually and reluctantly, he would summon a 'Hexpert.' Percy did not much care for 'hexperts,' they had a nasty habit of sending him bills in the aftermath of their visits and his preferred currency was a bit of pig or a pheasant rather than the shillings and pence variety.

Percy didn't invest heavily in machinery, nitrogen, organophosphates or anything else much – except betting slips – and he didn't overgraze his land; nor did he try to wrench from the land a level of productivity it would not yield naturally. I have no idea how he would have felt about diversification into tourism, an organic system, farmers' markets, horsiculture or telephone masts.

So, why am I telling you all this?

Well, whilst I am not deluded enough to suggest that we turn the clock back to the Sixties, when everything was less efficient, less slick and less mechanised I am enough of a romantic to hope that the past occasionally casts shafts of light that illumine the future. And besides, a look over our shoulder to a gentler, slower time can't possibly do us any harm. That's why.

I did not rush to restock as I wanted to feel confident that we were not going to see a resurgence of FMD. A farmer in Shropshire telephoned me and generously offered me some of his own sheep – Manxes of course – to 'help me get started again.' It was impossible to accept so tight were the restrictions on movement then and those sheep have long since been sold, but his fine and noble gesture left me totally lost for words. Recently, we heard of some old bloodlines lurking in the Trough of Bowland in Lancashire and I am hugely looking forward to having sheep running about Rowfoot again. It has not been quite the same without them.

I Wool Never Find Another Ewe

That nice Mr Fish said it was going to rain. He stopped short of warning that we would be overtaken by ducks in the outside lane when the M6 became tidal, or telling us that it might be best if we strapped a canoe to the roof rack but on the prospect of rain the man was unequivocal. It would pelt first, then rain some more.

We set out in bright sunshine. It was not that thin, mean sunshine that shafts through cloud illuminating chosen patches of fell in the colours of a deftly dealt bruise; this was the real stuff – rich, benevolent and warm, sunshine redolent of ripe peaches and heady blossom and sand between your toes. Though we had the brolly in the boot. You just never know in the north of England do you?

Travelling south, Eden's mellow pink sandstone yields to rockier Lake District grey slate. The railway snakes alongside us a while, and then I look out for that little heart-shaped wood on the lower slopes of the open fell. Planted in memory of someone loved and lost, I have never failed to notice it and be touched by the sweet romance of such a gesture. When we used to drive south in the lorry bound for some distant competition, I used to look out for the wood as a kind of talisman for the day ahead – all part of the mad superstitious ritual which also, very unromantically, involved wearing Snoopy socks, the one with the hole in the heel always on the left foot. And did the ritual bring any luck? Of course it didn't, don't be silly. But who knows what additional, compounded disasters might have befallen us if I hadn't stuck to it.

As the traffic gets heavier and lorries get so close that they look as if they are trying to hitch a ride in the one in front's trailer, we turn off into the Trough of Bowland. I've only been here once before and then it was too foggy to see anything. This time, the sheep out in the fields are loving this weather; strong lambs bask threequarter prone in unaccustomed warmth, eyelids half closed against the sunshine. Twins sit upright, facing one another like bookends.

We arrive at Portfield Farm about five minutes ahead of schedule. Ponies graze in the surrounding paddocks, a fat ginger cat yawns welcomingly and a very elderly ewe gives a benign nod in our direction. Sheelagh Holmes has been breeding Manxes for 'ever' – about 26 years. She has four-horned sheep and two-horned sheep, some young, some older and some past breeding age and so ancient that they will see out their days here. The first time mothers are in the nursery pens; their lambs are about the size of pet rabbits on stilts. I had forgotten how tiny new born Manxes are.

We walk among the flock grazing in the field. The inquisitive lead sheep – every flock should have one – pushes her dark nose into our hands and snuffles about hopefully as the rest weave about, curious but not completely convinced that hand to nose contact is such a smart move. Sheelagh says that they will follow a bucket almost anywhere and they duly follow her and her bucket obligingly through one gateway, then another. Just one makes a break for freedom and curiously, she has curly horns. My first Manxes were mostly hoggs but I included one or two older sheep to set a good example. It was a stupid idea; setting a good example is a concept entirely foreign to sheep and the renegade amongst mine was one of the two older ewes with very curly horns indeed. She was a menace, was Curly Horns.

CH Mark II, who is I think, second cousin twice removed to my original, careered about for a minute or two in her capacity as professional decoy, maybe seeing the wrong sort of leaves on the line of her progress. When the family dog came to join in the fun, though, she conceded defeat graciously. The dog is not really a sheepdog at all, apparently, it just pretends to be but it was good enough pretence to persuade Sheelagh's whole flock, Curly Horns included, through the orchard and into the pens. My sort of sheep, these.

Then I saw the geese. There are some things more alarming than meeting a goose I suppose. But apart from an asteroid taking a wrong turn and falling out of the sky, I can't think of any. Geese are the devil's work, ferocious, disagreeable, lumps of grit in the oyster of life. I worked, briefly, on a farm which had geese instead of guard dogs and I still have the scar to prove it. So, regrettably, does a retired postie somewhere, a worm rep, a milk recorder, the cook, the gardener, two tractor men, several charity collectors who came to appeal to the Boss' better nature and social conscience (a complete waste of time because he possessed neither) and the Boss himself, who richly deserved any savaging he got, by geese, ganders or persons unknown.

Geese have an uncanny sense of knowing when you are terrified of them too. And this one knew. I could tell. I tried hiding behind a sapling but since I was wider than it, this was none too successful. The gander stared beadily at me.

'Run,' shouted my husband.

'Not on your life,' I squeaked. Sotto voce, but not so sotto that he couldn't hear me, I hissed at the gander (since hissing is the language ganders understand best): 'Delia Smith, Chapter 6 The Christmas Book.' It sounded almost Biblical. The gander, obviously familiar with Chapter 6 – it's the one for Geese, Poultry and Game – glared at me, then quite suddenly lost interest. I ran.

The sheep were now penned and fused into one fleecy multipeded mass and the advantages of having seen them in the field first apparent. We sifted through them for closer inspection of breed points – hairy legs (as undesirable on a Manx female as on the human sort), rough tails (ditto), good dark fleeces, fine bone etc. As we did so, the inquisitive lead ewe who had been so friendly came over all combative and did her level best to beat up all the others one by one in the corner of the pen. That's Manxes for you – no more predictable than geese or men. Finally, we settled on six to come to Rowfoot, two from the nursery with babies, three more juniors and a shearling – a mix of four and two-horned sheep. By now we were rather enjoying ourselves and it seemed a shame to dash home.

'Let's go to Downham for lunch,' suggested Malcolm, on the grounds that it appeared in the Good Pub guide, was two miles and a caber toss from nowhere at all and the road looked seductively wiggly. We wiggled onwards, upwards. In the valley to our left a couple of burnished mahogany Shire horses grazed under a canopy of sweeping boughs and flicked their tails idly at midges – the final piece in the jigsaw of chocolate box perfection. Then the signposts disappeared altogether and at the crossroads we wondered what to do next. Left? Right? Straight on?

'How do I know? You were the Boy Scout,' I grumbled. And anyway, I have all the sense of direction of a supermarket trolley and a propensity to get maps upside down. On the basis that two vehicles were heading along the road to the right, we took that one. We went ten miles in completely the wrong direction but reached Downham in time for an excellent lunch and a walk round the village. And about the signposts – there aren't any. It's deliberate and it's because Downham is a village so frozen in time that it is often used as a film set. It's very, very lovely, Downham. So is the rest of the Trough of Bowland without fog.

We didn't encounter any of the Pendle witches and we had an ice cream on the way home. Six lovely new sheep, England at her best, no peck on the bum from a gander, a total absence of spooks or rain and an ice cream. What more could anyone want?

I'm off to sharpen up the foot trimming knife, rinse out the worming gun, check on supplies of sheep mix and set up a deckchair and a parasol in the handling pens. I shall sit there, reading a book while they mill about getting to know me before I let them go off exploring so I needn't trust to luck or dogs to get them in. If they are very good, I'll even have a selection of sheepy oldies playing on the radio: Mouflon Up, Please ReFleece Me and I Wool Never Find Another Ewe . . .

2002 was as good a year as 2001 had been catastrophic. The silent days had passed. As the year drew to a close, flushed with her success as a Cover Girl and still svelte as a whippet, Tess was negotiating a transfer fee from Rowfoot to Capital Models (Canine Division). Only an offer of increased Chum rations and a new flea collar prevented her, well, fleeing really . . . Gyp, meanwhile, went a bit grey and the vet made some rather unflattering comments about her developing middle-aged spread. Gyp glared at him with her very special Dumb Insolence look. The vet is recovering slowly, I hear.

Taking Stock

Well. What a year 2002 was.

The hardback version of *The Funny Farm* was inflicted on an entirely innocent public in July. Amongst the predictable side-effects of the scribbling life are squinty eyes (all that staring at a computer screen), sore fingers (writer's cramp) and walking around with a brick blue-tacked to your head (writer's block). Among the less predictable though, is becoming a page three girl. And I did, if page three of the *Cumberland and Westmorland Herald* counts. At the launch the young reporter, rather ungallantly I thought, asked my age. He excused his impudence by saying that his readers like to know these things. And, as Tess reminded me, it is a common (if not vulgar) journalistic tool brutally applied to ageing starlets, serial bigamists or feminists with an inventive line in revenge. I should just like to make it clear that I am none of these and that she is very well informed for a dog.

Border TV's Eric Wallace asked me at the launch why Tess was on the front cover. 'Well,' I said, 'she's prettier than me.' Knowing my place and having the ideal face for radio if not for book covers, I did the radio interviews as Tess finds them a bit tricky. Both she and Gyp relished meeting their public at book signings though they are both still struggling to master fountain pens and are only now kicking their motion discomfort pharmaceuticals habits. G&T do not travel well, you see. The vet said they would grow out of it. They are ten now. They haven't grown out of it. You need no further information on this, truly.

Earlier in the year, on a fine Friday morning in June, we had trundled down the M6 to Whalley to collect our new flock. The inside lane was as empty as the Marie Celeste on a quiet day. Very occasionally, when it became irksome to stay in the slipstream of a wagon driver with a Ginster's giant Cornish pasty in one hand, a mobile phone in the other and a varicosed road map of Birmingham propped up on the steering wheel in a spirit of forward planning, we ventured out in to the middle lane. We did Whalley and back, including a loading/coffee break in a little over four hours. How? Well, you see, it was the Friday that England whimpered out of the World Cup and things like working and travelling seemed to have been put on the national back-burner. A weekly World Cup could, I think, solve this country's traffic problems at a stroke.

At home, I put the new sheep in a cage. The Rare Breeds Survival Trust will tell you that Manx sheep are decorative, hardy little beasts yielding low-cholesterol meat but what they don't tell you, lest you change your mind, lose your bottle and decide to keep stick insects instead, is that they are also accomplished high jumpers with a surprising talent for escapology. Hence the cage. After the first day's incarceration they had overcome their Orwellian two-legs-bad-four-legs-good attitude, chiefly because of the troughs brimming with Bob's Mix. I met the eponymous Bob at Penrith show in August. We talked of ships and shoes and sheep instead of sealing wax and the cabbages and kings didn't get so much as a passing mention. As we parted he said: 'You know that other Bob, Bob Martin the dog wormer bloke? I'm nothing to do with him.' I was glad he cleared that up for me.

On the second day I sat in their grassy pen and read them bedtime stories though I didn't do *Three Billy Goats Gruff* because Manx sheep can only take so much excitement. In no time, two fed happily out of my hands, two Don't Knows hung about trying to look insouciant and two affected panic attacks at my approach. Now I know I'm not as pretty as the dog – I said as much to Eric Wallace – but I'm not THAT bug-ugly.

A fortnight later, it was clipping time. I've clipped plenty of horses in my time, the only difficulty there being strong-willed enough to resist the temptation to write 'BUM' in an appropriate spot on their hindquarters. Don't try it: it is very, very difficult to eradicate completely and graffiti does not look good on a serious competition horse.

It is no coincidence that Manx sheep have wondrous handlebars: it is something to do with their homeland being the site of the TT races I believe, but handlebars notwithstanding it is a job and a half keeping a Manx still enough to clip. When you fire up the clippers, they wriggle, squirm and threaten to gouge out your eyes with a carefully aimed handlebar. You become so anxious about 'nicking' them with the blades that you catch your own fingers instead. And fingers don't just bleed, they empty the rest of your body through the tiniest incision.

I just don't do blood, I'm afraid, not when it's my own and it's leaching wastefully away. My response is simple: first I feel nauseous and then I keel over. So, I stuck the injured index finger in my mouth in an effort to staunch the flow and return the loss whence it came. I sucked fiercely: no crunchy bits, ergo no bone damage. That's good then. Several cold-tap-running minutes later, it stopped and was wrapped up tightly. I was left with no alternative but to revert to writing everything in longhand – luckily it was my left hand – or type e-mails and what passes for work, with no Fs, Gs, Rs, Ts, Vs or Bs. Limiting, I'm sure you'll agree.

I'm steering clear of clippers in future.

In July too, Mickey was despatched to Blackdyke where he finally realised that there was more to life than ornamenting the back field at Rowfoot. Truth to tell, Blackdyke came as a bit of a shock for the darling boy. He knew there were two other horses in the world, his field-mate Sam and Sherry across the road and he was relaxed enough if another occasionally passed by. When horsy holidaymakers Irish Jake and exotic Arabian Mia arrived at Rowfoot, poor Mickey had a nasty, if brief giddy spell. Bit of shock, that was, two at once.

But nothing had prepared Mickey for his arrival at Blackdyke. He minced down the ramp of the wagon to find fifty more horses and ponies, scattered all over the place in boxes, yards, fields and schools. Mickey's flabber was finally and irreparably ghasted. He nibbled his mum's remaining good fingers the next day and looked her pleadingly in the eye. 'Take me home, mummy I don't like it here.' The hard-hearted, bug-ugly old bat (47), was completely unmoved and he cried big salt tears that night.

He soon settled down. Roughly about the same time as he started achieving straight sixes for artistic merit and women started prostrating themselves at his hooves in awe of his nifty movement. He has a new lady in his life, Sarah and together they will conquer the world.

But all this about books and blood and Blackdyke is so much blatherskite.

We in Cumbria will remember 2002 for simply this: it was the year that stock returned to our fields. And for that, we give thanks.

*I always worry far less about my sheep being worried than about
the fate of any dog daft enough to take them on. Manxes take no
prisoners. The challenge, to Rottweilers and Jack Russell terriers
alike is 'Come on then, if you think you're hard enough . . .' And
they're not, any of them, though Jack Russells, whopping great
dogs in very small packages, come closer than most.*

Sheep Terrorise Terrier

Why Manxes, people ask me. Why not some other
fleecy creature? What's wrong with pleasingly
crinkly Wensleydales or North Ronaldsays, aka Ronnies –
you could even have Two Ronnies – or Soays, clever little
sheep that shed their fleeces without human intervention?
The answer has less to do with complex principles of conservation and genetic diversity than the simple fact that I
like the look of Manxes. All those horns, funny little
brown faces, nothing more complicated than that, I'm
afraid. It helps too that they are completely mad.

I have always liked barmy animals. It started with the
black rabbit I had as a kid. I used to take it for walks in a
red leather collar and lead, in an effort to make the
parents feel absurdly guilty about denying me a dog. It
didn't work. I felt absurd all right, but they failed to show
any signs of guilt about the dog-denial thing.

I moved on to hard animals in my teens: my old friend
Kathy appeared with three orphan lambs one Easter and
as we had a redundant outside loo and her family didn't,
we parked them in ours for the duration of Kathy's college
holidays. There is logic in there somewhere. We called the
lambs Hop, Skip and Jump and fed them fantastically
smelly lamb milk. Our unholy ovine trinity chewed

electrical flex, piddled on carpets and on one occasion caused an uncomfortable exchange with a policeman who berated us energetically for having a dog in the front seat of Kathy's mini. The smelling salts Kathy unaccountably kept in the front of the mini came in handy too when he realised that it wasn't a dog at all but a sheep and that there were two more in the back.

I spent the next decade trying to find parking spaces in Bedale main street, investigating the principles of gravity with particular regard to saddles and my bottom and acquiring first a family and later a dog who slept on the kitchen table.

Then, in 1987, we bought a Jersey cow called Pixie and transported her to Cumbria from sub-tropical Oxfordshire before she had time to grow herself some proper cladding. Pixie was cold. And cold cows produce little milk. So, I wrapped her up in a horse's cast-off New Zealand rug and yes, in her knee length, sludge-green, waterproof frock she looked a very silly cow indeed. But now that she had the right sort of clothes for the wrong sort of weather, Pixie's productivity progressed. By Spring, Pixie's output no longer needed paragraphs lifted from Professor Henry Higgins training manual to describe it, the rug was in the advanced stages of decomposition and the weather had improved no end.

Now the problem wasn't Cold or Comfort on the Farm but sunburnt pigs. Austin and Morris from Tamworth had delicate skin. Cheap lotions brought them out in spots – not the Gloucester Old variety, obviously, but nasty sore ones instead. A special sort of hogwash was called for: Ambre Solaire, especially behind the ears and on the snout.

See what I mean: I have been systematically stalked by very, very odd animals indeed. And we haven't even started on sheep yet.

The latest wave of weirdness started with Sam, who started shuffling about on the other three legs his Maker had thoughtfully equipped him with and using his off-hind as little as equinely possible. After a fortnight's dossing about as unproductively as Pixie ever managed, he was still not level. I rang Bob the Back Man and although he found a couple of things 'out' and put them back, neither, he said accounted for the lameness. But since Bob had troubled to trek across to Rowfoot I uttered those three little words certain to strike dread into the hearts of back men (and probably plumbers) everywhere 'while you're here . . .' and pointed him in the direction of the husband who, you will be glad to hear, trotted up sound in no time flat.

A couple of days after Bob's visit, a stranger – one stranger than fiction, certainly – materialised. He was accompanied by a very fine packhorse called Troy with a back so flat and so expansive that you could have played bar billiards on it; a back loaded to the gunnels or whatever it is that you load horses to, with sundry collapsibles – tent, water bucket, sleeping bag and probably a widget for unscrewing resistant jamjar lids for all I know. This pair needed a billet for the night, somewhere to tether the Falstaffian Troy and somewhere to pitch an uncollapsed tent. The top field was just the spot.

Our happy camper took one look at Sam and beamed. 'I am a horse healer. I'll have a look at him.' Out came the crystals, the wands, the beads, the shaky-maracas, the pendulum, the water, and allegedly, anyway, all Sam's nasty negative energy. I don't know what went in, but almost immediately Sam galloped up the field like a two year old. Then he went lame again. So, working on the principle of trusting in Allah but rowing way from the rocks, I dosed him with MSM and that didn't work either.

We had tried the Back Man, Horsery Sorcery and

herbalism so finally, we tried a long rest. And now that it is far too cold to go out driving, he is scampering about as friskily as he did after his brief encounter with the Witch Doctor.

What came to plague me next? A sheep-worrying dog. These can be a real problem if you have normal sheep but for the average Manx Loghtan who regard dogs as mere playthings, this is a bit of harmless (for the sheep anyway) fun. This, dear reader, is what happened.

A little white terrier trotted alongside its owner in perfectly matched step: a jaunty little dog with a stumpily perpendicular rudder. Then it saw the sheep, went selectively deaf and into overdrive, hurtling towards them as fast as its Queen Anne legs would carry it. The sheep, realising they were supposed to flee – being Manxes and congenitally contrary – stood firm. The lead sheep fixed the terrier with a glare that would have peeled a tangerine at forty paces and gave the secret signal for the flock to go into attack formation. Accordingly, the First Battalion of the 100% Pure New Wool Infantry circled the terrier and closed in. Menacingly and very, very slowly. The terrier could go neither forth nor back; its tail, that oh-so-sure barometer of the doggy mind, drooped pathetically. Quite soon and with impressive velocity, a rugby ball emerged from the sheepy scrum into the peaceful afternoon sky. Only it wasn't a rugby ball but a very small, very chastened dog.

I saw the dog again, later in the week. His legs were still going like pistons but now he looked neither left nor right, just straight ahead lest he should make eye-contact with his former combatants.

I am not sure, but I think I saw one of the Manxes smirk. Not a lot of sheep can do that.

The statutory five years were up. It was time to go to London again. And now that I go back as a tourist, I have rekindled my love affair with London. We stayed at the Howard Hotel where Paula, Malcolm's middle daughter, works. The night time views over the Thames were so dramatic – the Oxo Tower almost opposite, the London Eye to the right and Tower Bridge to the left – that it seemed rather a waste to go to sleep at all. And one morning, Spiderman went upriver crouched on a barge – we thought it was all very surreal but apparently it was just publicity for a film.

The Gateway to London

'Did you see that advert in the *Cumberland News* for miniature sheep?'

'They're not miniature, they're just stunted.'

'No, proper miniature, they are. Like poodles.'

'Why aren't those huge poodles "Large" not "Standard"?'

'Because they're poodles not eggs, that's why.'

'Medium eggs are standard size though. Those poodles are LARGE. Enormous in fact.'

'Old Betsy had miniature poodles. Used to give them a teaspoon of whisky a day to keep 'em small.'

'They weren't miniature poodles. They were p...d poodles, them . . .'

'And what about toy poodles? Are they toys like those dolls that pee and cry when you hold them upside down?'

'You try holding dogs upside down and you'll have the authorities after you, waving writs and summonses and Lord knows what else . . .'

This conversation proves beyond all reasonable doubt that mending a gate on a wet Saturday morning messes with your head. Freddie and John were taking a break from the hammering, bashing, whacking and using some words I did not understand while I just got on with making the tea (I know my place).

'Sugar?'

'One.'

'Two.'

I was tempted to start on 'buckle my shoe' but I bit my tongue and ruminated silently on the unfairness of nature. Why exactly is it that chaps who take two sugars in tea (blacksmiths always take three, for some reason) are built like bootlaces?

There was no time to unravel this particular injustice as we had to get a bit of a wriggle on with re-hanging the gate. Manxes, you see, regard gates, walls and perimeter fencing sufficient to contain kangaroos come to that, not as barriers but challenges, and I was anxious to get to London with a clear conscience. I freely admit that I usually find the lure of the capital entirely resistible but on this occasion a birthday treat, reunion lunch and a trip on the London Eye at night conspired to make it worthwhile. Just. Anyway, every so often it's good for me to leave the countryside – a place where people don't wear smog shields and can't get pizza delivered – for the capital where you can do both; the only significant obstacle to departure was an unapologetically prostrate gate.

The first time as it crashed to the ground it flattened me and that takes some doing. Heroically, I crawled out from underneath it, my left arm as colourfully bruised as the surrounding ether. After the gate's second unprovoked attack upon my person, I decided to get it dendrologically analysed. And, just as I thought, it turned out to be distantly related to that tree beloved of male drivers – you know, the one that stays in the same place for four hundred years and then leaps out in front of a woman driver. The gate, though, failed to utter anything along the lines of 'it's a fair cop, guv, I'll come quietly . . .'

So I guess this proves the old adage that most accidents occur in and around the home and if your home is a farm you are at risk from more than your egg whisk beating you up instead of t'other way round: it's the gates you need to watch out for.

Gate-fixing had become a matter of considerable urgency not just because of the Manxes but more importantly to keep borrowed Bob securely caged up.

'Who is Bob? What is he?' I hear you ask.

Bob is a Welsh Section C pony, half of a driving pair. He's not mine, he's Tommy Thomlinson's and he is allegedly sixteen. I don't believe this. I think he lied about his age, or possibly that he has a picture in his attic, or more likely in Tommy's attic, because he behaves more like a four or five year old. He walks like Nijinsky – the racehorse and probably the ballet dancer too – and he resembles nothing more in colour and texture than a guardsman's bearskin: prune black, dense and furry. He looks like the rocking horse Alice Hovenden had in her loft in 1958, although I am not sure that this observation is of much help to anyone not fully conversant with Alice, her loft or 1958, and if he had a snook, he'd cock one at tractors, buses and high rise sheep transporters but he doesn't like push chairs much.

Bob's lack of height has invited comment along the lines of 'he's not as big as horses you've had in the past, Jackie.' And for good reason: Jackie is getting older, and likes being reassuringly near the ground these days. I have implored all concerned observers not to ring the welfare agencies just yet, as a horse's load-bearing capacity is not dictated by its height but by the circumference and density of bone immediately below the knee joint. And Bob has a lot of it. His ancestors would have carted Welsh shepherds, their pack, plus the occasional slothful sheep trying to keep its feet for Sunday best – often all at once – up and down Welsh mountains.

Welsh mountains being too far away, we sauntered into a Cumbrian forest. Tendrils of ice hung from bare branches like jewels. Higher up, twiggy fingers clawed silvery scars into a crystalline sky. A lonely buzzard soared in the topsy-turvy stillness beneath us, far down the cleared hillside of the gorge. Regaining the level and breaking the silence I rousted Bob along. 'We'll have a nice little trot along here.' But Bob doesn't do nice little trots, not when he can see half a mile ahead and has a bit of old turf under his dinky little hooves, anyway. If he could have said 'don't patronise me you old bat,' he would have done but he put me in my place instead – very nearly on his rump but not quite.

Now you see why I had no wish for him to go off exploring the highways and byways, as he might have done if the gate had not been secure.

John and Freddie swigged their tea and fixed the gate with just a brief hiatus when a cry went up for something stout and dense to wedge the new stoop. As there were neither politicians nor pop stars handy, they found an adequate substitute and finished the task. And we went off to London where we saw lots of people drinking skinny latte but none, as far as I could see, taking two or three sugars in their tea. And then something occurred to me: while John and Freddie's photographs would have no need of Winslet-style digital remastering, all the London skinny latte imbibers had bottoms the width of Lincolnshire.

Could it be that Saturday gate-hanging is the missing X Factor in dieting, I wonder?

From a land far, far away where beer is called neck oil, a spunk bucket is rather a good-looking chap and anyone with red hair is called 'Bluey', comes the notion that your neighbours can double up as good friends. It may be the theme of an Antipodean teatime soap but it is no less true of Eden. Good neighbours, good friends don't come any better than Freddie and his wife Joan. And just in case you were wondering, I do not answer to Bluey.

A Perfect Day

A spring sun hangs like a topaz pendant in a clear sky, cloudless save for a wisp of mare's tail here and a puffball of cumulus there. As perfect a morning as you could possibly wish for, especially for having a sort through your sheep.

The sheep are well trained, easily lured by a bucket of coarse mix, the hours – no, make that days – I spent hanging about with them when they first came to Rowfoot now yielding rich dividends. It has taken them no time to get back in the old routine of coming into the pen for feed, usually with Bob trotting briskly behind them, herding them very neatly for a pony untutored in the noble art of shepherding. Gyp's nose has been put just slightly out of joint by Bob's superior competence; Tess, on the other hand, watches from the vantage point of the muck heap and just looks relieved to be spared the bother. She is having much more fun having a poke around in search of weapons grade emetics. If her search is fruitful and has quite hideous consequences for the kitchen carpet, she may be looking for a new home very soon indeed.

Freddie has come to help and we have to crack on: he

has to seek out a pet lamb for one of his ewes and I am off to watch Mickey show jump. So, no messing about: we clamp the sheep in to a corner of the pens, securing the hurdles tightly with Michael. Michael doesn't mind: he's baler twine: I have no idea why he goes under the epithet of Michael round here and John Robert in the west of the county, but perhaps someone will illuminate me one day. And while they're at it, some thoughts on how the Hawaiian nation manage with only twelve letters in their alphabet would not go amiss either.

One by one, we turn the ewes upside down. This is the royal 'we', because Freddie is doing all the turning. It is a precision skill, this, though probably not one that normal people need to develop. Its execution is all in the timing. Over they go, flipped as neatly as pancakes.

Some demonstrate an unexpected talent for break-dancing but it's token resistance. Or at least, I think it is. We do what's necessary now. While they can't argue. They have wintered well. Their fleeces are tight as doormats, though one or two have gone in for a shabby chic look, snagged on hedging. Their feet, designed to cope with rocky outcrops and rough ground, grow long on soft low-land pasture and need attention from the sheep chiropodist. That's me.

I have a pair of serrated secateurs, thoughtfully equipped with bright orange handles by the manufac-turers lest I drop them in the grass. I do, frequently. I would never have made a blacksmith: I am far too cautious. As I persevere, Freddie roars at one of the ewes: 'Give ower fightin' wumman.' She looks over her shoulder, scowls and lays into her neighbour with renewed vigour. Manx sheep are not for the lily livered: there may be blood spilt here though not by me, as I snip and snap and pare. What I do not do is slice, not deliberately anyway.

As we work through them, I become more positive,

clipping longer shards of horn away. I straighten up and say with a certain finality and satisfaction: 'There. Look at that. Perfect.' 'Yes,' says Freddie, 'except that you've only done three feet and these are four legged animals . . .' I never was much good at maths, but usually I only start to make mistakes when I've run out of fingers.

'I like a nice sharp knife myself,' says Freddie. I worry about him sometimes. And anyway I would not trust myself with a nice sharp knife. The only time I mixed sheep and a nice sharp knife, it ended up with my husband waiting a very long time in casualty and me moaning that it would have been altogether quicker if we had called in at the vets' surgery on the way through Penrith instead. Vets, he had pointed out, do not do their stitching on the National Health. I'll stick with my secateurs.

They all get a dose of vile-tasting multivitamins. I know it is vile because some of the liquid finds its way under my thumb nail and I spend most of the afternoon wondering about the persistent smell of doggy-do before realising that it is not doggy-do but multivit and it's under my thumb. Since most things that smell horrible taste worse – I'm thinking boiling cauliflower here – I am pretty confident that it is filthy stuff. Still, they should think themselves lucky since it is not only good for them, it is also well within its use-by date and that is a great deal more than can be said for many of the pots and packets festering in my pantry.

Close inspection indicates that they are all in lamb, all that is, with the exception of the young tup, who's been a very busy boy indeed, proving, if proof were needed, that size is not everything. He doesn't much care for his pedicure and tries very hard to give me a Glasgow kiss, but hey, he's been so productive that I hardly mind.

This really feels like something to look forward to, the first lambs in three years.

The sun is still shining when we let them out again. Freddie goes off to do some rural problem solving vis-à-vis his pet lamb or his spare triplet and we set out for Blackdyke.

Mickey looks touchingly grown up these days. He is clipped and fit and pays far more attention to Sarah, the new lady in his life, than he does to me. And that is just as it should be. He won his first rosette for coming fifth in a dressage competition last month and today jumps brilliantly, having a clear round in the first competition. Sarah and he are forging a real partnership: it is good, heartening stuff to watch and no more than either of them deserves.

And that, for me, wraps up a perfect day. Only the discovery of calorie-free Chunky KitKat could have improved my good humour.

Talking of Perfect Days, someone asked me recently what mine would be. I am not one of your 'breakfast in New York, lunch in Paris' merchants, not least because my track record suggests that my luggage would almost certainly be in Turkmenistan. But a day on which I discover that all my sheep are in lamb, Mickey jumps a superb clear and one of the Sunday supplements informs me that an octopus keeps its testicles in its head, I really feel that my cup runneth over.

Next morning, though, my husband has toothache and Bob has a cough. Doesn't do to get too complacent does it?

Epilogue

We came to Rowfoot in 1982. So much has changed since that if we were moving now, I do not think we could do what we did then. Rules, regulations and restrictions abound and farming itself has polarised, with agribusiness at one extreme and hobbyists at the other. In the middle, though, Cumbrian family farms remain: dairy, sheep, beef or an amalgam of all three, holdings small in modern terms but still huge by comparison with those of fifty years ago.

All farms, bar the very smallest, are machinery rather than manpower dependent. Modern tractors have jousting spikes on the front and an array of fearsome folding stuff mounted on the Power Take Off drive. I still have my gripe and shovel.

Still, this much I have learned over the past twenty years:

1 Sheep are not nearly as stupid as you think.
2 Politicians, on the other hand, are as stupid as you think, though far craftier than you had imagined.
3 Never stand behind a cow when she coughs.
4 A horse is a very dangerous conveyance. A unicycle is safer and cheaper to keep.

5 A dog is not just for Christmas. A pickled walnut ought to be.

Most importantly, I have reached the inescapable conclusion that while growing older is inevitable, growing up isn't.   *Jackie Moffat*

THE STREAM
Brian Clarke

Winner of the BP Natural World Book Prize and the Authors' Club
Best First Novel Award

'A SECOND *SILENT SPRING* . . . A MARVELLOUS, TIMELY AND
BEAUTIFUL WORK, IRRESISTIBLE FROM THE FIRST PAGE'
Lynne Reid Banks

'MAGICALLY WROUGHT . . . *THE STREAM* IS A PARABLE FOR
OUR TIMES; IT'S ALSO SERENDIPITY AND A DELIGHT'
Godfrey Smith, *Sunday Times*

A few protesters aside, the announcement of an industrial park in
a depressed rural area is widely welcomed. It promises new jobs,
new blood and a return to prosperity.

A few miles away, in a valley with a stream running through it, a
farm passes from father to son after years of wrangling between
them about the way it should be run.

Over time – and unnoticed by anyone – the impact of the new
development on the surrounding land and the effects on the
valley of the way the farm is now managed begin to compound
one another. The pressures are felt most powerfully in the stream
itself. Little by little, the small creatures that live there, and the
birds and animals dependent on its clear, fast-flowing waters,
become sucked into a mute and desperate struggle for survival. . .

There are no villains in this story. What happens occurs quite by
chance. But as the drama unfolds, this remarkable and affecting
novel raises powerful questions about priorities and choices:
about the kind of world we want – and are creating.

'AN EXTRAORDINARY BOOK THAT MAKES YOU CARE . . .
MOST BEAUTIFUL . . . AND PAINFUL, AS THE BEST BOOKS
ARE, YET WITH NOT A TRACE OF SENTIMENTALITY'
Fay Weldon

'DEVASTATINGLY EFFECTIVE . . . OUGHT TO BE REQUIRED
READING FOR SCHOOLCHILDREN, GOVERNMENT MINISTERS,
BUSINESSMEN, ENVIRONMENTALISTS AND ANYONE ELSE'
The Times

'BRILLIANTLY ACHIEVES . . . A RENEWAL OF OUR
PERCEPTION AND EXPERIENCE OF NATURE, AND OUR ROLE
IN SUSTAINING IT' *Guardian*

0 552 77077 9

BLACK SWAN